OBJECTIVE

first certificate

Annette Capel
Wendy Sharp

Student's Book

CAMBRIDGE
UNIVERSITY PRESS

Map of Objective First Certificate Student's Book

TOPIC	LESSON FOCUS	EXAM SKILLS	GRAMMAR	VOCABULARY
Unit 1 **Fashion matters 8–11** Fashion; describing people	1.1 Speaking and listening 1.2 Grammar	Paper 5 Speaking: 2 Comparing photographs Paper 4 Listening: 3 Matching Paper 3 Use of English: 3	Comparison Adverbs of degree	Appearance and clothing Phrasal verbs
Exam folder 1 12–13		Paper 3 Use of English: 3 Key word transformations		
Unit 2 **Only for nerds? 14–17** Computer games; the Internet	2.1 Reading 2.2 Grammar	Paper 1 Reading: 1 Skimming and scanning; matching headings	Review of present tenses -ly adverbs	Computers Compound nouns Positive and negative adjectives
Writing folder 1 18–19		Paper 2 Writing: 1 and 2 Informal letters		
Unit 3 **Going places 20–23** Travel	3.1 Listening Pronunciation: word stress 3.2 Grammar	Paper 5 Speaking: 2 Paper 4 Listening: 2 Sentence completion Paper 3 Use of English: 3	Modals 1: Obligation, necessity and permission	Travel and holidays Verb–noun collocations Expressions with *do* Prepositions of location
Exam folder 2 24–25		Paper 3 Use of English: 5 Word formation		
Unit 4 Our four-legged friends 26–29 Animals; pets	4.1 Reading 4.2 Grammar and vocabulary	Paper 1 Reading: 4 Matching	*as* and *like*	Animals and pets Compound adjectives Expressions with *time*
Writing folder 2 30–31		Paper 2 Writing: 1 Transactional letters 1 (formal)		
Unit 5 Fear and loathing **32–35** Narration: frightening experiences	5.1 Listening Pronunciation: past tense endings 5.2 Grammar	Paper 4 Listening: 1 Short extracts Paper 3 Use of English: 2	Review of past tenses: Past simple Past continuous Past perfect	Fear Irregular verbs
Exam folder 3 36–37		Paper 3 Use of English: 2 Open cloze		
Unit 6 **What if? 38–41** Winning prizes	6.1 Reading 6.2 Grammar and vocabulary	Paper 1 Reading: 3 Gapped sentences Paper 3 Use of English: 1	Review of conditionals with *if* Adverbs of frequency	Winning Phrases with *in* Parts of speech
Writing folder 3 42–43		Paper 2 Writing: 2 Stories 1		
Revision Units 1–6 44–45				
Unit 7 **Life's too short 46–49** Sport	7.1 Grammar 7.2 Listening Pronunciation: question tags	Paper 4 Listening: 3 Matching Paper 3 Use of English: 3 and 5	Gerunds and infinitives 1 Question tags	Sport Phrases expressing likes and dislikes
Exam folder 4 50–51		Paper 3 Use of English: 1 Multiple choice cloze		

TOPIC	LESSON FOCUS	EXAM SKILLS	GRAMMAR	VOCABULARY
Unit 16 Good, plain cooking 102–105 Food and drink	16.1 Listening and reading 16.2 Grammar	Paper 1 Reading: 3 Gapped sentences	The article Possession	Food Prepositions of time
Writing folder 8 106–107		Paper 2 Writing: 1 Transactional letters 2 (informal)		
Unit 17 Collectors and creators 108–111 Hobbies	17.1 Speaking and listening 17.2 Grammar Pronunciation: contrastive stress	Paper 5 Speaking: 2 The long turn Paper 4 Listening: 1 Short extracts Paper 3 Use of English: 4	Relative clauses	Hobbies Phrases with *look* Phrasal verbs with *look*
Exam folder 9 112–113		Paper 4 Listening: 4 Choosing from two or three answers		
Unit 18 What's in a book? 114–117 Books	18.1 Reading 18.2 Grammar	Paper 1 Reading: 2 Multiple choice Paper 3 Use of English: 2 and 3	*enough, too, very, so, such*	Books Phrasal verbs with *come* and *go*
Writing folder 9 118–119		Paper 2 Writing: 2 Question 5 The set book		
Revision Units 13–18 120–121				
Unit 19 An apple a day ... 122–125 Health and fitness	19.1 Grammar 19.2 Listening Pronunciation: silent letters	Paper 4 Listening: 4 Multiple choice Paper 3 Use of English: 1 and 5	Modals 3: Advice and suggestion *have/get something done*	The body *It's time* Phrases with *on*
Exam folder 10 126–127		Paper 1 Reading: 1 Multiple matching		
Unit 20 No place to hide 128–131 Crime and punishment	20.1 Speaking and reading 20.2 Grammar	Paper 5 Speaking: 3 and 4 Shared task and related discussion Paper 1 Reading: 1 Summary sentences	Gerunds and infinitives 2	Crime Verbs with a change in meaning: *try, stop, regret, remember, forget, mean, go on*
Writing folder 10 132–133		Paper 2 Writing: 2 Stories 2		
Unit 21 To have and have not 134–137 Shopping	21.1 Listening and vocabulary 21.2 Grammar and reading	Paper 4 Listening: 3 Matching Paper 1 Reading: 1 Headings Paper 3 Use of English: 3	Clauses: Concessive clauses Purpose, reason and result clauses	Money Goods and services Adjective-noun collocations Phrasal verbs with *cut*
Exam folder 11 138–139		Paper 1 Reading: 2 Multiple choice		
Unit 22 A little night music 140–143 Music	22.1 Speaking and reading 22.2 Grammar	Paper 5 Speaking: 2 Paper 1 Reading: 3 Gapped paragraphs Paper 3 Use of English: 4	Complex sentences	Music and concerts
Writing folder 11 144–145		Paper 2 Writing: 2 Reports 2		

TOPIC	LESSON FOCUS	EXAM SKILLS	GRAMMAR	VOCABULARY
Unit 23 Unexpected events 146–149 Natural disasters	23.1 Listening Pronunciation: intonation 23.2 Grammar	Paper 4 Listening: 2 Sentence completion Paper 3 Use of English: 2 and 3	*I wish/If only wish/hope* Intensifiers	The natural world Phrasal verbs with *off* Verb-noun collocations
Exam folder 12 150–151		Paper 1 Reading: 3 Gapped text		
Unit 24 Priceless or worthless 152–155 Art	24.1 Reading 24.2 Grammar and vocabulary	Paper 1 Reading: 2 Multiple choice Paper 3 Use of English: 5	Adverbs and word order	Art Verb collocations Confusable words
Writing folder 12 156–157		Paper 2 Writing: 2 Articles 2		
Revision Units 19–24 158–159				
Unit 25 Urban decay, suburban hell 160–163 Cities	25.1 Listening and speaking 25.2 Grammar	Paper 4 Listening: 4 Who says what? Paper 3 Use of English: 1 Paper 5 Speaking: 4	Mixed conditionals	City life Words with *up* Words with *re-*
Exam folder 13 164–165		Paper 1 Reading: 4 Multiple matching		
Unit 26 Getting around 166–169 Transport	26.1 Reading 26.2 Grammar and vocabulary	Paper 1 Reading: 1 Headings Paper 3 Use of English: 4	Inversion Relative pronouns: *who, whom, whose*	Means of transport Phrases with *get*
Writing folder 13 170–171		Paper 2 Writing: 2 Compositions 2		
Unit 27 Material girl 172–175 Famous people	27.1 Listening Pronunciation: intonation 27.2 Grammar and vocabulary	Paper 4 Listening: 4 Multiple choice Paper 3 Use of English: 5	Revision of tenses	Famous people Phrasal verbs and expressions
Exam folder 14 176–177		Paper 5 Speaking: Complete test		
Unit 28 Sense and sensitivity 178–181 Popular psychology	28.1 Reading and vocabulary 28.2 Grammar	Paper 1 Reading: 3 Gapped paragraphs Paper 3 Use of English: 4	Number and concord	Colour Verbs/adjectives with prepositions Phrasal verbs with *out*
Writing folder 14 182–183		Paper 2 Writing: 2 Applications 2		
Unit 29 Newshounds 184–187 The media	29.1 Listening 29.2 Vocabulary	Paper 4 Listening: 3 Matching Paper 3 Use of English: 1		The media English idioms
Exam folder 15 188–189		Paper 2 Writing: 1 and 2		
Unit 30 Anything for a laugh 190–193 Urban myths and jokes	30.1 Reading 30.2 Grammar and vocabulary	Paper 1 Reading: 4 Matching Paper 3 Use of English: 2	*rather* The grammar of phrasal verbs	Humour
Writing folder 15 194–195		Paper 2 Writing: 1 Transactional letters 3 (formal)		
Revision Units 25–30 196–197				
Grammar folder 198–207				

Content of the First Certificate Examination

The Cambridge First Certificate examination consists of five papers, each of which is worth 40 marks. It is not necessary to pass all five papers in order to pass the examination. There are five grades: Pass – A, B, C; Fail – D, E.
As well as being told your grade, you will also be given some indication of your performance i.e. whether you have done especially well or badly on some of the papers.

Paper 1 Reading 1 hour 15 minutes

There are four parts to this paper and they are always in the same order. Each part contains a text and a comprehension task. The texts used are from newspaper and magazine articles, advertisements, fiction, guides, manuals and reports.

Part	Task Type	Number of Questions	Task Format	Objective Exam folder
1	Multiple matching	6 or 7	You must read a text preceded by multiple matching questions. The prompts are either headings or summary sentences.	**10** (126–127)
2	Multiple choice	7 or 8	You must read a text followed by multiple choice questions with four options A, B, C or D.	**11** (138–139)
3	Gapped text	6 or 7	You must read a text with paragraphs or sentences removed. You need to use the missing paragraphs or sentences to complete the text.	**12** (150–151)
4	Multiple matching/ multiple choice	13–15	You must answer the questions by finding the relevant information in the text or texts.	**13** (164–165)

Paper 2 Writing 1 hour 30 minutes

There are two parts to this paper. Part 1 is compulsory, you have to answer it. In Part 2 there are four questions and you must choose one. Each part carries equal marks and you are expected to write between 120–180 words for each task.

Part	Task Type	Number of Tasks	Task Format	Objective Writing Folder
1	Question 1 • a transactional letter • formal/informal	1 compulsory	You are given a situation which you need to respond to by letter. You may be given two or three different types of information which you need to use in your answer.	**2** (30–31); **8** (106–107); **15** (194–195); **Exam folder 15** (188–189)
2	Questions 2–4 • an article • an informal non-transactional letter • a letter of application • a report • a composition • a story Question 5 Writing one of the above types of task on a set book – choice of two questions	4 choose one	You are given a choice of topics which you have to respond to in the way specified.	Compositions **4** (56–57); **13** (170–171); Articles **5** (68–69); **12** (156–157); Reports **6** (80–81); **11** (138–139); Letters of Application **7** (94–95); **14** (182–183); The set book **9** (118–119); Stories **3** (42–43); **10** (132–133); **Exam folder 15** (188–189)

Paper 3 Use of English 1 hour 15 minutes

There are five parts to this paper, which test your grammar and vocabulary.

Part	Task Type	Number of Questions	Task Format	Objective Exam folder
1	Multiple choice gap-fill mainly testing vocabulary	15	You must choose which word from four answers completes each of the 15 gaps in a text.	4 (50–51)
2	Open gap-fill, testing mainly grammar	15	You must complete a text with 15 gaps.	3 (36–37)
3	'Key' word transformations testing grammar and vocabulary	10	You must complete a sentence with a given word, so that it means the same as the first sentence.	1 (12–13)
4	Error correction mainly testing grammar	15	You need to identify any extra words, which are wrong, in a text containing some wrong lines and some correct lines.	5 (62–63)
5	Word formation	10	You need to use the right form of a given word to fill the gaps in a text containing 10 gaps.	2 (24–25)

Paper 4 Listening about 40 minutes

There are four parts to this paper. Each part is heard twice. The texts are a variety of types either with one speaker or more than one.

Part	Task Type	Number of Questions	Task Format	Objective Exam folder
1	Multiple choice	8	You hear short, unrelated extracts, each about 30 seconds with either one or two speakers. You must choose an answer from A, B or C.	6 (74–75)
2	Note-taking or sentence completion	10	You hear either one or two speakers and this part lasts about 3 minutes. You must write a word or short phrase to complete the notes or sentences.	7 (88–89)
3	Multiple matching	5	You hear five unrelated extracts with a common theme. Each lasts about 30 seconds. You must choose the correct answer from a list of six.	8 (100–101)
4	Choosing from 2 or 3 possible answers	7	You hear either one or more speakers talking for about 3 minutes. Task types may include yes/no; true/false; 3-option multiple choice; who said what, etc.	9 (112–113)

Paper 5 Speaking about 14 minutes

There are four parts to this paper. There are usually two of you taking the examination and two examiners. This paper tests your accuracy, vocabulary, pronunciation, and ability to communicate and complete the tasks.

Part	Task Type	Time	Task Format	Objective Exam folder
1	The interviewer asks each candidate some questions.	3 minutes	You are asked to give information about yourself.	14 (176–177) Complete speaking test (Parts 1–4)
2	Each candidate talks to the interviewer for about 1 minute.	4 minutes	You have to talk about two pictures and then comment on the other candidate's pictures.	see above
3	Candidates have to discuss a task together.	3 minutes	You are given some material – diagrams, pictures, etc. to discuss with the other candidate.	see above
4	Candidates offer opinions relating to the task they've just completed.	4 minutes	The interviewer will join in with your discussion.	see above

UNIT 1 Fashion matters

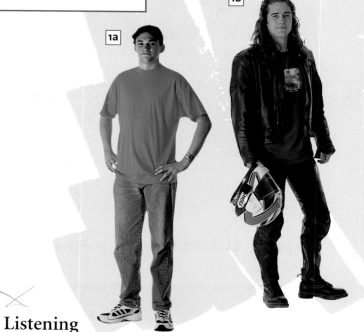

1 What sort of clothes do you prefer to wear? Do you ever have to wear things you don't really like? If so, why? Talk with a partner.

2 In pairs, describe what people in the class are wearing today. Then list topic vocabulary under these headings, adding to the words given.

Clothes: suit, sweatshirt, ...
Footwear: (flat/high-)heeled shoes, ...
Jewellery: bracelet, pendant, ...
Headgear: beret, helmet, ...
Materials: woollen, leather, ...
Hairstyle: curly, spiky, ...
Appearance: stylish, smart, ...

V ocabulary spot

List topic vocabulary in sets like these, using headings to help you learn the words and their meanings.

3 Work in pairs. Each student chooses a pair of photos, for example, 1a and 1b. Take it in turns to describe what each person is wearing and say something about their appearance.

E xam spot

In Part 2 of Paper 5, each candidate is given a pair of photos to talk about on their own. The task will involve comparing and contrasting the two photos, rather than just describing each one.

4 In the same pairs, compare the two people in your pair of photos. Talk about their age, their clothes, their hair, or even imagine their personality! These examples may help you.

The one on the left is younger than the one on the right.
This girl's clothes are not as stylish as the other one's.
He/She has longer hair than the other one.
This man seems to be less serious than the man in glasses.

5 As a class, summarise what you said about the people.

Listening

6 🎧 **You are now going to hear some short** recordings, where five of the people in the photos talk about what they like to wear. Say who is speaking in each case.

Here is an example: Speaker 1 is the man in picture 3b. Look at the photo of him as you listen.

In this transcript of what Speaker 1 says, some words and phrases are highlighted. This is to show that parts of an exam recording may make you think that other answers are possible. This is why you must listen carefully and check when you listen a second time.

__I'm not a suit man__ – even for work, I can get away with casual stuff, though I still __like my clothes to look smart__. I love shopping – my favourite place is Paul Smith in Covent Garden. I bought a really nice woollen shirt there recently. Clothes are important to me, but they need to be comfortable as well as __stylish__.

7 🎧 Now listen to the other four speakers and match the correct photo to each speaker. Note down any words and phrases that help you to decide. Compare your answers with another student when you have finished.

Speaker 2 [ ]   Speaker 4 [ ]
Speaker 3 [ ]   Speaker 5 [ ]

Vocabulary

In the recordings, there are several examples of phrasal verbs.
For example, Speaker 1 says:

> ... *even for work, I can **get away with** casual stuff.*

Phrasal verbs are commonly used in informal English, particularly in speech.

8   Listen to Speakers 2–5 again and list all the phrasal verbs you hear. There are nine in all. Then match the nine phrasal verbs to these short definitions.

a be seen very clearly
b join or combine things
c return
d wear smarter clothes than usual
e keep money for something special
f reduce
g get dressed in something
h go somewhere for entertainment
i know the most recent facts about something

9 Now choose six of the phrasal verbs to complete this letter, using each of them once only.

What advice would you give the writer? Discuss in pairs.

Dear Jayne

Last night, Maria, Sally and I
(1) .... clubbing.
Because I was late back from work,
I quickly (2) ....
that black skirt of mine and a
T-shirt, but the other two really
(3) .... ! Maria
chose a beautiful purple dress and
sprayed her hair gold. Sally
(4) .... the
most outrageous outfit - red leather
shorts, a bright green top and high-
heeled, knee-length boots with stars
on. When we got there, they both
(5) .... on the
dance floor and I looked very
ordinary in comparison.

Honestly, I can't (6) ....
.... them -
they're so fashion-conscious. What
would you do in my position?

Comparison

1 Read this short text about the fashion industry. Do you agree with its viewpoint?

> Why is it that fashion houses design their clothes for the youngest and skinniest men and women? We may not actually want to look like supermodels, but it is a fact that the most emaciated figures have dominated the world's catwalks for a very long time. It seems it is not in the interests of the fashion industry to represent an 'average' person. Although 'slimmer' may not always mean 'more desirable' in the real world, fashion succeeds because it carries with it that image of the least attainable figure.

2 All these comparison structures have occurred in this unit, including some superlative forms in the text above.

-er than	*more … than*	*the most …*
the -est	*less … than*	*the least …*

Why do we say *younger than* but **less serious** *than*; and the *youngest* but *the **most emaciated**?
Which common adjectives can we either add *-er/-est* to or use *more/most* with?
What are the spelling rules for words like *slim* and *skinny*?
Check the Grammar folder whenever you see this:

G ⋯⋮ page 198

3 Give the comparative and superlative forms of these adjectives. Some examples are given to help you.

bright	brighter	(the) brightest
large	....	....
thin	....	....
dirty	....	....
quiet	....	....
casual	....	....
outrageous	more/less outrageous	....
good	....	(the) best
bad	worse	....
far	....	....

4 Now complete the following sentences by using one of the adjectives above, choosing either the comparative or the superlative form, whichever makes the best sense.

a There's no way you can fit into my shoes – you take a .... size than I do!

b Jake wears .... clothes of any of us – take his pink and purple ties, for example!

c Don't dress up for the club tonight – everyone's looking .... there nowadays.

d You can't put those jeans on again – they're .... pair I've ever seen!

e I'm a bit worried about Sally. She doesn't eat a thing and so she's getting .... than ever.

f Australia is .... place I've ever travelled to.

g Have you painted this room recently? Everything's looking a lot .... than before.

h Market stalls often offer slightly .... value for money than shops.

G rammar extra

Note the use of *a lot* and *slightly* in sentences *g* and *h*. These are adverbs of degree, which are commonly used with comparative adjectives. Some adverbs of degree are also used with superlative adjectives, as in this example:

*Kate Moss is **by far** the most famous model of the 1990s.*

Put these adverbs of degree into the following sentences. Which one can be used with both comparative and superlative adjectives?

a bit	a great deal	much

a This ring is only .... more expensive and it's .... nicer than the others.

b Tracksuits may be .... warmer, but shorts are .... the best for running in, whatever the weather.

G ⋯⋮ page 198

5 *not as … as/not so … as*

You used this structure to compare the people in the photos in the last lesson. Now compare these photos of cars in the same way, choosing suitable adjectives from the ones below to describe them.

EXAMPLE: *The Beetle is not as fast as the Ferrari.*

| comfortable | elegant | fast | practical | sexy |

Comparison of adverbs

6 Identify the comparative adverbs in this short newspaper article and then explain how they are formed.

G ···> page 198

BOY MEETS GIRL

Androgenous clothing design is a familiar idea nowadays, although it is perhaps the term 'unisex' that is more commonly used by the fashion industry. Traditional dress restrictions for men and women are becoming blurred, largely because gender roles in today's society are defined less strictly than they were.

With menswear designer Lee Copperwheat, Pam Blundell produces the *Copperwheat Blundell* label. She says, 'I design trousers for women and Lee will re-cut them for men. We have even started doing unisex pieces, such as trousers and raincoats, in six different sizes to fit everybody.' Many other designers work in this way, with the result that similar lines for men and women are now much more readily available.

What do you feel about these sorts of clothes? Do you think that unisex clothing will still be in fashion in five years' time? Why?/Why not?

7 Now practise using all these comparison structures. Complete the second sentence so that it has a similar meaning to the first sentence, using the word given. **Do not change the word given.** You must use between two and five words including the word given. There is an example at the beginning (0).

0 Mary is shorter than her brother.
not
Mary is ....*not as tall as*.... her brother.

1 These sunglasses cost a bit less than my last pair.
were
These sunglasses .... than my last pair.

2 Coco Chanel was an extremely talented designer.
most
Coco Chanel was one of .... in the world.

3 That supermodel is only 17 – I thought she was older.
as
That supermodel is not .... I thought.

4 It takes much less time to travel by train than by car.
lot
Travelling by train .... travelling by car.

5 The piece of music by Genzmer is easier to play than it looks.
less
The piece of music by Genzmer is .... it looks.

6 Suzanne's host at the dinner party wasn't as elegantly dressed as she was.
more
At the dinner party, Suzanne was far .... her host.

7 I prefer swimming to football.
interesting
For me, football .... swimming.

8 John wears smarter clothes now he has a girlfriend.
less
John dressed .... he didn't have a girlfriend.

Exam folder 1

Paper 3 Part 3 Key word transformations

In this part of the Use of English paper you are tested on both grammar and vocabulary. There are ten questions and an example at the beginning. You can get up to two marks for each question.

1 Read the Part 3 exam instructions below and then look at the example (0).

Complete the second sentence so that it has a similar meaning to the first sentence, using the word given. **Do not change the word given.** You must use between two and five words, including the word given.

Here is an example **(0).**

0   This is the most exciting holiday I've ever had. < *First sentence*

   exciting < *key word – this never changes*

   I've never had a .... one.

The second sentence must mean the same as the first when it is complete.

The gap can be filled by the words 'more exciting holiday than this', so you write:

0	more exciting holiday than this

ANSWER:
I've never had a ...*more exciting holiday than this*... one.

   1 mark   +   1 mark

Write **only** the missing words **on the separate answer sheet.**

2   Think about what is important in this exam task. What advice would you give another student about answering Part 3 in the exam?

3   Now read the advice given in the bullet points.

Advice

- Read the first sentence carefully.
- Think about how the key word given is commonly used.
- Complete the gap with a possible answer. You can use the question paper for rough answers.
- Count the number of words you have used in the gap. You must use not less than two and not more than five, including the word in bold. Note that a contracted form such as 'don't' counts as **two** words.
- Read the completed second sentence to check it means the same as the first.
- Ask yourself whether the words in the gap fit the sentence grammatically.
- Transfer your answer (just the words in the gap) to the answer sheet.

4 Complete these transformations, using exactly the number of words in brackets (this includes the word given). There is an example at the beginning (0).

---

0 Have you got a brooch that is cheaper than this one?
less (4)
Have you got *a less expensive brooch* than this one?

1 'A club has just opened in Leeds,' said Maria to Sally.
told (5)
Maria .... club in Leeds.

2 I returned the dress to the shop because it was badly made.
took (3)
Because the dress was badly made, I ....
to the shop.

3 Some shops try really hard to help you.
effort (3)
Some shops really .... to help you.

4 Fifty years ago, cars were slower than they are nowadays.
as (5)
Fifty years ago, cars .... they are
nowadays.

5 Every concert I had attended had been better than that one.
the (4)
It .... I had ever been to!

6 People wear casual clothes where I work.
up (4)
People .... where I work.

7 It's a lot easier to learn a language by visiting the country where it's spoken.
much (4)
You can learn a language .... you visit
the country where it's spoken.

8 Peter Høeg writes the best novels in Danish today.
far (4)
Peter Høeg is by .... of Danish novels
today.

9 The stall didn't sell much jewellery because of its high prices.
highly (3)
The jewellery on the stall was so .... not
much was sold.

10 You can get away with wearing jeans nearly everywhere nowadays.
wear (4)
It .... jeans nearly everywhere nowadays.

UNIT 2 Only for nerds?

1 Do you agree with the following statement? Talk to another student, giving your opinion.

Computer games are anti-social and violent, and their users are mindless nerds.

nerd, *Aus also* **nurd** /£nɜ:d, $nɜ:rd/ *n* [C] *infml* a person, esp. a man, who is unattractive and awkward or embarrassing socially ● *People who work with computers are often dismissed as spotty nerds.*
nerd-y (**-ier, -iest**), *Aus also* **nurd-y** (**-ier, -iest**) /£'nɜ:·di, $'nɜ:r-/ *adj infml* ● *I switched to contact lenses because I felt so nerdy wearing glasses.*

2 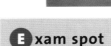 Now listen to this extract from a radio interview with a university lecturer. Does he have the same view of computer games as you have? What are his reasons?

3 When you are looking for specific information, you can ignore any parts of a text that do not relate to this task. Running your eyes over a text in this way is called scanning.

Scan the four short articles about computer games, to decide quickly which game is:

a the worst   **c** the least expensive
b the best   **d** the most informative.

Where did you find this information? How much of each article did you need to look at?

1

The idea is brilliant: set in the Wild West, this is a clone of perhaps the most popular game ever, *Doom*. Probably the best thing about this game is its introduction, with unusual camera angles, excellent sound effects and just about every Western cliché there ever was. It goes downhill when you get into the game itself. You spend your time creeping around deserted buildings, endlessly shooting at hundreds of bad guys. You collect ammunition, health points and other things that you can use to solve puzzles. But once you finish one level of the game, on you go to another one which is remarkably similar. It's a case of 'Been there, done that' – eight times! However, while you're playing, you can always listen to the background music, which is great. Turn up the volume and enjoy it.

THE VERDICT: *Makes you yawn at times, but good fun for fans of Westerns.* *** £45

2

Did you know that car games have a poor relation? Yes, it's their motorbike cousins! Somehow motorbike games never provide the same thrill as car games. But this version comes very close and is easily the best available. There are eight different bikes, nine long tracks and a choice of race styles: Grand Prix or the muddier scrambling type. The intelligence and speed of your 23 computer opponents is high, which guarantees a game demanding enough for the most advanced racer. So get on your bikes!

THE VERDICT: *A super-slick bike racer that does not disappoint.* ***** £40

3

Ice is very useful. It keeps food cold in your freezer and combines perfectly with Coca-Cola. Tragically, of course, the passengers of the Titanic experienced the downside of ice. Namely that if a ship hits a big piece of ice, the ship comes off worse. The real-life setting of the Titanic disaster may seem a joyless subject, but there is plenty of historical fact and, thankfully, no gory detail. This is a first-person adventure, with a real sense of atmosphere. Unfortunately, though, just as you start solving a few puzzles, the ship goes down. As the technology improves, games of this type are becoming more and more elaborate, but here there is just too little to do. What a missed opportunity!

THE VERDICT: *If you're interested in the history of the ship, you will definitely learn something – if not, give it a wide berth!* ** £40

4 To get an idea of what a paragraph or whole text is about, you should read it through quickly, rather than word by word. This is called skimming.

In groups of four, choose one article each and skim it to find out what sort of game is described. Briefly describe the game to the others.

5 Now look at A–E below, which include the four article headings and one extra heading. Read the articles (1–4) on your own and decide which heading fits each one. Underline the words in 1–4 that helped you to decide.

> **A** Doomed at sea
> **B** Reach for your guns
> **C** Failure on all points
> **D** Two-wheeled fun
> **E** Fast and exotic fantasy

6 Find words or phrases which mean the same as a–j. The article number is given in brackets.

a an exact copy (1)
b a frequently-used idea (1)
c deteriorates (1)
d bullets (1)
e a feeling of excitement (2)
f challenging (2)
g gloomy (3)
h complex (3)
i walk with heavy steps (4)
j vulnerable to (4)

7 In article 3, the writer talks about the *downside of ice*. What exactly does this mean? Here are some more compound nouns using 'up' and 'down'. Which three words are used in connection with computers?

upturn	breakdown
upgrade	crackdown
set-up	let-down
back-up	downloading

Check the meaning of the other words in a dictionary if necessary. Then use the words to complete the sentences a–h.

a This game is a complete ....! It cost me over £40 and it is really boring.
b I can't find the original file and I forgot to make a .... , so I'm starting the whole document again.
c Keep an eye on your phone bill – .... from the Internet can be expensive, especially when a file includes sound effects.
d Jean is new to the department and doesn't understand the .... yet.
e The .... in the economy is good news for all of us.
f There was a serious .... in communication and the peace talks collapsed.
g You should buy this .... for your software. Then your computer wouldn't crash so often!
h 'Zero tolerance' means a total .... on crime.

4

This game is so bad that I am sitting here unwilling to even write about it! But the magazine pays me to, so I must. Here goes … You are a bird-headed robot and you want to control a number of cities. To do this, you have weapons, a shield and the ability to jump higher than the non-bird-heads. You stomp around at a slow pace, searching for something to shoot at. When you do find something, you end up at the mercy of the interface as well as the enemy. The control system is useless. The graphics are appalling. The cities are flat and bare. The task is truly boring. What more can I say? It's coming out next month!

THE VERDICT: *Avoid.* ∗ **£35**

Review of present tenses

1 Here are some examples from the articles on computer games. Look at the underlined tenses in a–j and identify them as present simple or present continuous. Then complete the statement about present tenses, using the letters a–j once only.

a It goes downhill when you <u>get into</u> the game itself.

b While <u>you're playing</u>, you can always listen to the music.

c Motorbike games never <u>provide</u> the same thrill.

d It <u>keeps</u> food cold in your freezer.

e If a ship <u>hits</u> a big piece of ice, the ship <u>comes off</u> worse.

f Games of this type <u>are becoming</u> more and more elaborate.

g I <u>am sitting</u> here unwilling to even write about it.

h But the magazine <u>pays</u> me to.

i You <u>stomp around</u> at a slow pace.

j It<u>'s coming out</u> next month.

The present .... tense is used for permanent situations (examples .... and ....) or to talk about actions which are habitual or repeated (examples .... and ....). This tense is also used in time clauses, introduced by words such as *if, until, once, as soon as,* .... (example ....). Note also that it is used in both parts of zero conditional sentences, as in this example and in example ....

On the other hand, the present .... tense is used for temporary situations (example ....), situations that are changing or developing (example ....), and for events or actions happening now (example ....). This tense can also be used to talk about the future (example ....).

G ⤑ page 198

2 Read these sentences and correct any tense errors.

a Home computers are becoming more and more popular.

b This week, the shop sells all software at 20% off.

c Don't use the phone downstairs for the next twenty minutes as I am surfing the web.

d As soon as you are using a computer, you realise how helpful it is.

e When you buy a new computer, you are getting a lot of free software.

f Many children prefer computers to books.

3 Choose the correct present tense for each of these sentences, using the verbs in brackets.

a My new game is sensational – as soon as you .... a level, you .... something completely different to do. (finish, get)

b Generally, computer manuals ...., although some are still very long and difficult to follow. (improve)

c A System 8 upgrade .... soon. (come out)

d In the latest version, a dragon .... overhead and .... dramatically when you .... it. (fly, explode, hit)

e The downloading of sound and images from the Internet .... increasingly sophisticated each year. (become)

f Back-up disks .... time to prepare, but they are essential. (take)

g It is said that computers .... life easier. (make)

h If a computer ...., you .... the file you .... on unless you .... it regularly. (crash, lose, work, save)

4 Skim this review of Internet software. Then fill each space with a suitable present tense of one of the verbs below. Use each verb once only. There is one extra verb you do no...

[handwritten note overlapping:]
Grammar Practice : Unit 2 p. 16-17

allo...	①	Coin 1 :	Simple pres	vs	pres Continuous
cor...		Coin 2 :	He/She/It	vs	They/I/You
hav...		Coin 3 :	Statement	vs	Question
put...		3 Dice :	Number of words in sentence
sha...				

Com...
ano...

In w... *Production:*
pres ① *Discussion of computers.*
con ② *Brainstorm various computer websites/games/activities*
cha...   *Then in pairs, compare & contrast.*
          Then, design a video game.
Wh...
not have a present continuous form?
Do you know any more verbs like this?

Verbs not normally used in the continuous tenses are called 'stative' verbs.

G ┄┄⯈ page 199

5 Read these statements and say whether you agree or disagree with each one, giving your reasons.

a Some people hate computers because they don't understand them.

b Computers belong to the 21st century; books don't.

c The Internet seems to offer an enormous amount of helpful information, but in fact, a lot of it is dangerous, particularly for children.

d People forget that computers may have a health risk.

Microsoft v Netscape: **battle of the browsers**

The Internet is undoubtedly one of the fastest-moving technologies in the computing world. It (1) .... the way we (2) .... with each other and (3) .... us to access a huge amount of information quickly and cheaply. ... full advantage of what the Internet (4) .... you (5) .... a good browser.

...oducts (6) .... the market at present: ...oft's *Internet Explorer*® and Netscape's ...unicator®. In an effort to be the best, each one .... extra features apart from the core browser. ...these products are remarkably similar, showing that ...ompany (8) .... it must keep a close eye on ...e other (9) ....

...is the usual unfortunate trade-off: the inclusion of ...eatures (10) .... less user-friendly products. When you (11) .... about their e-mail facilities, for example, they (12) .... really good – but if you (13) .... an e-mail to anyone with less sophisticated software than your own, they won't be able to read it! However, both products (14) .... to be fully usable when it (15) .... to Internet browsing itself and both can be recommended here.

Vocabulary

6 These adjectives have all come up in this unit.

appalling	brilliant	demanding	elaborate	excellent
joyless	popular	sensational	sophisticated	terrific
tremendous	useless			

Divide them into two basic meaning groups, positive and negative. If you are not sure which group to place a word in, use a dictionary.

Some of these adjectives may be useful in the next writing task on pages 18–19.

Vocabulary spot

List new words in a vocabulary notebook and add to them when you can. It can be helpful to include a sentence showing how the word is used.

Writing folder 1

Informal letters

1 Look at the extracts from three letters below. Which two would you describe as informal? How did you decide?

A

I want to let you all know about our staff get-together last week. It's a pity more of you weren't there as it was a terrific occasion. Why not come along next time? There's free coffee and biscuits!

B

This is to inform you of the decisions taken at last week's meeting. Please note that all members of this department are strictly required to be present at such meetings and action may be taken in future to ensure this.

C

Anyway, let me tell you about the party Jack is having on Saturday. Well, just about everyone is coming – even that weird guy Sam from college! Jack says he wants us all to be there, so you'd better not miss it. Why not come down for a few days? You can stay at my place if you want.

Decide for each extract who could have written the letter, who it was probably written to and why.

Exam spot

In Paper 2, you may have to write an informal letter in Part 1 or Part 2. Think carefully about who you are writing to and why, before you decide whether to use informal language. You may be given an extract from a letter to reply to, which can also give you clues about a suitable style.

2 Read this writing task and find the style clues.

Here is part of a letter from an English friend:

Guess what? My parents have given me some money for passing my exam, so I can splash out on something really special. I can't choose between buying a new computer game or saving up a bit more and getting some clothes. Which do you think would be better? And can you suggest what exactly I should get?

Write a suitable reply to your friend. (120–180 words)

3 The sample answer below would get a low mark, for several reasons. What are they?

Dear Frankie

What brilliant news in your letter! I wish to offer you congratulations about the exam. Moreover, how nice to have some spare cash.

You say you can't decide if to buy a computer game or some clothes. Don't you think that if you choose some new clothes you must save up a bit more money first? Clothes are not as cheap than computer games and I know you like expensive designer outfits. If you choose computer game, which one? There are so many available and to my mind they are all the same. In my opinion you should spend the money in something else. Why don't you get yourself a new dictionary, for example? Then it would be easier for you to study, wouldn't it?

I hope you will consider my suggestion seriously and I look forward to receiving a reply from you in due course.

Yours sincerely

Correct the errors in paragraph 2 and rewrite paragraphs 1 and 3 in an appropriate style.

4 How will you answer this task? Work in pairs.

Content ideas
Decide whether you think your friend should buy a game or clothes and note down some reasons to support your view. Then think about one specific game or item of clothing. What is special about it? Compare your ideas.

Game: topic, best points, price
Clothes: material, colour, style

Language input
You need to include these functions:

Congratulations   Opinion   Advice/Suggestion

Think of some informal examples of each function. Then read the informal expressions from sets 2–4.

Organisation

A letter needs adequate paragraphing, to make it easy to follow. In the sample answer, paragraph 2 is too long and the ideas in it are muddled. It is important to plan what you are going to say in note form before you start writing.

- Use this plan for your letter.
  - Opening formula
  - Paragraph 1 Initial greetings and congratulations
  - Paragraph 2 Opinion about which item the friend should buy
  - Paragraph 3 Description of one specific item
  - Paragraph 4 Final remarks
  - Closing formula
- Try to use linkers within each paragraph, to improve the flow of the letter. Choose appropriate ones from set 5 to present your ideas in a clear order.
- Do not include any postal addresses, as they are not needed in the exam.

Style

Here are some typical features of informal writing. There is at least one example of each in the sample.

Contracted forms, for example, *I'm, don't*
Phrasal verbs
Phrases with *get, take, have*, etc., for example, *take a look*
Short sentences
Simple linking words, for example, *Then*
Direct questions, for example, *What about …?*
Some exclamation marks (not too many!)

Editing your work

It is important to read through what you have written and put right any mistakes. Check your work for the following:

a Is the grammar accurate?
b Is the spelling correct?
c Is there enough punctuation?
d Is the style consistent?

The first letters of the five headings above spell out the word C-L-O-S-E. It is important to think about these five elements (Content, Language, Organisation, Style, Editing) for all FCE Paper 2 tasks. And the word 'Close' will also remind you to finish a piece of writing, for example by signing off a letter. Some candidates in the exam forget to do this and lose marks.

Formal or informal?

Write *Inf* next to the expressions that are informal.

1 Initial greetings
   It was great to hear from you. ....
   I am writing with reference to your letter. ....
   Thanks for writing to me. ....

2 Congratulations
   Well done! ....
   I would like to offer congratulations on ....
   Let me congratulate you on ....

3 Opinion
   In my opinion ....
   To my mind ....
   I hold the view that ....
   Personally, I have no doubt that ....
   My own thoughts are ....

4 Advice/Suggestion
   Why not try ....
   What about trying ....
   It is recommended that you ....
   You could ....
   I urge you to ....
   I suggest that ....
   If I were you ....

5 Linkers
   Moreover ....
   Also ....
   Then again ....
   Furthermore ....
   Better still ....
   As well as that ....
   What's more ....
   Additionally ....

6 Endings
   Do drop me a line if you have time. ....
   I look forward to hearing from you without delay.
   ....
   Hope to hear from you soon. ....
   Keep in touch. ....
   I hope to hear from you at your earliest convenience.
   ....

7 Opening and closing a letter
   Match these opening and closing formulae and say when you should use each of them.
   Dear Jayne   *Yours faithfully*
   Dear Sir   *Yours sincerely*
   Dear Ms Jones   *Love*

UNIT 3 Going places

1 Discuss these photographs with a partner. What types of holiday do they show?

2 Now compare the two photographs.

Student A	Student B
What sorts of people would enjoy these holidays?	What are the advantages and disadvantages of each of these holidays?

3 Where do you usually spend your holidays? Why?

E xam spot

In Part 2 of Paper 4 you may be asked to complete some sentences. You will need to write a word or short phrase and you will hear the passage twice. The words you write down are in the order you hear them. There is no need to make any changes to these words.

NOT DONE

Listening

4 You are going to hear a man being interviewed on the radio about a cruise he recently took to the Antarctic. In groups note down the kind of travel vocabulary that you think you will hear. Explain your words to the rest of the class. For example:

Cruise: ship, captain, ...
Trip: voyage, journey, ...

5 🎧 Read through the questions 1–10 very carefully and, in pairs, try to predict what word or words you might need to fill each gap. Now listen to the interview.

1 The temperature was usually around ....
2 The name of the ship was the ....
3 The cupboards in the cabins were situated ....
4 The nationality of the expedition leader was ....
5 The weather in this area is sometimes ....
6 Steve enjoyed seeing the different types of ....
7 The only people, besides tourists, in the region are working at a ....
8 The only evidence of the fishing industry is empty ....
9 The cruise ships are forbidden to get rid of ....
   in the area.
10 It's important that tourists don't disturb the ....

6 Do you approve of tourists being allowed to go to unspoilt areas of the world? Would you go to these places if you had the opportunity?

Vocabulary

7 All the words in the box below are to do with travel and holidays. With a partner, put them into the following categories:

a boats
b movement
c seaside
d people
e accommodation

journey	caravan	campsite	canoe
flight	courier	hotel	yacht
cliff	bed and	crossing	sightseers
liner	breakfast	holiday-makers	coast
shore	voyage	travel agent	sand
ferry			

Vocabulary spot

It is useful to remember words which go together. These are called 'collocations'. For example, you *go on holiday, on a trip*, etc.

8 Link the verbs in list A with suitable nouns in list B. There is sometimes more than one answer.

A
take   book   catch   set   board   get   go

B
skiing   a trip   sightseeing   sail   a ship
a plane   a tan   a hotel   a flight

9 In the listening, you heard the expression to *do more good than harm*. Now look at some other expressions with *do*. Complete the sentences below, putting *do* into the correct tense.

do someone a favour	do your best
do your homework	do business with
do military service	someone
do the shopping	do something for a living

a I've always found that they are a very good company to ....
b What does your father ....?
c We don't have to .... in Britain.
d I usually .... at my local supermarket.
e I'd run out of change for the telephone so Pete .... and lent me some.
f I always try to .... when I have to ...., but I'm not sure I always succeed.

Pronunciation

Look at this word from the interview: ANT**ARC**TIC
The middle syllable of the word is stressed. This means that it is slightly longer when you say it. It doesn't mean you need to make it louder!
In English the stress pattern in words is variable.

10 In pairs decide where you would put the main stress on these words from the listening. If you're not sure, listen again to the interview.

recent	expedition	deserted
temperature	injection	untouched
comfortable	scientists	excursions
passenger	biscuits	permitted
atmosphere	industry	experience

11 Read this dialogue through to yourself and mark the stress on the words in italics. Then work with a partner. Take a role each and read out the dialogue.

Travel Agent: Good morning, can I help you?
Customer: Yes. Have you got any *brochures* on *Africa*? I'm a keen *photographer* and I'd like to spend some time *photographing* the *animals*.
Travel Agent: Well, we can offer you *various package* deals. What kind of *accommodation* would you prefer?
Customer: Oh, a good *hotel*. I don't like to be *uncomfortable* – I'm not the camping type.
Travel Agent: Well, I think we have *something* here to suit you. Let's see. We have two weeks in *Kenya*. It looks very *attractive*, I don't think you'll be *disappointed*. They also *guarantee* plenty of *wildlife*.
Customer: That sounds good. Thanks. I'll take the *brochure* and have a look at it tonight.

12 ∩ Listen to the cassette to check your pronunciation.

Modals 1: Obligation, necessity and permission

1 Look at the extracts (a–g) from the listening and then decide which extract goes with phrases 1–6.

a you should take warm clothes
b you really need a windproof coat
c you don't have to socialise if you don't want to
d cruise ships are not allowed to go where they like
e they have to carry scientists to lead the excursions
f small parties are permitted to land
g you've got to keep away from the wildlife

What word or phrase in a–g means:

1 There's no choice.
2 It's necessary.
3 It's forbidden.
4 It's allowed.
5 It's not necessary.
6 It's a good idea.

2 In small groups talk about the following sentences. Decide why some sentences use *must* and others use *have to*.

a I must remember to buy a newspaper on my way home.
b The doctor says I have to try to take more exercise.
c All cars must be left in the car park, not on the road.

G ⋯⟶ page 199

3 Imagine you are **extremely** rich. In pairs discuss your holidays in the places shown, using *must*, *have to*, and *don't have to*. Talk about transportation, accommodation, food, activities, entertainment and people.

> When I go to Los Angeles I tell my secretary that I *must* stay at the Beverley Wiltshire hotel. My suite *must* have a private swimming pool and jacuzzi. Luckily I *don't have to* queue at the airport as I have a private jet, and a limousine to meet me. Even though I'm very rich I still *have to* take a passport like everyone else.

4 Which is the correct alternative in these sentences?

a You *needn't / shouldn't* have a lot of money to enjoy life.
b Travel agents *don't have to / aren't allowed to* produce inaccurate brochures.
c You *mustn't / needn't* smoke in this part of the restaurant; it's a no smoking area.
d I *must / have to* show my passport at the frontier.
e Full board *is compulsory / optional* at this hotel, but that's OK because I like their food.
f You *have to / don't need to* wear a seat belt in a car in England.

5 With a partner, talk about the following situations.

EXAMPLE: *I'm going to travel abroad.*
- *I need a new passport.*
- *I have to have an injection.*
- *I must pack my bag.*
- *I should buy a new pair of sunglasses, but I don't think I have time.*

a It's the weekend tomorrow.
b I'm 18 today.
c My friend is getting married soon.
d I started a new job last week.
e I've won the lottery.
f I'm going to learn to drive a car.

6 You can use *permit, allow, let* and *can* to express permission. Notice that both *permit* and *allow* are followed by *to*, and *let* and *can* aren't.

What did your parents let you do when you were younger?
What are you allowed to do when you are 18 in your country?

Using *permit, allow, let* or *can* once only, complete these sentences. You may need to add other words.

a I wasn't .... to go on holiday with my friends until I was sixteen.
b You .... stay at this camp-site without booking in advance.
c Peter .... me borrow his large suitcase when I went shopping in New York.
d They .... us to board the plane early because we only had hand luggage.

7 There are two past forms of *need*. One is *didn't need to do* and the other is *needn't have done*. Look at these examples and in pairs discuss what you think the difference in meaning is.

a I didn't need to go to the bank this morning, as I had enough money to do the shopping.
b I needn't have rung to tell him about the air traffic control strike because he told me he had already heard about it on the radio.

G ⋯⋗ page 199

G ⋯⋗ page 199

E **xam spot**

Remember that a contraction – *don't, isn't* – counts as two words.

8 Complete the second sentence so that it has a similar meaning to the first sentence, using the word given. **Do not change the word given. You must use between two and five words, including the word given.**

1 The travel agent said, 'All passengers for Marseilles must change trains in Paris.'
to
The travel agent said that all passengers for Marseilles .... trains in Paris.

2 I went to the bank but it wasn't really necessary.
gone
I .... the bank.

3 I wasn't allowed to go on holiday with my friends last year.
let
My parents .... on holiday with my friends last year.

4 This is a 'no swimming area'.
permitted
You .... in this area.

5 It's a good idea to have health insurance when you go on holiday.
get
You .... before you go on holiday.

6 British passport holders no longer need a visa to visit the USA.
have
British passport holders .... a visa to visit the USA any more.

G **rammar extra**
Prepositions of location

Complete the following sentences with these prepositions of location.

on	in	into	off	at	across

a The hotel had a swimming pool .... its roof.
b I arrived .... the airport very early in the morning.
c When I walked .... the hotel I was amazed by the decoration.
d I arrived .... Spain last Tuesday.
e We showed our passports as we went .... the frontier.
f I found a bank .... the town centre.
g We sat .... the terrace drinking coffee.
h There was a notice .... the wall telling us about trips.
i I jumped .... the pool to cool off.
j Singapore is an island .... the coast of Malaysia.

Exam folder 2

Paper 3 Part 5 Word formation

In this part of the Use of English paper you are given a short text with ten gaps and an example. At the end of each line there is a word which you will need to change so that it will make sense when it is put in the space in the same line. In the example below, you are given the verb 'arrive' and it needs to be changed into the noun 'arrival' in order for the sentence to make sense.

EXAMPLE:	Their plane's late ..... was due to a thunderstorm during the flight.	**ARRIVE**
ANSWER:	Their plane's late _arrival_ was due to a thunderstorm during the flight.	

You need to read the sentence carefully to decide what kind of word is missing – is it a noun, a verb, an adjective or an adverb? In English we often use prefixes (words that go in front of a word) and suffixes (words that go at the end of a word) to change the type of word it is.

Prefixes

1   The following prefixes all give the meaning of NOT when they come before a word. We often put *il-* before words beginning with *l*, *ir-* before words beginning with *r*, and *im-* before words beginning with *p*. Take care with this rule though as there are exceptions.

il-	un-	in-
dis-	ir-	im-

Which prefix do we use to make these adjectives negative?

a   satisfied
b   relevant
c   patient
d   complete
e   legal
f   possible
g   comfortable
h   honest
i   popular
j   legible
k   accessible
l   responsible
m   pleased
n   realistic
o   perfect
p   regular
q   literate

2   What meaning do you think these prefixes give to the word that follows? Can you think of some more examples?

a   *mini*-skirt
b   *non*-stop
c   *re*train
d   *sub*way
e   *un*tie
f   *under*done
g   *anti*-freeze
h   *ultra*-conservative
i   *out*live

Suffixes

3   NOUNS – Typical noun suffixes are:

-ation	-ion	-ness	-ship	-ity
-ism	-ence	-ment	-al	

Make these words into nouns.

a   happy
b   intelligent
c   approve
d   repeat
e   inform
f   popular
g   friend
h   social
i   pay

4   Not all nouns follow the above pattern. Make nouns from these words.

a   true
b   succeed
c   die
d   high

5   ADJECTIVES – Typical adjectival suffixes are:

-ible	-able	-y	-al
-ive	-ful	-less	-ous

Make these words into adjectives.

a   wind
b   attract
c   hope
d   peace
e   eat

6 VERBS – Typical verb suffixes are:

-ve	-ist	-en
-ise	-ize	-ify

Make these words into verbs.

a wide   **c** sympathy
b behaviour   **d** clear

In British English you will nearly always be correct if you use *-ise*.

7 ADVERBS – Adverbs are usually formed by adding the suffix *-ly* to the adjective. However, there are some exceptions.

Make these words into adverbs.

a hard   **d** peace
b good   **e** fast
c slow   **f** true

8 Read through the passage on the right and think about what kind of words you need to make. For example, 0 is a noun (publication). List the parts of speech for 1–10 and then complete the task.

1 = a verb
2 =
3 =
4 =
5 =
6 =
7 =
8 =
9 =
10 =

Advice

- Read through the passage carefully to get an idea of what it is about.
- Decide what kind of word is missing – is it an adjective, verb, noun or adverb?
- Make sure that your choice makes sense in the sentence. Some words may need to have a negative prefix.
  EXAMPLE: The waitress took ages to bring us the menu and I found her very rude and .... HELP
  ANSWER: Unhelpful
- Check that you have spelt the words correctly.

A MAP MAKER

The (o) <u>publication</u> of the first atlas was in 1595. The man   **PUBLISH**

who (1) ..... this collection of maps was called Gerardus   **PRODUCT**

Mercator. Born in 1512, he spent his (2) ..... in Flanders   **YOUNG**

where he became known as an (3) ..... talented map-maker   **EXTREME**

and maker of (4) ..... instruments. In 1544 he was   **SCIENCE**

briefly imprisoned for his (5) ..... beliefs and, fearing   **RELIGION**

for his family's (6) ..... he went to live in the Rhineland,   **SAFE**

where he lived for the rest of his life.

His atlas was so (7) ..... that it was translated into a   **SUCCEED**

(8) ..... of European languages. However, his map of the   **VARY**

world is (9) ..... because the earth is round. As maps are flat   **ACCURACY**

it is virtually (10) ..... to have correct scale, area   **POSSIBLE**

and direction on one map.

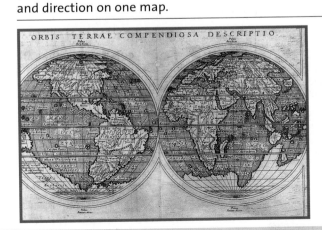

ORBIS TERRAE COMPENDIOSA DESCRIPTIO

1 Before doing this questionnaire, discuss your feelings about animals in general and having a pet.

Pet Questionnaire

1 Which kind of pet would you prefer to have and why?

a A dog
b A cat
c A budgerigar
d A goldfish
e Something exotic like a snake or a tarantula
f None. I object to people keeping animals as pets.

2 Which country keeps the most dogs as pets?

a The UK
b The USA
c France

3 Which country keeps the most cats as pets?

a Sweden
b The UK
c Germany

4 If someone owns a dog, do you think that they should

a be made to buy a licence for it?
b have to do a training course?
c only allow the dog out on a lead?
d be allowed to keep it in an apartment?
e be free to do what they want as dog owners?
f do none of these?

2 What do you think would be the best pet for the people in pictures 1–4?

3 You are going to read four texts about different pets. Read the introduction below to find out who the four pets have been to see recently.

Nowadays more and more pet owners are spending their hard-earned money on sorting out their pets' psychological problems. 'Owners come to us when they've tried everything they can with no result,' says Dr Mugford, one of Britain's leading animal behaviourists. 'We find that most owners can be trained to deal with behavioural problems in one 90-minute session, although it does take a lot of hard work and commitment to see the results. Dogs are the most receptive to therapy. Cats can be tricky, and the chances of success with anything more exotic depend on the problem and the creature's personality.'

4 Skim texts A–D. Where are they from?

a an article
b an encyclopaedia
c a pet-care book
d a novel

Exam spot

In Part 4 of Paper 1, you are asked to find information in a number of separate texts. First of all read through the texts quickly to get an idea of where they come from and what they are about. Remember this is called 'skimming'.

5 Now scan the texts A–D to find the information to answer questions 1–11. Underline the words or phrases that give you the answers.

EXAMPLE: *Which owner was embarrassed by a pet?*
     A Brett   **B** Rosemary
     C Fiona   **D** Vicki
ANSWER: D (*I spent the whole time going red in the face and apologising to people.*)

Which owner

1 had some trouble with accommodation because of a pet? `1 ☐`
2 thinks the pet is completely cured? `2 ☐`
3 was attacked by a pet? `3 ☐`
4 got a pet when it was very young? `4 ☐`
5 had to learn new ways of behaviour? `5 ☐`
6 wanted a pet because of loneliness? `6 ☐`
7 believed the pet might die? `7 ☐`
8 had to teach a pet who was the boss? `8 ☐`
9 wasn't given any help by the therapist? `9 ☐`
10 wasn't worried about the pet's health? `10 ☐`
11 bought nice things for their pet? `11 ☐`

A Brett

Brett got his pet Doberman, called Sonny, from an organisation which rescues dogs that have been badly treated by their previous owners. The day after he arrived he refused to let me into the house after work, and when I fought my way in he bit me. It was like an all-out war. I didn't know what to do, but I'd had Dobermans before and I know they're very bright dogs and I felt he deserved a chance. I finally went to see an animal behaviourist and although it took over two years of tremendously hard work, Sonny is much better. The therapist started by retraining me. I had to ignore Sonny's bad behaviour. He had to learn that I was in charge. It's been the hardest job I've ever done, and although Sonny can still be a bit tricky, he's a different dog these days.'

C Fiona

Fiona, who works as a nurse, has a Siamese cat called Tooting. She's spent over four years trying to cure Tooting of anorexia, a problem you have if you don't eat. 'There was a time when I thought Tooting wouldn't survive, he was so painfully thin. His previous owner told me that Tooting had been on antibiotics because he had problems with his teeth and gums. I'd do everything to tempt him to eat – buy him fresh prawns and salmon, then hand-feed it to him. In the end I saw an animal behaviourist who said that Tooting had profound anxiety about eating because he now associated it with pain. So I had some of his teeth extracted and I was given a pain-relieving electrical device that he wears when he eats. It's been pretty successful, and Tooting is eating fairly normally again.'

B Rosemary

Rosemary had always wanted a parrot, so a year ago she acquired William from an advertisement in a newspaper. 'I needed a bit of company as I'm a pensioner living on my own, so at first I was delighted to get William. Well, three weeks after I got him, he suddenly started barking like a dog. The flats where I live don't allow dogs and William made such a loud barking noise that my neighbour reported me. Then William started repeating the arguments he must have heard at his previous owners. They were a young couple getting divorced. William shouted "Steve you're a liar! Don't go Steve, I love you Steve" (Steve was the husband's name). I took William to see an animal behaviourist who said he was in good condition, but she couldn't do anything for him and she thought that in time he'd forget his past owners and start copying the noises I make. In fact, I like opera and William has now started to sing along, as I do when I'm listening, although he can only manage the high notes at present.'

D Vicki

Vicki has a dachshund called Yoda. 'At about six months Yoda suddenly became really wild. She'd rush up to anyone – especially if she thought they were doing something she regarded as odd, such as sitting on the grass or sunbathing – and start barking. She'd chase passers-by, particularly if they were carrying umbrellas, and stand and bark at objects like post-boxes and tin cans on the pavement. I spent the whole time going red in the face and apologising to people. But I knew enough about dogs to suspect that Yoda's problem was due less to being very aggressive than to excessive fear. As I'd got her as a puppy from a reputable breeder, I knew there was nothing basically wrong with her. I only had one consultation and Yoda was immediately better. I was given a device called an Aboistop, which fits on a dog's collar. Each time Yoda barks it squirts lemon essence, which isn't at all harmful but dogs don't like the smell. It has worked like a dream.'

---

6 What do you think about behaviour therapy for animals? Is it popular in your country? What would you do if:

   a your dog kept barking at people?
   b your dog tried to bite people?
   c your cat clawed the furniture?
   d your parrot wouldn't speak?

7 What adjectives come from these nouns? Check your answers by looking back at texts A–D.

   a sanity (A)   **e** aggression (D)
   b a trick (A)   **f** excess (D)
   c a difference (B) **g** reputation (D)
   d a success (C)

as and like

1 Read the explanations below. All the examples are taken from the article you have read in 4.1.

- *As* is used to refer to a person's (or animal's) profession:
  I knew he'd been trained as a guard dog …
  Fiona, who works as a nurse, …

- *Like* is only used for comparison or similarity:
  He suddenly started barking like a dog. (He's actually a parrot.)
  It was like an all-out war.
  It has worked like a dream.

- *Like* and *such as* can be used to mean *for example*:
  … and bark at objects like post-boxes …
  … such as sitting on the grass or sunbathing …

- Some verbs can be followed by *as*:
  … something she regarded as odd …

  Other verbs of this type are *refer to, use, to be known, describe, class, accept* and *treat*.

- *As* is normally followed by a subject and verb, while *like* is followed by a noun or pronoun:
  … as I do when I'm listening …
  He was crying like a baby.

  (In British English it is becoming more common to hear *like* followed by a subject and verb. This is acceptable in American English.)

2 Now decide whether the following sentences are correct or not. If not, correct them.

a He is usually described like 'a charming young man'.
b He worked as a butler for a very rich family when he was in the USA.
c I've no time for people as hypocrites and liars.
d She could play the piano like a professional.
e One of the Russian Tsars was known as *Ivan the Terrible*.
f She went to the traditional wedding dressed as a tramp.
g Will went to the fancy dress party dressed as a knight.
h Like I always say, nothing good will come of lowering taxation.
i Paul McCartney has written a lot of good songs – like *Yesterday* and *Let it be*.

j You'll find it difficult to make a living like a writer.
k As a boss he was very unpredictable.
l Camping is best when it's hot, as in spring and summer.

G ⋯⋗ page 199

Compound adjectives

3 A compound adjective is an adjective which has two parts and is usually written with a hyphen. Many have a present or past participle in the second part of the compound, as in this example from 4.1:

hard-earned money – money which you work hard to earn.

Work through the questions in a–d with a partner.

a
1 Who do you think our 'four-legged friends' are?
2 What is a man-eating tiger?
3 How would you describe a cat which has blue eyes, long hair and a bad temper?
4 What about an animal with two toes and a back covered in scales?

b
Do you know anyone who is:
1 left-handed?
2 cross-eyed?
3 bad-tempered?
4 sharp-tongued?
5 narrow-minded?

Compound adjectives are very useful for describing people, both for character and physical characteristics. Describe someone in your family.

EXAMPLE: My mother's a brown-eyed, curly-haired, right-handed woman. She's a broad-minded and self-confident person.

c

Some compound adjectives have a preposition in the second part of the compound, as in this phrase from 4.1:

'all-out war' – total war.

1 Where would you sit at a drive-in movie?
2 How would you feel if you were hard-up?
3 How much money do you need to have to be well-off?

Can you think of some more examples?

d

The article in 4.1 talked about a '90-minute session' with the therapist. Notice that *minute* is singular not plural.

How would you describe:

1 a journey which was fifty kilometres long
2 a girl who is twelve years old
3 a film which lasts 75 minutes
4 a car which costs £35,000
5 a pause which lasts ten seconds

Listening   NOT DONE

4 🎧 You overhear some conversations about animals. For Questions 1–3, decide which is the right answer, A, B or C.

1 Which animal does the man own?
  A a bird
  B a snake
  C a rabbit

2 What problem does the woman have with her dog?
  A The neighbours are frightened of it.
  B It is always ill.
  C She hasn't time to take it for walks.

3 What does this man think about zoos?
  A He likes visiting them.
  B He thinks they should free the animals.
  C He believes they are doing a good job.

Vocabulary

Ⓥ ocabulary spot

Use an English-English dictionary to look up words you don't know.

5 Decide which of the words below belong with each of these animals.

parrot   cat   dog   horse

perch	foal	mane	feather
hoof	fur	neigh	purr
bark	paw	kennel	puppy
stable	whiskers	kitten	wing
squawk	claw	beak	

6 There are many common expressions with 'time' in English, as in this example from the article about the four pets.

… *that in time he'd forget his past owners*

to spend time	to kill time
to pass the time	to have a good time
to take time off	to tell the time
time for breakfast/lunch	ten times three
in time	behind the times
at times	from time to time
four times as much	a time when
to waste time	

Complete the sentences a–h with one of the expressions above.

a Her ideas on women working are completely
  ....
b I usually don't have enough ...., so I grab a sandwich on the way to work.
c He says he never puts on weight, but he eats three .... as I do.
d .... people will realise that not spending enough on education will only lead to disaster.
e Although Peter decided not to come to the concert with us he said he hoped we would ....
f I always take a book to the doctor's surgery to .... while I'm waiting.
g She was given a watch as soon as she learnt to
  ....
h I really hate .... doing stupid exercises.

Writing folder 2

Transactional letters 1

Question 1 in Paper 2 is compulsory – all exam candidates have to answer it. 'Transactional' means that the letter has a particular purpose, and will require further action by its reader, usually in the form of a written response. The letter must be based on the information given in the question. Examples of transactional letters include: writing to a school to request details about a language course; complaining to a company about a holiday; replying to a friend about arrangements for a party. The letter could be formal or informal.

1   Look at the following extracts and decide what the writer is doing in each. (Some may be used twice, while others are not used at all.)

a complaining   d giving information
b suggesting   e asking for information
c correcting information

1

I must point out that the article in your newspaper about our International Club gave some misleading information. We actually meet once a week, not once a fortnight and we begin at 8 o'clock, not 9 o'clock. You also gave the impression that the club was just for young people. In fact, we are very happy to welcome people of all ages.

2

I have always enjoyed working with animals and have spent every summer working as a riding instructor at a local stable. I am available for interview from May 19th this year and I include the names and addresses of two people who would be willing to give me a reference.

3

As I've already said I think the general standard of accommodation in your hotel is good. However, I think that you should spend more time on staff training as I found some of your staff, especially those in the restaurant to be unhelpful and on one occasion, quite rude.

2   Read this example of a Part 1 task.

You have just returned from a trip to Florida. You flew there and back with Ocean Air. You decide to write to the airline to complain about your flight and ask for some money back.

Read the advertisement and the notes you made and then, using the information, write a letter to the airline. You may add other relevant points of your own.

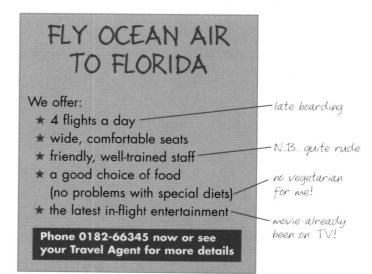

FLY OCEAN AIR TO FLORIDA

We offer:
★ 4 flights a day — *late boarding*
★ wide, comfortable seats
★ friendly, well-trained staff — *N.B. quite rude*
★ a good choice of food — *no vegetarian for me!*
   (no problems with special diets)
★ the latest in-flight entertainment — *movie already been on TV!*

Phone 0182-66345 now or see your Travel Agent for more details

Write your **letter** in 120–180 words. Do not include any postal addresses.

3   In pairs, discuss what you are being asked to do.

- Do you need to write a formal or an informal letter? How do you know?
- Do you know the name of anyone at the company? How will you begin and end the letter? What kind of tone will your letter take (rude, polite, etc.)?
- How are you going to organise the letter? For example: How many paragraphs? What kind of linking words?
- Which points do you think are the most important?
- Are there any points you think you can leave out?
- Is there anything you think it would be a good idea to add?

4 With a partner decide what is wrong with the following letter. For example, there are punctuation mistakes so *a* is ticked (✓). Do the same with b–j.

a punctuation ✓
b paragraphing ☐
c length ☐
d grammar ☐
e vocabulary ☐
f opening and closing phrases ☐
g content points ☐
h spelling ☐
i tone (level of politeness, formality) ☐
j linking words ☐

Dear Sir,

I am writing to complain about the flight to Florida that I made with your airline on 12th June this year. We were three hours late boarding the plane. No one was able to tell us why. Another problem was the air hostess. She was very unhelpful. I had problems with my hand luggage. She told me she was too busy to help me. When she came round with the lunches there were no vegetarian meals left. I had ordered one when I had booked my flight. I think this is disgusting. All I had to eat in eight hours was some bread and cheese. I demand some compensation for the problems I had flying with your airline, especially for not having a hot meal during a long flight. If you don't send me the money immediately, I will call my lawyer.

Yours faithfully

5 With a partner decide which of these sentences you would use in a formal letter and why. You must remember that your letter must have a 'positive effect' on the person reading it.

a I want you to give me back my money.
b I look forward to hearing from you in the near future.
c The food was OK.
d I have decided not to fly with your company again.
e I would be grateful if you could send me a refund.
f The service was satisfactory.
g If you don't do what I tell you, there's going to be trouble.
h I would appreciate an apology from your company.
i Hi Steve!
j See you soon.
k Dear Sir or Madam
l And, another thing, I won't fly with you again because it wasn't very comfortable.

Abbreviations

6 You will sometimes find abbreviations given in the Part 1 task. Decide what the following common abbreviations mean. Use your English-English dictionary to help you.

a RSVP
b e.g.
c etc.
d N.B.
e tel.
f Sq., Ave, St, Rd
g PTO
h kgs, kms
i nos.
j max., min.
k Dr
l c/o
m approx.
n cont'd
o mins.

7 Another type of transactional letter task is correcting information, usually from a newspaper article. Look at this task.

In the summer you had a job at a workcamp in Kirby in England. A friend in Kirby has just sent you this article from the local newspaper. You decide to write a letter to the newspaper to correct some of the information in the article.

Read carefully the article and the notes you have made. Then, using this information, write a letter to the Editor of the newspaper. You may add other relevant points of your own.

Student Slaves at Workcamp

All summer some 30 foreign students, mainly from France and Sweden, were working long hours for little more than pocket money on a local farm. Sleeping in old tents and with only one shower between 30 people, the students spent their days picking fruit and vegetables. It's a disgrace that visitors to this country, who come to these so-called 'international workcamps', should have to put up with such dreadful conditions. I think that

Notes
- *max. 15 students*
- *many different nationalities*
- *mornings only, weekends free*
- *modern, wooden buildings with showers*
- *fun, great atmosphere*

Write a **letter** of between 120 and 180 words in an appropriate style. Do not include any postal addresses.

It is important not to waste time or space writing addresses. You must begin with *Dear ......*, and finish appropriately with *Yours sincerely* or *Yours faithfully*.

UNIT 5 Fear and loathing

1 **What frightens you?** Say how you feel about the things in the picture.

2 **Have you personally ever had a frightening experience?** If so, describe what happened to another student. If not, try to imagine a frightening situation and tell the story as though it really happened to you. You can use some of the words and phrases below.

> a bit uneasy/anxious/nervous/shocked/jumpy/
> tense/on edge
> scared stiff/scared to death
> absolutely terrified/petrified
> hair-raising/spine-chilling/creepy/scary/spooky
> to panic/to become hysterical/to go to pieces
> to go white/pale/to go rigid with fear

3 Write a title on the board that summarises the experience or story you have just heard. Look at all the titles as a class and choose the three most frightening ones. The students who have listened to these accounts should tell the class what happened.

NOT DONE

Listening

4 🎧 Listen to this recording, where a man is talking about something frightening that happened to him. Say where the man was and how long he spent there.

Now listen again and describe in detail what happened to the man. Use these questions to help you.

1 Why was he in the building?
2 What time of day was it?
3 How far did the lift go?
4 Which two things did he try to do?
5 Why was he there for so long?

E xam spot

Part 1 of Paper 4 consists of eight short extracts. For each extract, there is one multiple choice question. The eight questions will test different things, for example who is speaking, how he or she feels, where the recording is taking place, or what it is about.

5 Here is the question for the extract you have just heard.

   1 You will hear a man talking about something frightening that happened to him. What was his first reaction?
     A He sat down and cried.
     B He decided to call for help.
     C He tried to keep calm.

All three options are mentioned in the extract. Listening out for sequence words – that is, words which tell you what happened when – will help you to decide what his **first** reaction was.

🎧 Listen once more to the extract and note down any sequence words and phrases. Which one signals the answer?

6 🎧 Now look at these questions. Before you listen, think about the words in bold and decide what you will need to listen out for.

   2 You will hear a woman talking about something that happened in her home. When was she **most** scared?
     A When she heard a burglar upstairs.
     B While she was watching a horror film.
     C When she suddenly saw a frog.

   3 You hear a man talking about how to deal with fear. **Who** is he?
     A a teacher
     B an ex-pilot
     C an actor

   4 You hear a woman describing what happened to her on a journey. **Where** did she **end up** that night?
     A on a country road
     B in hospital
     C at her house

   5 You hear a man being interviewed about a sailing accident. What was the **worst** part of his experience?
     A becoming cold
     B feeling hungry
     C avoiding sharks

   6 You hear a woman talking on the radio about an incident abroad. **Why** was she able to **escape**?
     A She was by the door.
     B She wasn't noticed.
     C She had a radio.

7 🎧 How much can you remember about the last account? Discuss with a partner what happened and note down everything in the order it happened. Then listen to the recording again to check your notes.

Pronunciation

8 In the extracts you have just heard, there are a number of examples of verbs with regular past tense endings. Although the spelling of these is always the same, -ed, the pronunciation is different, according to which letter precedes the ending.

🎧 Listen to extract 1 again. All the regular verbs which occur in it are listed below in order. Underline the verbs which contain the sound /ɪd/, for example, *started*.

pressed	screamed
noticed	hammered
started	helped
shuddered	realised
pushed	happened
lifted	called
shouted	

Can you explain the reason for the /ɪd/ ending?

G rammar extra

This unit revises past tenses. Before the next lesson, copy and complete the table of irregular forms. All the verbs below have occurred in the listening extracts. An example is given.

Infinitive	Past tense	Past participle
become	became	(has/had) become

burst   buy   creep   drive   find   get   hear   hold
keep   know   run   see   shake   sink   spend   take
think   weep

Which verb has the same form throughout?
Do you know any other verbs which are like that?

G ⋯⟶ **page 200**

Review of past tenses

1 Look at examples a–j, which come from the listening in 5.1. Decide which tenses they contain. Where there are two different tenses in the same sentence, list both.

past simple	(PS)
past continuous	(PC)
present perfect tense	(P)
past perfect tense	(PP)

a I'd had this interview for a job.
b I got in the lift and pressed the button.
c I've never been in one since.
d I was watching a horror movie.
e It was her footsteps I had heard.
f While I was putting the books away, I found something else.
g The others were looking at a map on the table, but I was standing by the back window.
h I knew they hadn't seen me.
i When I realised they had gone, I ran inside.
j You have recently sailed around the world.

Look again at the examples containing two different tenses. Can you explain why each tense is used? Think about when each action happened.

Past simple/Past continuous

The most important difference between these two tenses is the duration of an action. For example, in example *f* above, the past continuous describes an action that happened over a longer time period than the second action, which happened at a specific moment and may have interrupted the longer continuous activity:

————————X————————

While I was putting the books away ... I found something else.

Like the present continuous tense, the past continuous is used to describe temporary situations, as in example *d*.

————————————————X

I was watching a horror movie. ... I turned off the TV.

Note that this use can be an effective way of setting the scene at the beginning of a story, as in example *g*.

————————————————X

The others were looking at a map ... Six of them burst in .

2 Complete this text using the verbs in brackets, in either the past simple or past continuous tense.

Quite late one evening I (**1**) .... (walk) home alone from college. The wind (**2**) .... (blow) hard and it (**3**) .... (pour) with rain, so there (**4**) .... (be) no one around. Anyway, this big black van (**5**) .... (drive) past me and (**6**) .... (stop), just where the road (**7**) .... (curve) round. I (**8**) .... (decide) to go on, though I (**9**) .... (feel) increasingly uneasy. However, as soon as I (**10**) .... (get) close to the van, it (**11**) .... (drive) off. This (**12**) .... (happen) twice more further down the same road. Each time, the van (**13**) .... (pull up) fifty metres ahead of me, (**14**) .... (wait) until I almost (**15**) .... (draw up) with it and then (**16**) .... (pull away) again. By this stage I (**17**) .... (be) absolutely petrified. So I (**18**) .... (stand) for a moment under a tree. The rain (**19**) .... (come down) in torrents now. I (**20**) .... (shake) and (**21**) .... (wonder) what to do next, when a policeman (**22**) .... (come) past. He (**23**) .... (push) his bike because of the heavy rain. I (**24**) .... (grab) him by the arm and (**25**) .... (make) him stop. Then I completely (**26**) .... (go) to pieces. While he (**27**) .... (try) to calm me down, I (**28**) .... (hear) the van drive off, thankfully for the last time. I've never walked home on my own since.

Past simple/Past perfect

The past perfect is used for actions in the past that occur earlier than the time period that is being described, as in example *i*:

When I realised they <u>had gone</u>, I ran inside.

3 Complete these sentences with the verbs in brackets, in either the past simple or past perfect tense.

a We .... (spend) the previous night in a really creepy hotel in the middle of nowhere, so we .... (decide) to stay in a place in town.

b Jenny .... (tell) us in great detail what .... (happen) to her on the mountain and .... (explain) why she .... (find) it so scary up there.

c I .... (keep) still for over half an hour and I .... (think) it .... (be) safe at last to come out of my hiding place.

G ⋯⋗ page 200

4 Look at this set of four film stills from an action movie. Describe what happened in each scene, starting with the last one (4), and making reference back to what had happened in the earlier stills. Remember to use a range of past tenses.

5 Read this extract from the thriller *The Big Sleep*, ignoring the spaces for the moment. Why do you think the man telling the story wasn't frightened of the gun? Turn to page 45 to find out if you are right!

The gun pointed at my chest. Her hand seemed to **(0)** ....be............ quite steady. I laughed **(1)** .... her. I started to walk towards her. I saw her small finger tighten on **(2)** .... trigger and grow white at the tip.

I was about six feet away from her **(3)** .... she started to shoot. The sound **(4)** .... the gun made a sharp slap, a brittle crack in the sunlight. I didn't see any smoke. I stopped again **(5)** .... grinned at her.

She fired twice more, very quickly. I don't think **(6)** .... of the shots would have missed. There were five in the little gun. She **(7)** .... fired four. I rushed her.

I didn't want the last one in my face, **(8)** .... I swerved to one side. She gave it to me quite carefully, **(9)** .... worried at all.

I straightened up. 'My, but you're cute,' I said.

Her hand **(10)** .... holding the empty gun and began to shake violently. The gun fell **(11)** .... of it. Her mouth began to shake. Then her whole face **(12)** .... to pieces.

6 Now fill in each space choosing a suitable word from the box below. There are three words you do not need.

and	any	at	because	had	has
not	of	out	so	some	the	was
went	when				

Can you put these words into grammatical categories? For example, *and* is a conjunction. These words are typical of the kinds of words that are tested in Part 2 of Paper 3.

Exam folder 3

NOT DONE

Paper 3 Part 2 Open cloze

In this part of the Use of English paper you are asked to complete a text containing 15 spaces. The missing word is usually a grammar word, but there may be one or two vocabulary items in this part of the paper. There is an example at the beginning of the passage.

It is very important to read through the text carefully before you decide to write anything down. Sometimes the answer to a space depends on what is said later in the paragraph. Many students lose marks for not reading through carefully enough. Also look at the title so you get some idea of what the text is about. The title is there to help you.

1 Read this text through at least twice and then choose the best title from the three below.

1 **DON'T TAKE THE RISK!**
2 **NOTHING TO WORRY ABOUT**
3 **BALANCING THE RISKS**

What are the chances of slipping (0) ...on... a banana skin, being hit by lightning or being struck by a meteorite? (1) .... are not the sort of unlucky events that most people (2) .... their time thinking about, (3) .... perhaps one has already happened to them.

However, (4) .... surprising number of people have, (5) .... some time in their lives, imagined aliens kidnapping them. Some even (6) .... recurring nightmares about it, whereas relatively (7) .... are afraid of dying from flu, even (8) .... it is a far more common experience. No doubt many people (9) .... go rock climbing or bungee jumping will be among the same people drinking bottled water on the grounds that it is safer (10) .... water from the tap.

Amazingly, our fear of flying outweighs our fear of driving, (11) .... the statistics show that going by plane is much safer. The best explanation is that people dread far (12) .... the possibility of dropping (13) .... of the air to being involved in a car crash.

(14) .... an attempt to educate us all in the real and imagined risks of life, the Department of Trade and Industry has asked scientists to construct a scale of risk that the public can use to compare any new and unfamiliar risks, (15) .... as those involved in taking new medicines, in terms of real events.

2   Now try to fill in the gaps. If you need help, look
    at the following clues.

   0 on (to slip on something)
   1 What is the subject of 'are'? 'They' isn't quite
          close enough, try something else.
   2 A collocation – 'to … time doing something'.
   3 A linker which means 'if not'– read the
          sentence very carefully.
   4 What kind of article should go here?
   5 A prepositional phrase. Which preposition?
   6 Which verb goes with 'nightmares'?
   7 'Some' began the sentence, now you have a
          contrast with 'relatively …'. How many?
   8 A linker – could be two possibilities here. Just
          write one down.
   9 Read the sentence carefully and you'll see that a
          relative pronoun is needed.
  10 A word used in comparisons.
  11 Another linker.
  12 A word used in comparisons.
  13 A preposition.
  14 A prepositional phrase. Which preposition?
  15 '… as' means 'for example'.

Advice

- Remember to think about what type of word is needed in the
  space, e.g. verb, preposition, article, pronoun.
- Check whether it should be singular or plural, past or present,
  etc.
- Check that when you add a word, it makes sense in the
  sentence and the text.
- You must only write **one** word.
- No contractions (*can't, don't*, etc.) are allowed.
- Your word must be correctly spelt.
- Always write something down, however difficult the gap may
  seem.

UNIT 6 What if?

E xam spot

In Part 3 of Paper 1, you will have to complete a *gapped text*, where sentences or paragraphs have been removed. This type of text has a clear development of ideas, and may also have a time sequence. You should look out for words that refer back and forwards in the text, such as *it* and *this*, as well as references to time. This will help you to fit the text together.

1 Read this quote from the article below and suggest what the article might be about. Which are the key words that help you to decide?

> **I normally arrive at the winner's home around Sunday lunchtime, having got up early and driven for hours. If I left on a Saturday, after the draw, I wouldn't get there until the middle of the night.**

2 Now read the article quickly to see if you are right. Ignore gaps 1–4 for the moment.

3 What is the writer's job? Read the article again and describe to a partner what the man does on Sunday. Notice the time references in the article.

4 These four sentences have been removed from the article. Which two include a time reference? Use this information to help you fit sentences A–D into the correct gaps (1–4).

> A The bigger the win, the more mood swings there are.
>
> B All this is very understandable.
>
> C My initial visit lasts about two hours.
>
> D Then the subject of publicity comes up.

Which sentence refers back to the previous paragraph?

I usually arrive to find about eight adults sitting waiting, plus a lot of kids. It's always a very crowded room and the atmosphere is pretty tense. My nerves are on edge, too. The first thing I say is 'Can I take my jacket off?' and they always say 'Would you like a cup of tea?'

1 [ ] Then I leave them to it, having given them a little handbook we've prepared called *Out of the blue – it's you!* They seldom bother to read it but they tend to feel that by holding it they've established some sort of bond with us – the whole thing becomes more real to them because they've actually got something in their hands.

I check into a local hotel, leaving them to talk among themselves, then return later that evening. On this second visit, I usually have to go over all the same points I did the first time around. It seems they can't take things in because of the shock.

2 [ ] Winners often burst into tears when the press call. If I'm still in the house, I always go to the door and deal with reporters. In many ways, the effect of a sudden win is similar to that of a sudden death in the family.

Immediately, everything in their life changes. There's confusion, anxiety, emotional panic – they don't know what to do next, what the future holds, how to behave or where to go.

The behaviour of jackpot winners the first week is fairly standard. They won't be able to sleep, they'll pick at their food. Curiously, there can also be a sense of guilt. They'll sometimes say 'I didn't want to win this much, you know. If I'd won less, I'd have been much happier. Why did it happen to me?'

3 [ ] Most people buy lottery tickets for the fun of it, they never really expect to win. If they do win big money, they don't know how to cope. So it's vital for me to take my time, go slowly, repeat everything. If I appear to be in control, it gives them more confidence.

The first important question I'm asked by winners is 'When will we get the money?' They're often surprised when I reply 'Tomorrow!' But it's true. If they take their ticket to Camelot's regional office on the Monday, they'll get the money, immediately.

4 [ ] I make it clear that it's completely their decision. I just try to point out the pros and cons. I go over the chances of them keeping their win secret. I ask how many friends and relations they've already told – which is usually lots – and they say 'But if any of our friends were asked for information, they wouldn't talk.' They don't like it when I suggest the opposite. Once, two tabloid newspapers were offering £10,000 for such information. There are very few people who can resist that kind of temptation, friends or not.

Personally speaking, if I won the jackpot I'd go public. With luck, you can control the publicity. Otherwise, eventually it leaks out and you have no control. One of my winners has managed to keep it a secret so far, but mentally he's in a really terrible state. He's paranoid – he thinks people are following him, he is suspicious of everyone, he can't sleep for recurring nightmares. He's scared to buy a new car in case people start asking him questions. The poor bloke's life has been turned upside down and he's gained nothing, except the money in the bank, of course.

Grammar extra

*I **normally** arrive around Sunday lunchtime ...*

Normally is an adverb, which gives you information about the frequency of the action.

Find six more adverbs of frequency in the article. Look at where they occur in each sentence and use this information to complete the statements below.

In sentences containing the present simple or past simple tenses, the adverb goes .... the verb, except for the verb .... When this verb is used to form continuous tenses, the adverb again goes .... it. Where an auxiliary verb is used to form other tenses, e.g. *have* and *will*, the adverb goes .... it.

Now insert suitable adverbs of frequency into these sentences and finish them so that they are true for you.

a On Sundays, I get up late, because ....

b I've been frightened of spiders, which is why ....

c When I was younger, I enjoyed playing board games, but now ....

d I'm good at remembering people's names and this is ....

e I wish I could win a lot of money because ....

G ⋯⟩ page 200

---

5 Scan the article to answer these questions about lottery winners. Use the time clues in the questions to direct you to the right part of the article.

a Why does the man have to repeat things during his second visit?
b How do jackpot winners behave initially?
c What usually happens when the man first arrives at the house?
d When can winners claim their prizes?

6 Explain the meaning of these words and phrases from the article, guessing their meaning from context if necessary. The line numbers are given in brackets.

a bond (14)
b cope (46)
c in control (49)
d resist (69)
e leak out (74)
f paranoid (77)
g suspicious (79)
h recurring (80)

Find the phrase *emotional panic* (line 32). What exactly does this mean?
Underline any other words connected with **emotion** in the same paragraph.

7 Look closely at the final two paragraphs of the article and discuss these questions.

Should lottery winners receive so much publicity?
What are the pros and cons of winning the lottery?
If you won the jackpot, would you go public?

Useful language
As I see it ...
To my mind ...
In my opinion ...
For one thing ... .
For another thing ...
On the one hand ... .
On the other hand ...
The main advantage is ...
One drawback is ...

Conditionals with *if*

1 🎧 You are going to listen to four short extracts, where people talk about winning the lottery. How would their lives change if they won?

2 These examples from the article in 6.1 are all conditional sentences. Say what the contracted verb forms are in each sentence and explain how the sentences differ in their use of tenses.

   a If I won the jackpot, I'd go public.
   b If I'd won less, I'd have been much happier.
   c If they do win big money, they don't know how to cope.
   d If they take their ticket to Camelot's regional office on the Monday, they'll get the money.

   Match a–d to these descriptions of conditional types 0–3.

   0 A situation that happens often.
   1 A situation that may happen in the future.
   2 A situation that is unlikely to happen.
   3 A situation that could have happened in the past, but didn't.

3 Here are some more examples of conditional sentences. Match the two halves of each sentence.

   1 If you did more revision, …
   2 If it snows, …
   3 If I have time, …
   4 If Helen comes round, …
   5 If there had been a vote, …
   6 If they finish early, …
   7 If you swam regularly, …
   8 If I'd known about the risk, …

   a we'll get the toboggan out.
   b she'll be able to tell you.
   c Sam and Bernie usually have a coffee.
   d you'd pass the exam.
   e I'd never have eaten seafood.
   f they would have lost.
   g I like to walk to work.
   h your body would be in better shape.

4 Find eight errors in this text, underline them and write the correct tense form at the side of each line. An example is given.

> Yesterday was a very bad day. If it <u>wasn't</u> raining, perhaps it   hadn't been
> wouldn't have been so difficult. But it poured all day and I had real
> problems. I needed to get to an important meeting, but the car broke
> down on the way. If I had it serviced regularly, I know it won't be so
> unreliable, but garages charge so much for servicing these days that I
> don't bother. Never mind, I thought, if I'll find a phone box, I'll be able
> to call the breakdown company. Well, I did find one – two, in fact – but
> they were both out of order. These days, if you need to phone someone,
> you really couldn't rely on public phone boxes. I thought to myself, if I
> would have a mobile phone, I wouldn't be in this situation now. By this
> time, I was in a panic. What will my boss say if I didn't get to the
> meeting? With him, if people are even five minutes late, he will really
> have it in for them. So I didn't waste any more time. Luckily, a taxi
> pulled up. 'Mason Square,' I shouted, 'and if you will do the journey
> in under ten minutes, I'll pay you double!' 'Forget it,' said the driver,
> 'there's total gridlock in the centre of town. If you would pay me
> twenty pounds, I couldn't get you there in time.' So I ended up late for
> the meeting and yes, the boss was furious with me. It was a disastrous day.

5 Talk to a partner. Take it in turns to finish these sentences in a suitable way. Then tell the class what your friend said.

a If I get up early tomorrow, …
b If I had enough money, …
c My life would be a lot easier if, …
d If I hadn't come to class today, …

G ⋯⋕ page 200

Vocabulary Phrases with *in*

6 All these phrases have come up in this unit. Check you know their meaning with a partner. Then choose four of them to complete the sentences below.

take (something) in	in fact
in control	in case
in a state/in a panic	have it in for (someone)
in time	

a I don't want to go to that restaurant tonight. ………………………… , I never want to go there again!
b Always take your umbrella ………………………… it rains.
c People who work at home often feel more ………………………… of their time.
d Are we ………………………… for the 7.15 performance?

Write three example sentences containing the other phrases.

e ……………………………………………………………
f ……………………………………………………………
g ……………………………………………………………

7 Look at the words in the box. They form four sets and each four words have a similar meaning. Can you group them into the four categories in the table? Be careful: some words can be more than one part of speech. Think carefully about their meanings when you decide which category to put them into.

Nouns	Verbs	Prepositions	Adjectives

on	tiny	received	experiment
by	light	in	accepted	trial
gathered	try	welcomed	delicate
to	gentle	attempt	

Now read the short newspaper article below. There are four spaces in it. Decide which part of speech is required in each space. Then choose the correct option to fill each one from your four sets of words.

Could it possibly be YOU?

THE NATIONAL LOTTERY

Camelot is to make a final **(1)** ………………… today to track down the winner of an unclaimed £2.1 million jackpot prize. A **(2)** ………………… plane will fly over Hull trailing the banner: '£2 million winner – is it you?' for two hours at lunch time.

The city became the focus of attention after a local newspaper **(3)** ………………… an unsigned letter from an elderly local widow saying she did not want the prize. Her reason was that 'the fuss would finish me off'. If the money is not claimed **(4)** ………………… 11pm it will go into the lottery's good causes fund.

Writing folder 3

Stories 1

In Part 2 of Paper 2, you may be asked to write a short story. The first or last sentence of the story is given in the question and you must remember to include this. Make sure that the story you write fits with the sentence.

1   Look at these two questions. Discuss with a partner what tenses you would need to use in each story.

a   You have been asked to write a short story for your college magazine. The story must begin with the following sentence:

If he hadn't answered the phone, it would have been just another ordinary day.

b   You have decided to enter a short story competition. The rules say that the story must end with the following sentence:

Suddenly, he woke up and realised it had been a nightmare.

2   Now read this sample answer, which works for both questions. Notice which tenses have been used. You can ignore the underlined words and spaces for the moment.

If he hadn't answered the phone, it would have been just another ordinary day. But he had lifted the receiver and had heard the news that turned his life upside down. His girlfriend had been taken hostage and her kidnappers were demanding $1,000,000.

He was in shock but he still moved fast. He found his father's gun and (1) <u>went</u> out of the flat. A bus was pulling away and he managed to jump on. He travelled downtown to the city's biggest bank. As he (2) <u>went</u> in through the glass doors, people looked at him (3).................................
Then someone noticed the gun and screamed. 'If you don't move, you won't get hurt,' he shouted (4).. 'I want a million dollars, now. Hand it over.' He waved the gun around (5)...

They stuffed the cash from the safe in a bag. He grabbed it, left the building and headed for the river, where the kidnappers were waiting. He ran and ran, endlessly, but the river got further and further away. He was crying now.

Suddenly, he woke up and realised it had been a nightmare.

3   Look at numbers 1 and 2 in the text. To get a good mark in the exam, you need to use a range of vocabulary. Choose suitable words to replace the ones given from the sets below. These words have all come in previous units so you should know them!

1   **A** rushed   **B** shuddered   **C** hammered
    D stomped
2   **A** carried   **B** threw   **C** burst   **D** turned

Now choose suitable adverbs for spaces 3–5, from the ones below. More than one answer is possible. Decide with a partner which three words fit best together.

anxiously	desperately	nervously
suspiciously	tragically	wildly

4 Look at the picture sequence below and re-arrange sentences a–i in the order of the pictures. Then include suitable sentence openers from 1–6 where needed. There is one extra.

a … a crowd of people had gathered and were watching her anxiously as she struggled to reach the bank.

b … she heard someone whimpering below her and when she looked down from the bridge, she saw a small boy in the deepest part of the river, waving his arms helplessly.

c … she thought he was dead but when he coughed and his legs started to move, she knew she had saved his life.

d It was a fast-flowing river and she had to swim harder than she had ever swum before, to get to him before it was too late.

e As Jean walked towards the bridge, she was thinking of all the things she could do now that the school holidays had arrived.

f Although he was panicking, she was able to grab him and she started to pull him back to the bank.

g It was a beautiful summer's day, the sun was shining and the birds were singing.

h … she jumped off the bridge and dived into the rushing water.

i … she managed it and threw both herself and the boy onto the warm grass.

1 Eventually
2 Suddenly
3 Without a second thought
4 By now / then
5 At first
6 Last but not least

5 Now do this writing task.

You have decided to enter a short story competition. The rules say that the story must begin with the following sentence:

As soon as he got out of the car, Martin felt uneasy.

Write your **story** in 120–180 words.

Spend a few minutes noting down ideas for your story and then discuss your notes with a partner. Suggest how your partner's story could be improved. Then list relevant vocabulary you could both use, including a range of verbs, adjectives and adverbs.

Write your story, being careful to include the given sentence accurately and where you are told to.

After you have written your story, remember to check the spelling, punctuation and grammar.

Topic review

1   Together with a partner, read these sentences and discuss which are true for you, giving more details. Try to use as much of the vocabulary and language as you can from the units you have just studied.

   a   I always get out of bed early in the morning.
   b   If I had some money the first thing I would buy is a fast car.
   c   I'm worse at English than I am at Maths.
   d   I'm always getting into trouble for forgetting things.
   e   I'm not afraid of anything!
   f   I think I'm broad-minded.
   g   I must try to work harder.
   h   I like to follow fashion.
   i   Books interest me more than computer games.
   j   Package holidays are not for me.

Grammar

2   Use only one word to fill each of the spaces in the following passage.

Most (1) .... us go a little crazy when we jet off (2) .... holiday but some, it would seem, go completely mad. They see giant rats eating through their luggage and even lose their mother-in-law in (3) .... back of a stolen caravan. So says WorldCover Direct, the holiday insurer.

These are just (4) .... of the claims the company (5) .... received in the past twelve months.

A director said: 'One of our policyholders skied into a tree (6) .... he was on holiday and made a claim (7) .... injuries. What he didn't mention was that he (8) .... blind and in the process of testing a new radar system for blind skiers.'

But what (9) .... you were in the Mediterranean in August and had had (10) .... sun for the day? Take a dip in the pool, sit in the shade for a while – or phone your holiday insurance company requesting repatriation (11) .... you are 'feeling a bit hot?' One holiday maker, (12) .... was in Spain, chose the last (13) .... was refused. Another policyholder made a claim because he and (14) .... wife had missed their flight. He failed to mention that she was prevented (15) .... boarding because she had a baby pig in her hand luggage!

Phrasal verbs

3   Complete the following sentences using the appropriate verb.

   UP
   a   If Elizabeth had been able to .... up just a little more money, she would have bought a faster computer.
   b   When you manage to find his address, ... me up and let me know what it is.
   c   Come just as you are, there's really no need to .... up.
   d   We followed the signs to the beach without having any idea of where the road would .... up.
   e   I don't know how you .... up with the noise from your neighbours – it would drive me mad!

   OUT
   f   Tourist guides often carry umbrellas so that they .... out in a crowd.
   g   Sheila decided to get a travel agent to .... out all her holiday arrangements, rather than trying to book the tickets herself.
   h   Pete spent a long time trying to .... out how to get his dog to stop barking.
   i   'I don't know how you can .... out looking like that,' Sue's mother said.
   j   It was so foggy last night I could hardly .... out the lines on the road.

Now look at these mixed examples and replace the verb or phrase in italics with a phrasal verb or compound noun. You may have to add another extra word.

k If you want to look good in that outfit, you'll have *to reduce* the amount of chocolate you eat.

l The newspaper is saying that there has been *an improvement* in British Airways' share price.

m I really hate shops that make you feel guilty when *you return* clothes that shrink in the wash or fall to pieces.

n We decided *to start the journey* to the castle at midnight, in the hope of seeing the ghost.

o He was in hospital for a while but he's now back at work – it didn't seem to take him long *to recover from* being bitten by that dog.

Revision of present and past tenses

4 Read through this text and put the verbs in the correct tense.

The statistics on the safety of flying **(1)** ...... (BE) immensely comforting. It **(2)** ...... (SEEM) that the chances of being involved in an accident **(3)** ...... (BE) a million to one – the equivalent of flying safely every day for 95 years. Try telling that to the white-faced, petrified aerophobic, who **(4)** ...... (SEE) every frown on a stewardess's face as a portent of disaster. For some years now, psychologist Henry Jones **(5)** ...... (TRY) to tell them, and he **(6)** ...... (DO) a lot more besides. He **(7)** ...... (DEVELOP) both a theory and practice for treating air travel anxiety. Apparently, it **(8)** ...... (BE) a widespread phobia. One American survey **(9)** ...... (PUT) it as the fourth most common fear, preceded only by snakes, heights and storms. Jones **(10)** ...... (HAVE) nearly 500 clients during the last decade. Before they **(11)** ...... (COME) to him, some of his clients **(12)** ...... (never FLY), others **(13)** ...... (HAVE) just one bad experience after years of flying. One man **(14)** ...... (TAKE) over 200 flights a year for five years and **(15)** ...... (never WORRY) up till then. Then, one day on a flight to Chicago the pilot **(16)** ...... (ANNOUNCE) that they **(17)** ...... (GO) to turn back because of an engine fault. The man **(18)** ...... (HAVE) a panic attack and **(19)** ...... (TRY) to get off the plane in mid-air. After Jones's course, the man **(20)** ...... (OVERCOME) his fears and **(21)** ...... (MANAGE) to fly again.

5 Complete the second sentence so that it has a similar meaning to the first sentence using the word given. Do not change the word given. You must use between two and five words, including the word given.

1 Andrea said she would only go dancing if her mother bought her a new outfit.
   unless
   Andrea said she .... her mother bought her a new outfit.

2 I have never seen such a terrible film before.
   worst
   This is the .... seen.

3 I'm sorry I didn't meet you at the airport – my car wasn't working.
   met
   I .... at the airport, if my car had been working.

4 This party is 'evening dress' only.
   allowed
   You .... dress casually for this party.

5 I'm not as frightened of flying as I am of ghosts!
   than
   I'm .... I am of flying.

6 It was a mistake for me to buy you that computer game.
   bought
   I .... that computer game.

7 The play started before we could get there.
   had
   The play .... when we got there.

8 I need to wear glasses to drive.
   see
   I can't .... my glasses.

5.2 exercise 4
The man talks about the incident later in the story. He says:
'All five chambers are empty. She fired them all. She fired them all at me. From a distance of five or six metres. Cute little thing, isn't she? Too bad I had loaded the gun with blanks.' He grinned nastily.

UNIT 7 Life's too short

Gerunds and infinitives 1

1 Identify the equipment in pictures a–n, and name each sport.

2 With a partner ask and answer the following questions, using a complete sentence.

   a What sport can't you stand watching?
   b What sports do you really enjoy watching?
   c What sportsperson are you keen on seeing play?
   d What sports have you either taken up or given up recently?
   e Do you mind watching a sport if the weather is cold and windy?
   f Do you feel more like playing sports on holiday than during the rest of the year?

3 A gerund, which is a verb used as a noun, always ends in *-ing*, but not all *-ing* forms are gerunds. They can be present participles or adjectives as well. What is the *-ing* form in these sentences?

   a John pulled on the climbing rope to show he was safe.
   b Anna was running along the track when she tripped and fell.
   c Snowboarding is a very popular sport.

4 Look at these sentences:

   a I enjoy going swimming.
   b After learning to ice-skate, I'm going to learn to play ice hockey.
   c I want to take up playing golf.
   d Climbing is a fairly safe sport nowadays.
   e It's not worth going to watch our local football team because they always lose!

Find an example of a gerund above which:
1 follows a preposition.
2 is the subject of the sentence.
3 follows an expression.
4 follows a verb.
5 follows a phrasal verb.

5 When we put a verb after a preposition, we usually use a gerund. Complete the following sentences with a preposition and one of the verbs below.

learn	teach	drop	get	do	play	swim

   a She had difficulty .... to the meeting on time.
   b Steve is very proud .... to do deep sea diving so quickly.
   c I'm very keen .... the children to ride their bikes.
   d The boy was in trouble .... his muddy sports clothes on the changing room floor.
   e No one seems to believe .... enough exercise these days.
   f You don't have to be good .... to enjoy it.
   g I'm looking forward .... against him again soon.

G ⋯⋗ page 201

6 Infinitives are forms like (*to*) *do*, (*to*) *say*. They are usually used with 'to', but not always.

Look at the following sentences which show the more common uses of the infinitive.

a I'm going to the pool *to have* my swimming lesson.
b I want *to enrol* for netball practice next term.
c They are unlikely *to hold* the Olympics in Cambridge.
d They let me *do* the judo classes even though I had never done it before.
e You must not *run* with the ball in some sports.
f We encouraged them *to run* faster by cheering loudly.

Now say which of the above:

1 follows an adjective?
2 follows a modal auxiliary?
3 follows a main verb?
4 is used to express purpose?
5 has an infinitive without 'to'?
6 follows the object of a verb?

G ···⟩ page 201

7 Read through this letter and put the verbs in brackets in the correct form and give your reasons. Some answers may need an extra word.

Dear Jill,

I've just got back from **(1)** .... (climb) Mont Blanc in the Alps and I must **(2)** .... (tell) you what a great time I had. On **(3)** .... (arrive) in Chamonix we were introduced to our guides. We were then kitted out with ice-axes, crampons and climbing boots and were sent straight out into two days' **(4)** .... (train) in and around the Le Tour glacier. The guides used this time **(5)** .... (assess) our ability **(6)** .... (make) the ascent and **(7)** .... (teach) us the basics of **(8)** .... (mountaineer), such as how **(9)** .... (make) an ice-axe and teamwork **(10)** .... (count) in our favour.

The first day consisted of **(11)** .... (climb) for five hours from the Nid d'Aigle to the Gouter Hut. I thought I'd be too cold **(12)** .... (sleep) but in fact that wasn't a problem at all! Day 2 started at 2 am with a four and a half hour walk to the summit. **(13)** .... (reach) the summit was only a third of the day's work. The descent route down included **(14)** .... (jump) across gaps in the ice and took seven hours.

I'm really looking forward **(15)** .... (see) you next weekend so I can **(16)** .... (tell) you all the details.

Love, Sue

8 Complete the second sentence so that it has a similar meaning to the first sentence, using the word given. **Do not change the word given.** You must use between two and five words, including the word given.

1 The newspapers said that he had pushed the other player.
accused
The newspapers .... the other player.

2 The pitch isn't dry enough to play on.
too
The pitch .... play on.

3 It wasn't easy for me to learn how to paraglide.
difficulty
I .... how to paraglide.

4 'I wouldn't go diving by yourself, if I were you,' the instructor said.
advised
The instructor .... diving by myself.

5 I prefer to go on walking holidays than lie on a crowded beach.
rather
I .... walking holidays than lie on a crowded beach.

6 'You must play by the rules!' the coach shouted at us.
insisted
The coach .... by the rules.

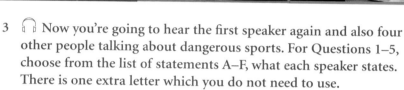

1 Discuss these questions with a partner.

a Who do you think is the greatest football player/swimmer/skier/athlete/tennis player/boxer of all time? Why?

b Do you think that some sports are easier than others? Why?

c What sports would you consider to be dangerous? Why?

d Have you ever seen or tried a dangerous sport? What was it?

Notice that when you talk about sport you usually ask 'Which sport do you do?' and you say, 'I go swimming', 'I play football'. Which sports do you use with 'go' and which with 'play'?

3 🎧 Now you're going to hear the first speaker again and also four other people talking about dangerous sports. For Questions 1–5, choose from the list of statements A–F, what each speaker states. There is one extra letter which you do not need to use.

Speaker 1 [1]   Speaker 3 [3]   Speaker 5 [5]
Speaker 2 [2]   Speaker 4 [4]

A I'm always looking for something new.
B I've always enjoyed taking risks.
C It's not as dangerous as some ordinary sports.
D Knowing I might be killed makes it more enjoyable.
E It puts some excitement in my life.
F I wanted to prove to everyone that I could do it.

4 What dangerous sports do they mention? Are they popular in your country?

5 Match the sport with the place.

a track   1 golf
b pitch   2 athletics
c course   3 tennis
d court   4 football
e rink   5 skiing
f slopes   6 ice-skating

Listening

2 🎧 Listen to this extract, where a woman is talking about a sport she has recently taken up. As you listen, try to work out what the sport is. What clues did you hear?

Pronunciation

6 🎧 In the extracts you have just heard there are some examples of question tags. Listen to these sentences.

That <u>could</u> be pretty scary, <u>couldn't it?</u>
I guess they <u>needed</u> to have a bit of excitement in their lives, <u>didn't they?</u>

Question tags are formed from the auxiliary verb and the personal pronoun. We use it when we are not sure of something or to ask for agreement. If the sentence is positive then the tag is usually negative and vice versa.

Steve's played football for ten years, <u>hasn't he?</u>
She couldn't get a place on the team, <u>could she?</u>

Quite often the tag isn't a real question.

EXAMPLE: *It's a nice day, isn't it?* →

This is usually used by English people to start a conversation at a bus-stop or on a train. Don't just answer with 'yes' or 'no'!

The following tags often cause problems.

a Somebody's here, aren't they? (*Somebody/everybody/nobody* take '*they*')

b Nobody's coming, are they? (*nobody* is negative)

c Let's go swimming, shall we? (*let's* means '*we shall*')

d It hardly/scarcely ever rains here, does it? (*hardly* and *scarcely* are negative)

e That's the man, isn't it? (Subject is '*that*')

f He'd rather go skiing, wouldn't he? (*would rather*)

g I'd better get some new trainers, hadn't I? (*had better*)

h I've got better at running, haven't I? (*have got* = possession)

i She has lunch at 12.00, doesn't she? (full verb)

j Don't do that, will you? (polite order)

🎧 The meaning of a question tag changes with the intonation. Compare examples a and b.

a 'It's a nice day, isn't it?'

b 'You haven't got change for £5, have you?'
In *a*, which isn't a real question, the intonation is falling, whereas in *b*, where it is a real question, the intonation rises.

7 You are the Editor of a local newspaper. Interview someone in the class for a job as a sports reporter on your paper. Find out as much as you can about them (where they live, what sports they play or enjoy watching, how old they are, etc.). First of all ask them questions to which you know the answer.

So, your name is ...., isn't it?
You're .... years old, aren't you?
You enjoy playing ...., don't you?

Then try asking some to which either you don't know or you're not sure of the answer.

You've worked in (country), haven't you?
You met (sportsman/woman) last year, didn't you?
You can play (sport), can't you?
You've visited (city), haven't you?

8 Decide what the question tag should be in these sentences.

a You'd rather go to the cinema than to a football match, ...?

b I'm awful at tennis, ...?

c You can't see where I hit the ball, ...?

d You will try to win, ...?

e Everyone wants to take part in the Olympics, ...?

f There will be a game on Saturday, ...?

g Don't forget the tickets, ...?

h You've got a racket, ...?

i You have a game tonight, ...?

9 Change the word in capitals to fit the sentence. Read through the text carefully before you do the exercise.

With some personal fitness trainers charging as much as £50 an hour, it's not surprising that only the rich and (1) .... (FAME) can afford the kind of one-to-one that will (2) .... (SURE) they work out enough to stay in shape. However, the idea that they are only for the elite is about to be shattered by *Get Motivated*, a new London-based company that charges just £15 for an hour with a (3) .... (QUALIFY) trainer. I decided to put this scheme to the test and asked *Get Motivated* to send a personal trainer to my home for a (4) .... (TRAIN) session. When 23 year old Stephanie arrived, I was sceptical about her (5) .... (YOUNG), but what followed was a very (6) .... (DEMAND) hour. Stephanie grew up in Australia and has a degree in human (7) .... (MOVE) studies and a diploma in (8) .... (EDUCATE) – the minimum (9) .... (QUALIFY) *Get Motivated* requires. Stephanie says that what appeals most to her about the GM scheme is that it gives her the (10) .... (FREE) to design her own sessions for clients.

Do you think you'd like a personal trainer? Why?/Why not?

10 You heard these words in the listening extracts. In pairs talk about what kind of words they are and then change them into nouns.

a dangerous
b frightened
c risky
d aggressive
e protective
f nervous
g terrifying
h exciting

Exam folder 4

Paper 3 Part 1
Multiple choice cloze

In this part of the Use of English paper you must choose one word or phrase from a set of four (A, B, C or D) to fill a space in the text. There are fifteen spaces and an example. The text always has a title, which will give you some help in telling you what it is about before you start reading.

Below are some examples of the type of words that are tested in this part of Paper 3.

Expressions

1 I .... to the conclusion, after failing to win any matches, that I would do better to give up playing tennis altogether.
   A drew   **B** got
   C formed   **D** came
   D is the right answer. The expression is to come to a conclusion. You can form a conclusion, draw a conclusion.

Verb/Adjective + preposition

2 I .... at the airport so late that my plane had already taken off.
   A got   **B** arrived
   C reached   **D** came
   B is the right answer. Came and get are followed by to; reached doesn't take a preposition.

Phrasal verbs

3 He was lucky to be kept .... at the factory when most of the other workers lost their jobs.
   A back   **B** on
   C off   **D** up
   B is the answer. To be kept on means to be retained in employment. The other phrasal verbs here, keep back, keep off and keep up all exist but mean something different.

Linking words

4 You'd better write your invitations to the party today .... you want people to reply by next week.
   A unless   **B** while
   C if   **D** otherwise
   C is the answer. Unless means if not, otherwise means or else and while is used in a different type of clause.

Vocabulary

5 I changed some of my money into foreign .... and also took some travellers' cheques.
   A income
   B funds
   C currency
   D revenue
   C is the right answer. All the other words are connected with money, but are used differently.

Advice

- Always read the text all the way through before you try to fill in any gaps.
- Make sure you read each sentence carefully so that you don't miss any important word.
- Always put down an answer even if you're not completely sure that it's correct.

For Questions 1–15, read the text below and decide which answer A, B, C or D, best fits each space. There is an example at the beginning (0).

Example:

0	**A** dates	**B** belongs	**C** exists	**D** comes

0	<u>A</u>	B	C	D

The History of Football

Football, or soccer, which is so popular all over the world, **(0)** .... back to the Middle Ages. At that **(1)** .... it was very different from the game we play today. Any number of players could **(2)** .... part and the matches usually developed into a free-for-all. In its modern **(3)** ...., football is less than two hundred years old.

In 1846, the first rules to govern the game were drawn **(4)** .... at Cambridge University. The number of players was **(5)** .... to 11 per side, which made things much more **(6)** .... than before. Later, in 1863, the Football Association was **(7)** .... up to help promote the game in Britain.

The game is played on a grass or artificial **(8)** .... with a goal net at each end. The **(9)** .... is to move the ball around the field, **(10)** .... the feet or head, until a player is in a **(11)** .... to put the ball into the net and score a goal.

Professional football is not only the most popular **(12)** .... sport in the world, **(13)** .... also more people actually play football themselves than any other team sport. In 1904 FIFA, the world governing **(14)** .... of football, was founded. It organises the World Cup tournament every four years. Other kinds of football are popular, but less **(15)** ...., for example American Football and Australian Rules Football.

	A	B	C	D
1	**A** season	**B** time	**C** term	**D** stage
2	**A** play	**B** make	**C** take	**D** do
3	**A** form	**B** shape	**C** fashion	**D** pattern
4	**A** out	**B** away	**C** up	**D** in
5	**A** limited	**B** checked	**C** counted	**D** defined
6	**A** tidy	**B** neat	**C** arranged	**D** orderly
7	**A** put	**B** set	**C** born	**D** called
8	**A** court	**B** pitch	**C** course	**D** track
9	**A** object	**B** reason	**C** focus	**D** purpose
10	**A** by	**B** to	**C** of	**D** with
11	**A** place	**B** point	**C** position	**D** spot
12	**A** witness	**B** audience	**C** spectator	**D** viewer
13	**A** because	**B** but	**C** while	**D** so
14	**A** body	**B** band	**C** collection	**D** group
15	**A** vast	**B** widespread	**C** enormous	**D** large

V ocabulary spot

When you learn new vocabulary, write it down in an organised way. Do not just write down an individual word with its translation into your language.

It's important to understand how a word is used, not just its meaning.

Verbs – Find out what comes after a verb. Is it a gerund/clause/infinitive with *to*/without *to*/a preposition?
Nouns – Is the noun countable or uncountable? This affects the grammar of the sentence.
Phrasal verbs – Learn the phrasal verb in context, that is, in a sentence.
Collocations – Organise these separately in sections according to topic or verb. For example, *to pay* – a bill, a compliment, attention *house* – household, housewife, housework

1 How do you feel about working conditions today? Do you think that things have got better or worse? Why?

2 Work with a partner and each look at one pair of photos. Say how you think going to work has changed in the last 100 years and why.

3 *Downsizing* is when a company reduces staff or offices in order to become more efficient. Skim the article to find out what **downshifting** is.

E**xam spot**

Part 2 of Paper 1 is a text with multiple choice questions, where you have to choose the answer to a question or finish a sentence from four given alternatives. You should read the text and the questions carefully, because this part of the exam tests detailed understanding. It is helpful to underline the words in the text which contain the answers to the questions.

4 Read the article again more carefully and answer question 1. Then look at the explanation below – were you right?

1 According to the writer, people are beginning to rethink their lives because
   A they feel too dependent on their possessions.
   B they are worried about the amount of rubbish they throw away.
   C they want to spend time doing other things.
   D their families object to their working so hard.

The answer is C. – 'leaving them precious little time or energy for family or leisure.'
A is likely but not the real reason.
B the writer is worried rather than the reader.
D is probably true but also not the answer to the question.

As you move around your home take a good hard look at its contents. It's likely that your living room will have a television set and a video, and your kitchen a washing machine and tumble drier, maybe also a microwave oven and electric toaster. Your bedroom drawers will be stuffed with almost three times as many clothes as you need. You almost certainly own a car and possibly a home computer, holiday abroad at least once a year and eat out at least once a week. If you could see the volume of rubbish in your dustbin over a year, you would be horrified.

Now, perhaps, more than ever before, people are wondering what life is all about, what it's for. The single-minded pursuit of material success is beginning to trouble large numbers of people around the world. They feel the long-hours work culture to make more money to buy more things is eating up their lives, leaving them precious little time or energy for family or leisure. Many are turning to alternative ways of living and downshifting is one of them.

According to a national consulting group, this new approach to work coincides with radical changes in the employment market, where a job is no longer guaranteed and lifetime employment can only be achieved by taking personal responsibility for your career.

Six per cent of workers in Britain took the decision to downshift last year, swapping their highly pressured, stressful positions for less demanding, less time-consuming work which they believe gives them a better-balanced life.

One couple who downshifted is Daniel and Liz. They used to work in central London. He was a journalist and she used to work for an international bank. They would commute everyday from their large house in the suburbs, leaving their two children with a nanny. Most evenings Daniel wouldn't get home until eight or nine o'clock, and nearly twice a month he would have to fly to New York for meetings. They both earned a large amount of money but began to feel that life was passing them by.

Nowadays, they run a farm in the mountains of Wales. 'I always wanted to have a farm here,' says Daniel, 'and we took almost a year to make the decision to downshift. It's taken some getting used to, but it's been worth it. We have to think twice now about spending money on car repairs and we no longer have any holidays. However, I think it's made us stronger as a family, and the children are a lot happier.'

Liz, however, is not totally convinced. 'I used to enjoy my job, even though it was hard work and long hours. I'm not really a country girl, but I suppose I'm gradually getting used to looking after the animals. One thing I do like though is being able to see more of my children. My tip for other people wanting to do the same is not to think about it too much or you might not do it at all.'

Now answer questions 2–4, underlining the words in the article that give you the correct answer, and saying why the other three choices are wrong.

2 What does the writer say about the employment market?
   A There aren't many jobs nowadays.
   B It's difficult to keep a company job for life.
   C You have to look hard to find a job yourself.
   D It's changing all the time.

3 When Daniel was a journalist he used to
   A live in central London.
   B dislike his job.
   C miss his children.
   D be highly paid.

4 Daniel and Liz both agree that the move
   A was difficult to organise.
   B has improved family life.
   C to a farm was expensive.
   D has been a total success.

There will often be a question on an item of vocabulary such as a word which is unusual or idiomatic, or one that is used by the writer in a special way. You should work out the meaning by looking at the context around the word itself.

5 What does the word 'tip' in line 64 mean?
   A a good idea   B a clue   C a word of advice
   D a warning

Sometimes a 'reference' question is included, which tests your understanding of words such as 'it' and 'this'. You must read the lines before and after the word carefully to decide what it is referring to.

6 What does 'it' in line 66 refer to?
   A her tip   B her job   C having animals
   D downshifting

You must read the lines before and after the 'it' carefully to decide what it is referring to.

The final question often asks 'Who was this text written by?' or 'Who is likely to read this text?', which tests your overall understanding.

7 Why was this text written?
   A To warn people of the problems of downshifting.
   B To tell people how to downshift.
   C To make people aware of a new social trend.
   D To prove that having a good job doesn't make you happy.

5 Do you think Daniel and Liz made the right decision? Why?/Why not? Are people beginning to downshift in your country? What are the advantages and disadvantages of downshifting?

6 Decide whether you think the following statements are true or false or whether you don't know. Then, in pairs, discuss your answers, using some of the expressions in the box opposite.

   a Modern working conditions are destroying the quality of life.
   b Most professional people suffer a great deal of stress.
   c Stress is worthwhile if you get what you want.
   d Success always brings happiness.
   e People are very materialistic nowadays.
   f Younger people see life completely differently from their parents.

7 Look at the article again and find words in each paragraph that are similar in meaning to the words below:

   Paragraph 1: amount   filled   appalled
   Paragraph 2: determined   hunt
   Paragraph 3: way   basic
   Paragraph 4: exchanging
   Paragraph 5: outskirts
   Paragraph 6: manage

Giving an opinion
Personally, I think that …
If you ask me, I …
On the one hand, I think that …, but on the other I think …
Well, first of all, … secondly …, finally …
Generally, I agree/disagree with …

Asking for an opinion
How do you feel about …?
Don't you agree that …?

Agreeing
I agree entirely.   You're right.
Absolutely!   Oh, quite!
Of course.

Disagreeing (Try not to say 'You're wrong!')
Well, I'm not sure I agree with you.
You have a point, but …
I understand your view, although I …
Mmm, I don't see it quite like that.

used to and *would*

1 Read examples a–c and then decide which rule(s) in 1–3 apply.

   a Daniel and Liz used to work in central London. (USED TO + DO)
   b They would commute every day. (WOULD + DO)
   c I'm gradually getting used to looking after the animals. (BE/GET USED TO + DOING)

   1 To talk about something in the past that doesn't happen now. This could be something permanent.
   2 To mean *to be/get accustomed to*.
   3 To talk about a repeated action in the past which doesn't happen now. Note that the action must be repeated and this form is normally used for narrative.

   Notice that *be used to* describes a state and *get used to* expresses a change in state.

2 Correct the following sentences, if necessary.

   a Some years ago the capital of South Vietnam would be Saigon.
   b People used to work very long hours in the steel industry.
   c Britain would have a large manufacturing industry.
   d I am gradually getting used to getting up early to get to work on time.
   e People are now used to working harder for less money.
   f It takes a long time to get used to do a new job.
   g Children would work down the mines in the nineteenth century.
   h My grandmother was used to work very long hours when she was a girl.
   i Families nowadays used to see less of their fathers.
   j When I worked for the BBC, I would have to start at 7.30 am.
   k John has never got used to having a woman boss.
   l I used to earn a large amount of money when I lived in New York.

   G ⋯⟶ page 201

Listening

3 🎧 In pairs, discuss what each of the jobs below involves. Then listen to the five extracts and decide which jobs the speakers used to do.

astronaut   chef   dentist   pop singer
detective   plumber   surgeon
window-cleaner   zoo-keeper

   Speaker 1 ☐ `1`
   Speaker 2 ☐ `2`
   Speaker 3 ☐ `3`
   Speaker 4 ☐ `4`
   Speaker 5 ☐ `5`

4 Imagine you have recently changed jobs. Tell your partner all about your old job, without saying what it was. Your partner has to guess the job.

Vocabulary

5 What jobs or professions are linked to these five places? For example, a bank has a manager, cashiers, secretaries, computer operators, a **security guard, etc.**

1 a cruise ship ....

2 a school ....

6 *Get* is a very common verb especially in spoken English and is often used instead of other verbs. Rewrite the sentences without using *get* either as a verb or in a phrase.

EXAMPLE: *Jon used to have a BMW, but now he's got a Mercedes.*

ANSWER: *Jon used to have a BMW, but now he owns a Mercedes.*

a Nurses have got to wear a uniform.
b They get breakfast in the canteen every morning.
c I'm getting promoted next month.
d We take it in turns in our department to get everyone coffee in the morning.
e I got a letter from my boss asking me to go to a conference in Los Angeles.
f Jane usually gets home from work about 7.30pm.
g Some students need to get their hair cut before they attend an interview.
h Sue has managed to get a man to come and service the photocopier on Tuesday.

3 a hospital ....

4 a department store ....

5 a sports centre ....

7 Phrasal verbs with *get*. Complete the sentences using the endings below.

my new boss   your exams
being made redundant   much money
his new job   his guards

a The prisoner got away from ....
b I get on well with ....
c I hope you get through ....
d He never got over ....
e My nephew is getting on well with

....
f While I'm doing an apprenticeship, I'll have to get by without ....

Now replace the phrasal verb in each sentence with a suitable form of one of these verbs.

making a success of	escape
like	manage
recover from	pass

8 Look back at the article in 8.1 and find four examples of compound adjectives. (These were covered in Unit 4.)

9 Make changes to these words, which have all come up in this unit.

a horrified ⟨ verb ....
                noun ....

b success ⟨ verb ....
               negative adjective ....

c energy ⟨ adjective ....
              adverb ....

d national ⟨ noun ....
                verb ....

e employment ⟨ negative adjective ....
                   verb ....

f responsibility ⟨ adverb ....
                      negative adjective ....

g decision ⟨ adjective ....
                verb ....

h commute ⟨ noun ....
               noun ....

Writing folder 4

Compositions 1

In Part 2 of Paper 2, you may be asked to write a discursive composition, that is one that argues for and/or against some topic, or one where you are asked your opinion. You are usually asked to write this composition following a class discussion on a topic. Here is an example of the type of question you may have.

Your teacher has asked you to write a composition giving your views on the following question:

Should companies give men and women equal opportunities to have time off work to look after their children?

Write your **composition**.

1   The following sentences are all from a composition on the subject above. Put them in the right order.

A This already happens in some parts of the world, particularly in Scandinavia, where both men and women are offered maternity leave.

B Not only would the family benefit from this flexibility, but also companies, which would have happier workers.

C In conclusion, therefore, I believe that both parents should be given the choice of deciding who will stay at home and who will go back to work.

D Although companies in my country, and men, might take a while to accept this idea, I think that it is an inevitable part of social change.

E In the past, and also nowadays in many countries, it was always the man who went out to work leaving his wife at home to take care of the children.

F I'd like to begin this composition by saying that I think both parents should be encouraged to take an active part in looking after their children.

G However, society is beginning to change and there needs to be more flexibility both at home and at work.

2   Now decide which sentences should go into:

Paragraph 1 – Introducing the topic
Paragraph 2 – Setting out the arguments or giving reasons
Paragraph 3 – Drawing a conclusion

3 Read this statement and the composition which follows:

People nowadays have to work too hard.

First of all, I'd like to say that, in general, the people in my country don't tend to work as hard as people in some other countries. Most of our population works in the service industry – in banks, hotels and insurance. **And** there is very little heavy industry and most manufacturing is fully automated. **And** they usually work about 35 hours a week and have four weeks' holiday a year. **But** in some countries the situation is totally different. People have to work in old-fashioned factories, which are dirty and likely to give them illnesses as they get older, or they work in the fields using animals rather than tractors. I think that people in my country have been lucky up until now. **But** things are beginning to change. There are fewer jobs and more people are out of work. **So** people have to work harder to keep their jobs and avoid being made redundant. **So**, in conclusion I'd like to say that I agree that people nowadays have to work too hard.

Decide which word or phrase you could use from the box below instead of the words in bold. For example for the first *And* you could use 'In addition', 'Moreover' or 'Furthermore', but you couldn't use 'As well as'. Why is this?

Think about other changes you may need to make to the text in order to use some of these linkers.

in addition	however
moreover	nevertheless
furthermore	in contrast
as well as	on the other hand
as a result	therefore

4 Where could you put the expression *not only … but also*?

5 Where do you think the composition should be divided into paragraphs?

Useful expressions

To begin
First of all, …
In my opinion, …
I'd like to begin by saying that, …
Many people think/believe/say that, …

To finish
In conclusion, …
I'd like to conclude by saying that, …
To sum up, …

Advice

- Read the question carefully.
- If the question asks for your experience, don't forget to give examples.
- Remember to organise your composition. It shouldn't be a string of sentences but a logical answer to the question.
- Don't forget to use paragraphs (three is about right).
- Check your spelling, grammar and punctuation.
- Use linking words.
- Check you have really answered the question.
- Count your words or make sure you know how many lines of your handwriting make 120–180 words.

6 In pairs, think about the following composition topic and make some notes using the questions below.

Your teacher has asked you to write a composition discussing the following statement.

Stress can be reduced by playing sport.

- Do you have any personal experience of this?
- Think about some examples.
- Can playing sport when you feel stressed be bad for your health?
- Are there other things to help reduce stress which are better than sport?
- How do you feel about the title – do you agree completely/partly/disagree totally?
- Any conclusions – in general/personally?

Now organise your notes into:

- an introduction
- some reasons/arguments/personal experience
- a conclusion

Which linking words are you going to use?

UNIT 9 The hard sell

Modals 2: Speculation and deduction

1 Look at the advert opposite. What do you think it is selling? Discuss your ideas with a partner, using some of these openers.

Well, it could be advertising …
Or perhaps it might be for …

I think it must be a …
It can't be for … because …

Look at page 83 to find out if you guessed correctly.

2 The modal verbs in the first pair of examples above indicate that the speaker is unsure about something. It is also possible to use *may*, though less common. However, *can* is **not** used in this way.

Is the speaker unsure in the second pair of examples? Which words tell you?

Now look at this example. Is the speaker unsure?

It couldn't possibly be an advert for chocolate.

Does the meaning change if the full stop is replaced by a question mark? Say the sentence and the question aloud to your partner. The question would sound better with extra words at the end. Which words?

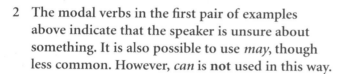 page 201

3 Now read the text about a TV advert and underline examples of the modals used in 1.

4 Explain the meaning of these words from the text.

  a voice-over   **d** verdict
  b jingle   **e** brand
  c celebrity   **f** cunning

Why is the title of Bob's article appropriate?

The best ad missed the boat at Cannes

This is the title of an article by Bob Garfield, an American expert on advertising. He was writing about the 1997 International Advertising Film Festival, which takes place at the same time as the main film festival in Cannes. 5

For Bob, the best ad of the year was from Delvico Bates, Barcelona, for *Esencial* hand cream. The ad shows a woman riding her bike, which has a very squeaky chain. The woman gets off the bike, opens her jar of *Esencial* and rubs some of the cream onto 10 the chain. Then she rides away – but the squeak remains. Why? Because, as the voice-over says, 'Esencial moisturizes, but it has no grease.'

Why is this ad so good? It can't be for its special effects, because there aren't any. Might it be the 15 music? No, there isn't even a jingle. Could it be that the woman is a celebrity? No. Bob's verdict: 'It's a vivid demonstration of brand non-attributes. Inspired. Cunning. Brilliant.' In other words, by showing failure in a different context, the quality of 20 the product is reinforced – grease is good for bike chains, but not for the skin.

So surely this ad must have won at Cannes? No. The simple truth is that it couldn't win, because the agency failed to enter it in time for the festival 25 deadline!

5 In the final paragraph, it says *So surely this ad must have won at Cannes?* Here, the modal is referring to a past action. Say whether the speaker is sure or unsure in sentences a–c below.

   a The latest Sony ad must have cost a fortune to produce.
   b There's one ad showing a man sitting in an armchair on a mountain peak. That couldn't have actually happened – it must be down to special effects.
   c Advertising has come a long way in the last thirty years. Television audiences of the 1960s might have been totally overwhelmed by an action-packed 1990s ad!

   G ····∴ page 201

6 Complete the second sentence so that it has a similar meaning to the first sentence, using the word given. Do not change this word. Use between two and five words, including the word given.

   1 It isn't possible for this to be a car advert.
      be
      This .... a car advert.
   2 If you read the slogan, it sounds as if it's about shampoo.
      must
      Reading the slogan, ... about shampoo.
   3 I'm not sure, but I think it's *Radiohead* singing that jingle.
      might
      That jingle .... by *Radiohead*.
   4 I'm sure that advert in 1984 for Apple computers had an enormous budget.
      must
      That advert in 1984 for Apple computers .... an enormous budget.
   5 I bet Ginola earned a lot for that Renault ad.
      paid
      Ginola .... a lot for that Renault ad.
   6 They didn't use Tom Cruise on the voice-over – the voice was deeper than his.
      been
      It .... Tom Cruise on the voice-over – the voice was deeper than his.

V ocabulary spot

Write down important collocations in your vocabulary notebook. Try using visual diagrams, like this one:

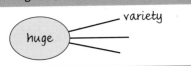

7 Look at the adjectives below. Which ones collocate with each of the nouns given? List the phrases that are possible, for example *huge variety*. You can use some in the role play that follows.

huge	variety
high	message
low	idea
deep	budget
shallow	market
narrow	character
wide	picture
	view
	voice

8 Role play: XK trainers. Get into small groups and read your instructions (A or B). Then spend a few minutes listing useful vocabulary, using a dictionary if necessary. When groups A and B are both ready, have a face-to-face discussion.

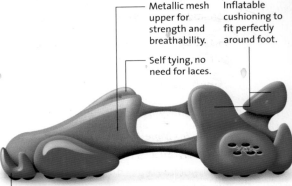

Metallic mesh upper for strength and breathability.

Inflatable cushioning to fit perfectly around foot.

Self tying, no need for laces.

Shock absorbing gel pumped into undersole to absorb impact.

Group A Advertising agency
A leading manufacturer of sports shoes, XK, is about to start selling a new type of trainer. Your agency hopes to get the contract for the TV commercial and you need to prepare your ideas. As there is a big budget for this, you should use famous people and exotic locations! Prepare to meet XK.

Group B turn to page 83.

Listening

1 Think about commercials you have seen recently on TV or at the cinema. Is there one that you really like? Or one that you just can't stand? Briefly describe a commercial to your partner and say why you like it or loathe it.

2 🎧 You are going to hear two people talking about some commercials they have seen. In Part 1, which of these aspects are mentioned by the speakers? Tick the ones you hear.

   a a puzzling beginning
   b a good storyline
   c a dramatic ending
   d an out of the ordinary setting
   e a surprising location
   f a well-known personality
   g a powerful slogan
   h an extravagant production

Grammar extra
Order of adjectives

The woman talks about *a graceful silver vehicle*. Which of the two adjectives is used to give an opinion? Can the order of these adjectives be changed?

Underline the adjectives used in slogans a–d and then identify them according to the types below. What is the rule for opinion adjectives?
a The classic British motorbike
b The sensational new CD from Jamiroquai
c Our popular full-length navy cotton nightshirt
d Bite-sized biscuits with a delicious creamy filling

OPINION
DESCRIPTION: SIZE SHAPE AGE COLOUR NATIONALITY MATERIAL
Descriptive adjectives are usually in the order above. It is quite unusual to have four adjectives in a row (as in example c). More commonly, any additional descriptive information is given in a separate phrase (as in example d).

Decide whether the following adjectives are in the correct order. Reorder them where necessary.
a a black huge dog
b an awful old woollen coat
c the Italian famous singer
d a red large apple
e an elaborate wooden square box
f a sophisticated new novel by a Scottish tremendous author

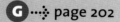 page 202

Pronunciation *Sentence stress*

3 🎧 Look at these sentences from Part 1. Certain words were stressed by the speakers for emphasis. Listen to Part 1 again and underline the stressed words.

   a It must have cost a fortune to make.
   b It's just another car advert!
   c The beginning is a bit misleading.
   d He eats it so it must be good.
   e … the one that had a whole team of top footballers from around the world!
   f The budget must have been huge … all for one advert!
   g But the company probably earned millions of dollars in increased sales …

4 🎧 Now listen to Part 2, where one particular advert is discussed. Answer the questions below by writing W for woman, M for man, or B for both of them in the boxes.

   1 Who didn't like the Bacardi advert? ☐ 1
   2 Who was surprised by part of the advert? ☐ 2
   3 Who thinks that adverts need to contain something unusual? ☐ 3
   4 Who agrees that Ray was an effective character? ☐ 4
   5 Who liked the music in the advert? ☐ 5

5 🎧 Listen to Part 2 again. Explain the following phrases in your own words.

   a brilliantly put together
   b a striking image
   c stick in your mind
   d the right ingredients
   e exotic location
   f made an impact on
   g getting the message across
   h dig into your pocket

6 In pairs, decide on the important factors that make a TV or film advert successful. You can include what you have heard but try to add ideas of your own.

Speaking

9 Think about how to structure the discussion so that you and your partner have equal opportunities to take part. Try to use some of the phrases below to achieve this.

Would you like to start?
What do you think about the second one?
Why don't you continue?
But what about you?
Is that your view too?
Okay, now we have to decide. Shall I summarise?

7 Look at the six photographs. Identify what product each billboard is advertising and discuss how effective it is at selling the product. Then decide which two adverts are the most effective, giving reasons for your choice.

8 Spend some time looking at the photographs and note down useful vocabulary for each one. Remember that when you do the task, you will have to give an opinion about them rather than describe them. Include relevant words and phrases from earlier in the unit.

10 Try to speak together for about three minutes. Make sure you allow enough time within this to decide on the two adverts, so that the task is completed. Give clear reasons for your choice.

11 Tell the class which adverts you both chose and say why.

Exam folder 5

Paper 3 Part 4
Error correction

In this part of the Use of English paper you will have to proof-read a short text which contains some errors. There are seventeen numbered lines, including two example lines at the beginning. In most lines there will be an extra word, which should not be there.

This part of the paper focuses on grammar. A range of grammatical areas are tested and a selection of these are practised below.

1 Work through each of the following sets of sentences (A–F) in turn. Cross out the error in each of the three sentences and then identify what type of word the errors represent, choosing from this list.

> articles   modal verbs   phrasal verbs
> prepositions   pronouns   quantifiers

A ....

  1 I explained them that I would be late for the party.
  2 The advert which was most famous it was the one set in the future.
  3 She felt herself scared stiff at the thought of having to jump.

B ....

  4 It was a hard work but we managed to finish on time.
  5 People planning to visit the Australia need to book flights well in advance.
  6 If you want to eat there, it is the better to phone for a table first.

C ....

  7 You do need not buy a copy to take part in the competition.
  8 It must to be difficult parking there during the day.
  9 If you paid more attention, you could have learn more.

D ....

  10 Jenny gave me a useful bit of some advice about how to apply.
  11 Many of people believe that cigarette advertising should be banned.
  12 I find his films are too much violent for my taste.

E ....

  13 When you reach to Seattle, let me know.
  14 I enclose their number, in case of you would like to find out more.
  15 The article suggests for that downshifting can be very beneficial.

F ....

  16 I try to keep my Italian up with, though I rarely get the chance to speak it.
  17 The company couldn't get over enough advertising time on television, so the campaign was delayed.
  18 Ellen made out a pair of earrings from sea shells.

2 Now look at this Part 4 task. Skim the text for its general meaning. Where do you think it comes from?

TELEPHONE SELLING DRIVES ME MAD!

0	I'm really fed up with telephone selling. I keep picking up on the	...on...
00	phone at home, only to find that the person on the other end is	✓
1	trying to sell me something. Most of these calls they seem to be	....
2	in the early evening, just when I'm trying to cook a meal, or take	....
3	a relaxing bath, or when that I'm getting ready for an evening out.	....
4	I never want the products or services that are being on offer, but	....
5	for some reason, I find it hard to say no and put the phone down.	....
6	If I say it is an inconvenient, they don't take any notice at all, but	....
7	continue putting their message across, explaining for why I must	....
8	buy immediately, before the special offer period ends up. I know	....
9	there is a too definite skill involved in dealing with these nuisance	....
10	callers, which is what they are. Although of I'm bad at hanging up	....
11	at the very beginning, I have tried simply walking away from the	....
12	phone, hoping so that when I finally return ten minutes later, the	....
13	caller will have given him up. This doesn't always work though!	....
14	Do other readers have the suggestions on how I could deal with	....
15	these calls more than effectively? They're driving me completely	....
	mad!	....

Advice

- Skim the text to get an idea of what it is about.
- Read it through sentence by sentence for meaning.
- Work through each line, crossing out possible errors in pencil.
- Make sure you have not marked more than one error per line.
- Read the text again without the errors to check that it makes sense.

3 Read the text through sentence by sentence. Then work line by line, crossing out any possible errors. If you find more than one error on a line, you have made a mistake!

4 Read the text through again without the words you have crossed out, to check that it makes sense. Then list your answers 1–15 in the spaces provided.

5 In the exam, you will have to transfer your answers to an answer sheet, part of which is shown below. Make sure you do this accurately.

Part 4		Do not write here
41		41
42		42
43		43
44		44
45		

UNIT 10 The final frontier

1 Describe what is happening in the pictures and compare the people. Will the general public be able to go into space by 2010? Why?/Why not?

2 Discuss these questions in small groups, explaining your opinions in detail.

- Do you think you will ever take a holiday in space?
- Should governments spend tax-payers' money on space travel?
- Why are there so many satellites orbiting the Earth? Will this technology become more important, in your view?

Exam spot

In Part 3 of Paper 1 you need to understand what the text covers, so first, you should skim the 'skeleton' text, (the main text, from which the paragraphs have been removed) and read the example paragraph (o). Then work through the skeleton again and predict what each gap might be about, to help you fit the missing paragraphs correctly.

3 You are going to read an article on space travel. Read its title and opening paragraph, and suggest what the article is about.

CHEAP ACCESS TO SPACE

Charles Conrad went to the moon with Apollo 12 and circled the Earth in Skylab. But from now on, he is going to aim high for himself. His company, Universal Space Lines, hopes to produce a more economical rocket, that will be able to go into space again and again.

4 Read the example paragraph and the one that follows it. Say how the words underlined link back to earlier in the article.

'Cheap' is an important word in space technology nowadays and re-usable rockets will be a key way of controlling costs. They will deliver things to orbit, bring stuff back to Earth and then go up again, perhaps with machinery for a space factory, or even carrying tourists.

NASA, the U.S. government-owned space program, plans to develop such a rocket. However, the immediate priority is missions to Mars, which will require different technology. So it is more likely that people outside the NASA program will develop re-usable rocket design. Rick Tumlinson runs an independent organization called the Space Frontier Foundation and firmly believes that it is time for businesses to get involved.

5 Now read the rest of the skeleton article to see how the text develops. Look at the handwritten notes predicting the content of each gap and then underline the words in the paragraphs above and below each gap that these notes are based on.

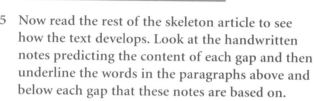

1 business/companies? Tumlinson/he? SFF?

So Tumlinson is also in business to prove a point. Space is our destiny, he says, so why not get on with it a bit more eagerly? To this end, the SFF is holding a conference in Los Angeles shortly, to be called Space: Open for Business.

2 LA conference? named company?

Another company, Kistler Aerospace, has similar plans: 'Our goal is to become a delivery service to low Earth orbit that will radically re-align the economics of doing business in space. Satellites will be our parcels; our vehicles will be operated in repeated flights with air freight efficiency.'

3 SFF? NASA program? opinions?

Their own view is that it is impossible for NASA, which is government-owned, to offer an 'open frontier'. This is not a matter of budgets or schedules, but of fundamental purpose and design. NASA is 'élitist and exclusive', whereas the SFF believe in opportunities for everyone:
'a future of endlessly expanding new choices'.

4 business? opportunities for all? astronauts?

Of course, the ex-astronaut and businessman Charles Conrad agrees. 'I'm trying to get affordable space transportation up and operative so that everybody can go enjoy space. And by the way, the Japanese are hard at work building a space hotel.'

5 tourism? he? future?

If he is right, mass space travel will have arrived by 2010 and space tourism will have become a viable industry. More importantly, the human race will have made serious progress in crossing that final frontier.

6 Paragraphs A and B both contain some of the predicted content for gap 1. However, one of these paragraphs does not fit anywhere in the article. Read both paragraphs and decide which one fits gap 1, saying why.

A
Companies will always be looking for profit. For this reason, the SFF is not in favour of American missions to Mars, claiming that there's nothing in it for investors. At the same time, they do accept that these missions could bring scientific benefits.

B
He sees the NASA program as a bit of a dinosaur. '25 years after the Wright Brothers, people could buy a commercial plane ticket ... but 25 years after landing on the moon, we sat around watching old astronauts on TV talking about the good old days.'

7 Now read missing paragraphs C–F. Say what each one is about and look again at the predictions. Then try to fit the paragraphs into gaps 2–5. Remember that each paragraph must tie in with the text above and below it.

C
In 1997, the SFF ran a survey on the Internet, called 'Cheap Access to Space', where it asked American taxpayers for their views on the U.S. space program and on what America's future priorities should be in space transportation.

D
U.S. government officials don't see a future for space tourism. Here again, private companies may well prove them wrong. David Ashford, director of Bristol Spaceplanes Limited, once said that space tourism would begin ten years after people stopped laughing at the concept. Recently, he added this striking comment: 'people have stopped laughing.'

cont.

E
Charles Conrad is due to speak there. But his company is in fact only one of several that already have blueprints for getting into space and back cheaply. Rotary Rocket is working on something that would be launched like a rocket but return like a helicopter. Pioneer Rocketplane believes there could be a billion dollar market in delivering packages from one side of the planet to the other in an hour.

F
They would like to see 'irreversible human settlement' in space as soon as possible and maintain that this will only happen through free enterprise. 'Building buildings and driving trucks is not what astronauts should be doing; that's what the private sector does.'

Vocabulary

8 Additional or contrasting information is often given in the article. The underlined words in extracts a–f are commonly used to signpost information in texts. Such words can be useful checks in the gapped text task.

a Another company ... has similar plans
b Their own view
c Charles Conrad agrees
d Here again ...
e only one of several
f he added this striking comment

9 Find words and phrases to do with money and business in the article. Compare your list with a partner and explain the words and phrases without the help of a dictionary. You will need these words and phrases for the speaking practice below.

10 Discuss these questions.

- Do you think the SFF is right to encourage the commercial development of space? Why?/Why not?
- What benefits and drawbacks might this bring?

Review of future tenses

1 Look at examples a–h from the article on space and identify the future tenses listed 1–5 below. What other tense is used in two of the examples to refer to the future?

1 *going to* future
2 present continuous
3 future simple
4 future continuous
5 future perfect

a Re-usable rockets will deliver things to orbit and bring stuff back to Earth.
b But from now on, he is going to aim high for himself.
c The SFF is holding a conference in Los Angeles shortly.
d Companies will always be looking for profit.
e NASA plans to develop such a rocket.
f If he is right, mass space travel will have arrived by 2010 and space tourism will have become a viable industry.
g Charles Conrad is due to speak there.
h Our vehicles will be operated in repeated flights with air freight efficiency.

2 Which of the examples mention the following?

1 a prediction about the future
2 a planned event that is expected to happen soon
3 an event that has not yet happened but will happen within a certain period of time
4 something that is certain to remain true in the future
5 an intention to do something

3 How are predictions about the future expressed in these two examples?

a Private companies may well prove them wrong.
b There could be a billion dollar market in delivering packages from one side of the planet to the other in an hour.

4 Why is *would* used in this example instead of *will*?

David Ashford once said that space tourism would begin 10 years after people stopped laughing at the concept.

G ⋯⟶ page 202

5 Choose the correct option in italics in these sentences and explain why it is correct.

a Within the next twenty years, the cost of space travel *will be falling / will fall* dramatically.
b In the near future, it's likely that adventure holidays *won't be / aren't going to be* limited to remote places on Earth.
c People *will / may* one day have the opportunity to go to distant planets, but first we need to discover a way of travelling faster than the speed of light.
d Our 7-day travel program is due to depart on December 1, 2001 and *will carry / will have carried* you 100 km into space.
e I've decided I *am going to book / will* book a trip into space as soon as there's one available.
f The Americans always said they *would fly / will* fly to Mars.
g Sooner or later people *will live / will be living* in space.
h Alpha, the International Space Station, *will have been / will be* up in space for five years this time next week.

Listening

7 🎧 You are going to hear three people talking about the future. Decide whether each speaker has a positive or a negative view of what life for human beings might be like.

Speaker 1 ....
Speaker 2 ....
Speaker 3 ....

Which speaker is closest to your own ideas about the future? Why?

Vocabulary Phrases with *at*

8 Speaker 2 used the preposition *at* in three different ways:

I'm reading one of his sci-fi ones at the moment.
They live for at least three hundred years.
There will always be some country at war with another.

Choose the correct phrase for each of these sentences and explain the meaning of the incorrect options.

a Hurry up, we'll be locked inside the building unless we leave

....

   A at first   **B** at once   **C** at last

b Jordi is looking forward to the move, but ...., I know he'll miss his friends here.

   A at least   **B** at present
   C at the same time

c For the first time in ten years, this war-torn country is now

..........................., thanks to the skills of the negotiators on both sides.

   A at peace   **B** at war   **C** at rest

d Journalists often get scientific facts slightly wrong, but this article is inaccurate reporting

....

   A at his laziest   **B** at its worst
   C at their best

Notice, as in the last example, that *at* is commonly used with a pronoun and a superlative.

6 Look back at the advice on Paper 3 Part 4 in Exam folder 5 before you complete this proof-reading task.

Read the text below.

If a line has a word that should not be there, write the word at the end of the line. If a line is correct, put a tick (✓) next to it. There are two examples (0) and (00).

HAPPY BIRTHDAY ALIENS!

0	We humans must be careful, because of the aliens are coming.	the
00	Already, strange beings walk our streets, their heads full of little	✓
1	green men. These are ufologists and it's their year. The one first	....
2	report of a 'flying saucer' was for fifty years ago next month and	....
3	thousands of UFO enthusiasts they are going to celebrate. As	....
4	well as new books and films, a series of the special conferences	....
5	will be taking place there. At one event in London, people will be	....
6	able to hear talks on such subjects as abduction by aliens. In	....
7	America, an estimated 150,000 people who are intending to visit	....
8	Roswell, the site of one of the most biggest mysteries in the UFO	....
9	world. In 1947 it was claimed that the U.S. military did found	....
10	parts of an alien spacecraft here, complete with the bodies of	....
11	extra-terrestrials. However, and some UFO watchers now view	....
12	this event as a deliberate misinformation, set up to hide the truth	....
13	about a top secret military project. 95% of UFO sightings turn out	....
14	to be cases of mistaken identity – though that still leaves more 5%	....
15	which cannot be explained. So why not to let the ufologists party on!	....

Writing folder 5

Articles 1

1 Look at these titles of articles about the future. Which article would you most like to read? Why?

2 Match the titles to the opening paragraphs A–D. Do all four paragraphs fit their titles well? Why?/Why not?

Aliens are coming …

3 – 2 – 1 Lift off!

Is anybody there?

A lifelong ambition

A

Imagine being launched in a rocket towards that final frontier. Strapped into your seat in a shiny silver capsule, you feel the power of the engines as they carry you up and away. And soon, you are orbiting around the earth, covering vast distances and looking down on the planet you call home.

B

I want to go up into space. I think it may be possible for ordinary people to go up into space soon. I read something about space travel. I want to be one of the first to go. I hope I can go up into space.

C

Our planet is going to be invaded – not by little green men but by a revolutionary new form of transport! Next week sees the launch of a worldwide advertising campaign, for a vehicle that could completely change our life on earth.

D

On some nights, I open my window and <u>watch</u> the stars. It's a <u>nice</u> thing to do. Sometimes I stay there for ages, wondering what the universe holds. It makes me feel <u>small</u>. Space is a <u>big</u> place. There are <u>a lot of</u> galaxies apart from our own – so there must be other life?

Hubble Space Telescope image of distant galaxies

3 Look again at paragraph D. How could it be improved? Choose words and phrases from the pairs below to replace the words underlined. In each pair, both a and b fit the text correctly, so the final choice is up to you!

a	b
stare at	gaze at
wonderful	brilliant
unimportant	humble
vast	huge
so many	an enormous number of

What parts of speech are the words in a–d below? Insert all these words into paragraph D where they fit best.

a cloudless   beautiful   twinkling
b forms of
c very   such
d truly   surely

Read through the paragraph once more. Could any sentences be joined together? Write out a final version.

4 Paragraph B is a poor attempt at an opening paragraph. Why? Rewrite it, making the following improvements, along with any others of your own.

- Order the ideas more clearly.
- Join any short sentences together.
- Include a first sentence that links back to the title.
- Replace any repeated words, e.g. *want: wish, hope.*
- Use a variety of sentence openers.
- Add suitable words to describe and emphasise.

Exam spot

An article is not a composition! It is written for a wider audience and will appear in a certain type of magazine. Read the exam question carefully to find out where the article may be published and who will read it. Choose a suitable style and use a range of language to make your article interesting to read.

5 Now look at this exam question.

You see this notice in an in-flight magazine and decide to enter the competition.

GALAXY TRAVEL COMPETITION

What forms of transport will we be using in 50 years' time?

Where will we take our holidays?

Write us an article, giving us your views on both of these questions. Science fiction writer John T. Price will choose the most original article, which will receive a prize of $1,000 and be published in our magazine next year.

Write your **article**. (120–180 words)

6 Answer these questions about the writing task.

   a Which **two** topics do you need to write about?
   b What is meant by 'forms'?
   c Should the style be serious or lively?
   d How many paragraphs should you write?

7 Plan your article before you start writing. Make content notes for each paragraph and think of a suitable title. Look back over Units 9 and 10 for relevant vocabulary and grammar. Then write your article in 120–180 words. Don't be afraid to use your imagination!

1 Look at these photos of famous people and their children. Do you think the children resemble their mother or father? What similarities or differences can you see?

E**xam spot**

In Part 1 of Paper 5, the examiner will ask you to give some basic, personal information about yourself. This is to help you to relax and 'loosen you up' for the rest of the Speaking Test. The questions will be about where you come from, your family, your studies or work, your hobbies or your future plans.

2 With a partner try to find out as much as you can about each other. When you ask about each other's family also ask these questions:

Who do you most look like in your family? Do you sound like anyone in the family when you answer the telephone? Who do you take after in character?

For extra practice take it in turns to think of a famous person but don't tell your partner who it is. Your partner has to ask you personal questions to try to find out your identity. Try not to make it too easy!

E**xam spot**

In Part 4 of Paper 4 you may have a multiple choice listening task. You will have seven questions with a choice of three different answers to each question. You have to listen very carefully to decide which is the right answer. You will hear the passage twice.

Listening

3 🎧 You are going to hear an interview with the daughter of a Hollywood film star.

The tape will be stopped when you hear the following words.

… *some of the kids I knew did.*

Now look at question 1.

1 For her 14th birthday, Hannah
  A took some friends to see a Harrison Ford film at the cinema.
  B went to watch the making of a film.
  C was given whatever she wanted.

Here are some things to think about.
• Did she go to the cinema? How do we know?
• Did she meet Harrison Ford?
• How did her parents treat her?
• Did she have any brothers and sisters?

4 Decide on the correct answer. Which sentence in the interview tells you?

Remember that a wrong answer often repeats the same vocabulary you hear in the passage, and might be true but doesn't actually answer the question.

5 🎧 Now continue listening to the rest of the interview and answer questions 2–7.

2 How did Hannah's mother feel when Hannah said she wanted to be an actress?
 A She wasn't keen on her doing it.
 B She wasn't discouraging.
 C She didn't think she was serious about it.

3 What does Hannah say about the comparison with her mother?
 A They have the same shaped eyes.
 B They are both tall.
 C Their noses are similar.

4 Hannah and her mother both think that
 A they look identical.
 B they do look a bit alike.
 C people are completely wrong.

5 How did Hannah feel about her mother's attitude to acting?
 A She was a bit upset.
 B She was angry.
 C She understood.

6 Why was Hannah encouraged to train to be an accountant?
 A Her mother had had a bad experience with money.
 B Hannah needed to learn the importance of saving.
 C Her mother considered it a useful profession.

7 How does Hannah's mother sound?
 A very demanding
 B slightly foreign
 C like her daughter

6 🎧 Now listen to the interview again. What adjective or adjectives does Hannah use to describe:
 a her childhood in Hollywood?
 b how her mother had felt when she first arrived in Hollywood?
 c part of her nose?
 d her mother talking about acting?
 e the quality they both possess?
 f her mother's attitude to money?
 g her mother's voice?

Grammar extra

You've heard already the expression *to look like* + a noun phrase which means *to resemble* or *to take after physically*.

EXAMPLE: *She looks like her mother.*

Now look at these two questions.
A What's he/she like?
B What does he/she like?

Decide which of the words below can be used to answer the questions.

| tall | swimming | friendly | hamburgers |
| watching TV | photography | amusing |

7 Find out who in your class is from a family the same size as yours, and then form a group. For example, if you are an only child, go to part of the room with others who are only children. Talk to the others in your group about what your family is like, how you feel about the size of your family and what effect, if any, it has had on you. Talk about your place in the family, and whether it's best to be the eldest, youngest, only one, middle child and so on.

8 Are there any special characteristics that run in your family? Is there anything you all like/dislike? Does it look as if you will:
 a grow bald/have white hair when still quite young?
 b get fat?
 c live a long time?
 d wear glasses?
 e follow in your parents' footsteps (do the same things as your parents have done)?
 f have good health?

Describing personality

1   Use one of the adjectives in the box to answer questions a–n.

> sociable   generous   bad-tempered   lazy
> considerate   optimistic   loyal   cheerful
> self-conscious   unreliable   conceited
> amusing   aggressive   sensible

How do you describe a person who:

a   has a very good opinion of him/herself?
b   is usually happy?
c   looks on the bright side of things?
d   buys you expensive presents?
e   never does anything stupid?
f   would never upset you?
g   never turns up on time?
h   really worries what people think of them?
i   gets out of bed on the wrong side in a morning?
j   tells jokes?
k   likes fighting with people?
l   doesn't want to get out of bed in the morning?
m will stand by you if you are in trouble?
n   enjoys the company of other people?

2   Which of the adjectives above are positive, and which are negative? What are their opposites?

In pairs, say which of these adjectives you would use to describe:

a   yourself
b   your parents
c   your brothers/sisters
d   your teacher
e   your best friend
f   your worst enemy

ⓥocabulary spot

Extend your vocabulary by thinking of adjectives with opposite meanings. Remember to use a negative prefix if necessary.

Phrasal verbs

3   Replace the words in bold with the correct form of one of the phrasal verbs in the box.

> fall out with   pick up   look on   grow up
> stand by   turn up   put off

EXAMPLE: *Fred **had an argument** with his best friend. Fred **fell out with** his best friend.*

a   I **learnt** a bit of Spanish when I was on holiday in Chile.
b   Susan **lived** in Shanghai **when she was young**.
c   He tried to **discourage** them **from** seeing the film, as it was very violent.
d   Pete usually **arrives** at work looking a bit of a mess.
e   My boss **supported** me when I had some trouble at work.
f   Most people would **see** film stars as being rich and spoilt.

I won't do it for less than 10 million and I want a helicopter and a kitten and a personal chef and a new hat and...

Adverb or adjective?

Normally adverbs are used with verbs.

EXAMPLE: *Hannah acts beautifully.*
        This tells you how she acted.
However, with certain verbs it's sometimes necessary to use adjectives. These verbs are usually connected with our senses – *look, sound, taste, feel,* and *smell.* Other verbs include *be, appear* and *seem,* and *become.*

EXAMPLE: *'Hannah is **beautiful**.'* and *'Hannah looks **beautiful**.'*

4   With a partner discuss what you would say in these situations.

EXAMPLE: *You're eating a lemon. It tastes sour.*

a   You're listening to a love song. It sounds …
b   You're walking by the sea. It smells …
c   You're walking home late at night. It feels …
d   You're eating spaghetti. It tastes …
e   You're looking through a travel brochure. It looks …
f   You're wearing a designer suit. It feels …

5 Some of these verbs can have two meanings. Look at the underlined verbs and explain the differences.

A The actress <u>looked</u> angry when she read the bad review.
B The actress had <u>to look</u> at her co-star angrily at one point in the film.

A I <u>feel</u> fine.
B I <u>felt</u> the water to see if it was hot enough.

In examples A, 'looked' and 'feel' mean 'seemed'. In examples B, 'to look' and 'felt' are both actions. If the verb means 'seemed', then an adjective is used after it. If the verb is used for an action, then it is followed by an adverb.

Complete these sentences using an adverb or an adjective.

a The food tasted ....
b I felt the soft fur on the rabbit very ....
c I don't feel very ....
d Ann looked .... to see if there was any traffic, before crossing the road.
e Noises can sound quite .... at night.
f Your coat looks ....
g He looked at her .... when she entered the room.
h The rabbit appeared .... out of the hat.

Past and present participles

6 When Hannah is talking about her mother and her attitude to acting she says 'she became quite embarrassed'. Hannah means that her mother became a bit red or maybe blushed and wasn't sure what to say. What would it mean if Hannah had said 'my mother became quite embarrassing'?

Can you finish these sentences which explain what the grammatical rule is?

1 to talk about how we feel about something we use ....
2 to talk about the person or thing that is causing the feeling we use ....

G···⟫ page 202

Look at the following pairs of sentences and decide which is correct.

a I'm interested / interesting in modern architecture.
b People are getting bored / boring with all the soap operas that are on the TV.
c It's exhausted / exhausting learning another language.
d I arrived at the cinema just as the most excited / exciting part of the film had finished.
e It's very worrying / worried how much violence seems acceptable in new movies.

Speaking

7 In pairs talk about how you feel when you watch the following:

a soap operas
b westerns
c Disney films
d Frankenstein movies
e films about aliens
f cartoons
g foreign films with subtitles

EXAMPLE: *I am bored by soap operas. They're so appalling.*

Use some of these adjectives.

bored/boring	excited/exciting
disturbed/disturbing	thrilled/thrilling
horrified/horrifying	appalled/appalling
shocked/shocking	revolted/revolting
moved/moving	gripped/gripping

Exam folder 6

Paper 4 Part 1
Short extracts

In this part of the Listening paper you will hear eight unconnected short recordings of about 30 seconds each. There will be either one or two speakers. For each question, you have to decide which is the correct answer from three possible options. Both the question and the options are recorded, which gives you time to think about the recording that is coming up. Each recording is repeated.

You should make the best use of the time available. Read through each question as you hear it and underline any key words. Think about what to listen out for during the pause before each recording starts. After you have listened once, choose the option that you think is correct. As you listen for the second time, check that the other two options are definitely wrong.

If you do not know the answer to a question, keep calm and move on to the next one. At the end of the Listening test, you will have time to transfer your answers to an answer sheet. For any questions you haven't been able to answer, make a guess – there is a one in three chance of your being right!

1   Look through these questions and underline the key words.

You will hear people talking in eight different situations. For Questions 1–8, choose the best answer, **A**, **B** or **C**.

1 You hear this advertisement on the radio for a new magazine.
   Who is the magazine aimed at?
   A gardeners
   B cooks
   C climbers

2 As you leave the cinema, you overhear this conversation.
   What is the man's opinion of the film?
   A It is longer than necessary.
   B It has a weak storyline.
   C Its actors are disappointing.

3 You overhear a woman talking on the phone.
   What sort of person is she?
   A unhappy
   B impractical
   C disloyal

4 You hear this interview on the radio.
   Why did the man give up his job?
   A to recover from stress
   B to reduce his expenses
   C to move somewhere quiet

5 You overhear this conversation in a hotel.
   Why has the woman come down to reception?
   A to ask for another room
   B to order some food
   C to complain about the service

6 You hear this radio report about a football match.
   What happened at the match?
   A Some fans ran onto the pitch.
   B A player was badly injured.
   C The referee stopped the match.

7 You hear this interview on the radio.
   Where is it taking place?
   A in a clothes shop
   B at an exhibition
   C on a beach

8 You overhear this woman talking about an evening course.
   What does she enjoy most?
   A doing maths
   B watching videos
   C having coffee

2   Now answer the eight questions. Remember that each recording is repeated. When you have finished, check your answers.

3   Fill in the extract from the answer sheet for Part 1 below with your answers.

Part 1			
1	A	B	C
2	A	B	C
3	A	B	C
4	A	B	C
5	A	B	C
6	A	B	C
7	A	B	C
8	A	B	C

Advice

- Think about possible contents for each question as you listen.
- Choose your answers at the first listening.
- Check your answers at the second listening.
- Keep calm and make a guess if necessary.
- Remember to transfer your answers to the answers sheet at the end of the listening test.

1 How technology-minded do you think you are? Try this questionnaire to test your response to modern technology. Answer yes or no to all the questions.

? ? ? ? ? ? ? ? ? ? ?

1 Have you ever felt anxious about:
   a down escalators stopping suddenly?
   b leaving a TV set plugged in?
   c putting food in a microwave oven?

2 Do you call an expert when:
   a the lights fuse?
   b the drains are blocked?
   c you need a plug putting on something?

3 Do you use:
   a an electric toothbrush?
   b the Internet?
   c a digital camera?
   d a PC?
   e a mobile phone?
   f an electric tin-opener?

4 When you speak to an answering machine do you:
   a talk naturally?
   b keep it brief?
   c put the phone down when you realise it's an answering machine?
   d keep repeating yourself?

5 If you put money in a vending machine and nothing happens do you:
   a kick it viciously?
   b put more money in?
   c walk away resignedly?
   d ring up the owners?

Scoring
1 2 points for Yes
   0 points for No
2 2 points for Yes
   0 points for No
3 2 points for No, 0 for Yes
4 a=0, b=0, c=2, d=1
5 a=2, b=1, c=0, d=0
The higher your score, the more uneasy you are with technology. In fact, you're a technophobe! A low score indicates you are at home with new developments and gadgets. You're a technophile!

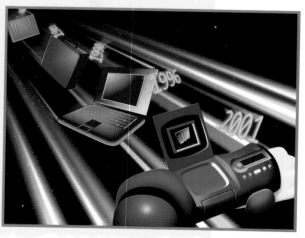

Guessing unknown words

Vocabulary spot

When you read a text you may find that some words are unfamiliar to you. Don't immediately reach for your dictionary! Try to work out the meaning of an unknown word from its context, that is, the words around it.

2 With a partner, work out the meaning of the words in italics in the following sentences.

   a Most houses in hot countries have *shutters* at the windows to keep out the sun.
   b The *forerunner* of ice-cream was frozen snow.
   c Batman wears *a mask* so no-one will recognise him.
   d Her flat was very *compact*, but everything fitted in very neatly.
   e You know when you reach Paris because you can see that famous *landmark*, the Eiffel Tower.
   f I think the *entire* film was a boring waste of time.
   g There were several *factors* in his decision to move abroad – the most important being that he could get a job more easily.

Exam spot

In Part 1 of Paper 1 you might be asked to match each paragraph of a passage to a summary sentence, that is, a sentence which summarises what the paragraph is mainly about.

3 Skim the text on the Kodak Camera quickly for general meaning. Ignore the missing summary sentences for the moment.

4 In pairs, read through the text again and decide what the topic of each paragraph is. Underline the key words in each paragraph that help you to decide. In the first paragraph the topic words have been underlined for you.

5 Now look at the summary sentences A–H. Identify any similarity in topic, referring to your underlined key words. For example, sentence H is 'Ordinary people took up photography when cameras became easy to carry', so there is a match with 'popular', 'small', 'light', and 'hand-held'.

   Match a suitable sentence (A–H) to each paragraph, using the key words to help you. There is one extra sentence which you do not need to use.

A The camera was not a new design, but it was an important development.

B The new camera was very similar to modern ones.

C An important decision about the camera couldn't be rushed.

D The camera was still not totally perfect in its design.

E Most households were now in a position to take up photography after the introduction of a camera at the beginning of the century.

F The invention of the camera was the beginning of photography.

G The new design overcame a former problem cameras had.

H Ordinary people took up photography when cameras became easy to carry.

THE KODAK CAMERA

0 H

Popular photography can properly be said to have started in 1888 with the introduction of the Kodak. The Kodak camera was the invention of an American, George Eastman (1854–1932). Advertised as 'the smallest, lightest and simplest of all Detective Cameras' (a popular term of the 1880s for hand-held cameras), it was a simple wooden box. It was small and light enough to be held in the hands while in use.

1

He chose the name for his camera with great care. 'The letter K had been a favourite with me – it seems a strong, incisive sort of letter. It became a question of trying out a great number of combinations of letters that made words starting and ending with K. The word Kodak is the result'.

2

Taking a photograph with the Kodak camera was very easy, requiring only three simple actions: turning the key (to wind on the film); pulling the string (to set the shutter); and pressing the button (to release the shutter and make the exposure). It was, in many respects the forerunner of today's point-and-shoot cameras. No viewfinder was needed, the camera was simply pointed at the subject to be photographed.

3

Poor definition at the edge of the image area, however, meant that a circular mask had to be used in the camera, placed in front of the film. This accounts for the distinctive round photographs which the Kodak camera produced.

4

Ingenious, compact and simple to use though it was, the technology of the Kodak camera was not particularly revolutionary. It was not the first hand camera, nor indeed was it the first camera to be made solely for roll film. The true significance of the camera, which makes it a landmark in the history of photography, is that it was the first stage in a complete system of amateur photography.

5

The Kodak camera was sold already loaded with enough film to take 100 photographs. After the film had been exposed, the entire camera was posted to the factory where it was unloaded and the film developed and printed. The camera, reloaded with fresh film, was then returned to its owner together with the negatives and a set of prints. Previously, photographers had had no choice but to do their own developing and printing. This, more than any other factor, had delayed the popularisation of photography.

6

The new convenience, however, did not come cheap. In Britain, the Kodak camera sold for five guineas (£5.25). The developing and printing service cost a further two guineas (£2.10). In 1888, £1 was a week's wage for many workers. However, in 1900 the five-shilling (25p) Brownie camera was introduced. For the first time, the pleasures of photography had been brought within reach of practically everybody.

The passive

1 Which of the verbs in bold in these sentences from the passage are in the passive?

   a The Kodak camera **was sold** already loaded with film.
   b This new convenience, however, **did not come** cheap.
   c It was small and light enough **to be held** in the hands.
   d After the film **had been exposed**, the entire camera **was posted** to the factory.
   e The letter K **had been** a favourite with me.
   f Popular photography **can properly be said to have started** in 1888.

2 How is the passive formed and why is it used?

G 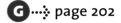 page 202

3 Fill the spaces in this newspaper article opposite with the passive form of one of the verbs below.

dissolve	store	fill	supply
persuade	disperse	encourage	use
talk into	ask	issue	hope make up

by or *with*?

4 What do you think the rule is for when we use *by* and when we use *with*?

Shakespeare wrote Romeo and Juliet; Romeo and Juliet was written by Shakespeare.
Money can't buy happiness; Happiness can't be bought with money.

Change the following in the same way.

   a Mud covered the kitchen floor.
   b A cat scratched him.
   c A car ran him over.
   d Bulldozers smashed down the old house.
   e They are rebuilding the school using a new type of brick.

5 It isn't always necessary to use *by*. Decide whether you would use it or not in the following and say why.

   a Jurassic Park was produced
   b A new road is now being built round the town
   c She was given a job
   d He was murdered
   e She is being operated on
   f The fire is said to have been started

G 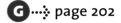 page 202

Shops with the sweet smell of success

It began with the smell of freshly baked bread. A supermarket with a sharp nose for business believed people (1) .... to spend more money if they smelled something pleasant. The idea was so successful that hundreds of other shops (2) .... to do the same. The smells of engine oil, leather and burning rubber (3) .... to launch and sell a new car, while banks and hotels (4) .... often .... with pleasant fragrances such as apple and lavender. Sports shops believe that customers (5) .... spending more money if they can smell the scent of freshly mown grass.

These business scents (6) .... by two companies, BOC Gases and Atmospherics. The fragrances (7) .... in carbon dioxide and (8) .... via air conditioning, or (9) .... in discreet cylinders and released when needed.

BOC Gases is working with British firms to see how well the fragrances are doing. Soon customers (10) .... with questionnaires, and it (11) .... their answers will provide a clearer idea of the relationship between scents and increased sales. A spokesman for the company said: 'Any smell you want (12) .... for you. We constantly (13) .... for the same smells, like coffee and bread, but we want people to think of other things.'

6 The passive is often used in notices and newspaper headlines. Look at this example of a newspaper headline.

Beef talks tomorrow

It means that discussions about beef are going to be/will be held tomorrow.

In pairs, explain the meaning of these headlines.

   a Dog comes to man's rescue
   b **Lost treasure found in garden yesterday**
   c Man held in police station for questioning
   d *Championships to be held in Japan*
   e **Chewing gum addicts face 'bin it' drive to clean up streets**

7 Where would you see the following notices?

a All crockery and cutlery to be returned after use.

b **You are requested not to smoke.**

c RESERVED FOR MEMBERS.

d Packet should be opened at the other end.

e NOT TO BE PHOTOCOPIED WITHOUT PERMISSION.

8 In pairs ask and answer these questions.

  a Has your photo ever been in a newspaper?
  b It is said that in the future most people will work from home. Do you agree?
  c Can you explain how paper is produced?
  d Where was your watch made?
  e What were you given for your last birthday?

9 Link the following pieces of information using a passive.

  a John Lennon – New York
  b Gunpowder – China
  c Telephone – half a billion people
  d Tutankhamun – Lord Caernarfon
  e Satellites – 1957
  f Olympic Games – Athens
  g India – 1947
  h Leather – cows

10 Complete the second sentence so that it has a similar meaning to the first sentence, using the word given. Do not change the word given. You must use between two and five words, including the word given.

1 Inventors don't like people copying their ideas.
  object
  Inventors .... being copied.

2 Why were the students mixing up those chemicals in the lab yesterday?
  being
  Why .... up in the lab yesterday?

3 They made her hand over her notebooks.
  was
  She .... her notebooks.

4 People say that the local camera shop is very good.
  supposed
  The local camera shop .... very good.

5 My boss told me of his decision yesterday.
  informed
  I .... decision yesterday.

6 Fewer people smoke these days.
  decrease
  There .... the number of people who smoke these days.

Listening

11 🎧 You are going to hear four people talking about different inventions. Decide in each case what you think the invention is.

12 In the article in 12.1, the collocations *to take a photo* and *to take a long time* are used.

Look at the words in the boxes and decide which of the verbs below each can go with. Some can go with more than one, but usually with a different meaning. Find out the meanings of the collocations.

come   **take**   **tell**   **fall**

a story	into money	turns	ill
a seat	advantage of	asleep	apart
a lie	the time	notice of	an interest
to a conclusion	to a decision	in love	the truth
the difference	offence		

Writing folder 6

Reports 1

In Part 2 of Paper 2 you may be asked to write a report. This will involve the presentation of information in a clear, factual way, using headings, and sometimes with some suggestions or recommendations.

1 Look at this task.

> Your local museum is quite old-fashioned and not many people visit it. Your local tourist board has asked you to write a report on the museum and to give some recommendations on how to improve its image. Write your **report**.

In the following report, the paragraphs are in the wrong order and they don't have a suitable heading. Read through the text deciding on the right order and then choose an appropriate heading from the list below.

Headings
A Purpose
B The museum today
C Suggested improvements
D Additional facilities
E Conclusion

Wademouth Museum

1
The museum mainly contains items connected with the pottery industry and various inventions connected with it. **Generally**, most of the items are displayed in glass cabinets with explanations on small bits of card. These aren't very easy to read and some of them are placed too high for small children. The lighting inside the building is also very poor.

2
To sum up, I found that Wademouth Museum could have a bright future if some time was spent up-dating the displays and opening some new facilities.

3
Finally, I spoke to some of the visitors and one thing that **most people mentioned** is having a good gift shop and a café in the building. The profits from these would help to pay for more interesting displays.

4
The aim of this report is to give an outline of what can be seen in this museum and to suggest ways in which the museum can change its image.

5
Although the museum gives the visitor a good idea of how the pottery industry developed through the ages in this area, it doesn't make the subject come alive. **I would recommend that** the museum puts in some working models or, even better, have people showing you how the pots were produced.

2 Reports are often written in an impersonal way. Look at these examples from the report.

   a Most of the items are displayed in glass cabinets.
   b … if some time was spent up-dating …
   c … of what can be seen …

The sentences above use the passive to make the report seem more impersonal and formal. Put the following sentences into the passive.

1 People say that the museum charges too much to get in.
2 Nobody ever dusts the exhibits.
3 The museum should open a café and a gift shop.
4 Someone will make the displays look more interesting.
5 They should employ more people to explain things to the visitors.

3 Complete the following sentences from different reports on cultural facilities, using one of the words or phrases in bold from the report.

   EXAMPLE: ***The aim of this report*** *is to give visitors to Doulton a clear idea of where to eat in the evening.*

   a ...., I believe that, with careful management, the shop will be able to attract more young people.
   b .... you visit the art gallery in the morning and take the open top bus around the town in the afternoon.
   c .... the fact that they would prefer to see a mixture of different types of film, not just the latest Hollywood films.
   d ...., most people I spoke to thought that the inventions on display were very interesting.

4 Read the expressions in 3 again. Which of the functions below are they using?

   a Introducing
   b Reporting an impression
   c Generalising
   d Making a recommendation or suggestion
   e Concluding

Do you know of any other expressions which you could add to each section?

5 Now look at these exam questions.

1 You regularly write a column in your college magazine on new films that are being shown in your town. Attendance at the local cinema is falling, and they have asked you to write a report, based on research at your college, on the cinema's facilities and to make some recommendations on how to attract more people to the cinema.

Write your **report**.

2 You belong to the College Science Club. The college authorities have asked you to write a report on the activities of the club to help them decide whether to increase the small grant they give to it every year.

Write your **report**.

UNITS 7–12 | Revision

Grammar

1 Read the text below and look carefully at each line. Some of the lines are correct, and some have a word which should not be there. If a line is correct, put a tick next to it. If a line has a word that should not be there, write the word at the end of the line. There are two examples at the beginning (0 and 00).

0	The best film I have seen this year it was *LA Confidential*, starring	*it*
00	Kim Basinger and Kevin Spacey. It was set in 1950s Los Angeles and	✓
1	although the budget wasn't particularly extravagant, so it had very	....
2	powerful images and seemed totally too authentic. For example,	....
3	the costumes looked just like what people must have worn; the cars	....
4	seemed to be exactly what people were used to drive around in.	....
5	All the actors played their parts extremely well, but while Kim	....
6	Basinger in particular who gave a truly outstanding performance.	....
7	The film was absolutely gripping, largely because of the storyline	....
8	was so carefully put together. There were several ingredients in.	....
9	Not only the obvious ones like murder and blackmail, but also as	....
10	corruption, Hollywood lifestyles, and, last but not the least, some	....
11	moving family histories. One leading character became into a	....
12	police detective to follow in his father's footsteps; the reason why	....
13	another took an interest in rescuing women from violent family	....
14	arguments was that his own father had badly been mistreated his	....
15	mother. In addition to, the ending is brilliant. This is an impressive film. See it!	....

Topic review

2 Read these sentences and say which are true for you, giving more details. Don't be afraid to use your imagination!

a I used to be different from how I am now.
b Next weekend I'm going to do something dangerous!
c I look like a famous film star.
d It must have been difficult looking after me when I was younger.
e I can't stand getting behind with my work.
f School used to be really boring.
g At home, I was always made to finish my food.
h By this time next year I'll have passed FCE.
i I really enjoy watching adverts on TV.
j I find it hard to believe that the Earth has been visited by aliens.

Vocabulary

3 Two common verbs are used in these sentences. Decide what they are and complete the spaces, using a suitable verb form.

a We're .... used to living in a village now.
b Jane .... on really well with her boss.
c Don't .... offence – I'm only trying to help!
d After Bill was made redundant, he soon learned to .... by with less money.
e You should .... advantage of the opportunity to go to America while your aunt is living there.
f I finally .... a letter from the company last week, offering me a refund.

g There's no point offering Jim any advice – he'll .... no notice of it!

h The engineer .... the whole thing apart and eventually found the problem.

4 Decide which is the odd one out in these sets and say why.

a disturbing, terrifying, cunning, appalling
b voice-over, jingle, slogan, campaign
c surgeon, sister, plumber, porter
d fancy, detest, loathe, hate
e deep, wide, huge, shallow
f pitch, rink, court, track
g intend, pretend, expect, hope
h extravagant, economical, affordable, cheap

Phrasal verbs

5 Complete these sentences with the correct verbs.

ON
a The property market is .... on favourably by investors.
b It must be really hard to .... on in advertising – it's such a competitive business.
c If you .... on going to the party, I suppose I'd better give you a lift.

OFF
d Sales of electric cars could .... off very soon.
e I'm going to use the exercise bike in the gym later to .... off that huge lunch!
f Jenny .... me off seeing that film; she said it was very shocking.

Writing

6 Read paragraphs A–C and decide what type of writing each one is, choosing from 1–4.

1 letter   **3** article
2 report   **4** composition

A

In my opinion, people should work fewer hours in the future. By doing this, unemployment could be reduced and working parents would be able to spend more time with their children. Moreover, life would be less stressful, which must be a benefit to society in the end.

B

Overall, there are good facilities in the town for students over the age of 18, but fewer opportunities exist for teenagers. Cinemas should be encouraged to show more 15-rated films. The local swimming pool should offer special prices to the under-18s. Finally, it would be worth opening new clubs for this age group, particularly for sport and drama.

C

Have you ever thought of joining a gym? I recently did and it changed my life. I used to come home from my job and just sit watching TV, but now, I work out every evening. My friends say my personality has changed. Before, I would be rather aggressive whenever my day had been bad, but now, they say I'm much better tempered.

Which paragraph

- is an opening?
- has a conclusion?

9.1 exercise 1

Isn't space the ultimate luxury?

(Advertisement for Renault Espace)

9.1 exercise 8
Group B XK Trainers
You are suspicious of advertising agencies, because two recent advertising campaigns failed. One used a famous basketball player, who was accused of taking bribes the same week the adverts appeared. Another, filmed at great cost in Antarctica, did not attract the public. Decide on the style you are now looking for.

1 Look at this pair of photographs, which show two different classrooms in Britain. Talk to a partner about the differences and say which school is closer to your own learning experience.

2 Now talk to each other about your schooldays. You should each describe:

a a school you attended (its size, location, atmosphere)
b a teacher you remember well
c something at school that you particularly enjoyed
d someone at school that you found really annoying

Report your partner's answers to the class.
For example:

X told me/said that he/she …
X spoke about/talked about his/her …
X thinks/feels/remembers that he/she …
X claims/believes strongly/is convinced that …

Which tenses did you use to report what you heard?

3 Report David's confession below as reported speech, being careful to use suitable past tenses.

EXAMPLE: *David said that it wasn't Simon's fault. …*

'It isn't Simon's fault! I want to describe what really happened. I was inside the classroom during break and I saw a group of my friends outside. I went over to the window and tried to get their attention. I waved at them but they didn't see me, so I hammered on the window. I know glass is breakable but I just didn't think. When my hand went through I panicked. I wasn't hurt and I wanted to avoid getting into trouble, so I put Simon's bag over the hole and left the room. I'm sorry I haven't told anyone the truth until now.'

Listening

ⓔxam spot

In Part 4 of Paper 4, you may be given seven statements about the recording, which will be true or false. Read these statements carefully in the time available before you listen, underlining any key words.

4 You are going to hear a radio interview with two work colleagues, Sandra Wilson and Mike Tripp, who also used to attend the same school.

First, read the reported statements 1–7 below.

1 Sandra explained that she had disliked Mike because of his attitude to school.
2 Sandra accused Mike of deliberately forgetting certain things he had done at school.
3 Mike explained that he had known at the time how irritating he was.
4 Mike wished he had worked harder at school.
5 Mike said that he had left the science exam because he couldn't answer the questions.
6 Mike felt that his father had expected him to do well when he left school.
7 Mike admitted that the school careers teachers had been quite helpful.

🎧 Now listen to the recording and decide whether the statements are true (T) or false (F). Then compare your answers with another student. Listen again to check your answers.

5   In the recording Sandra talked about some of Mike's friends who didn't *make it*. What exactly does this mean? In which other situations might you use this expression?

There are a number of other expressions with *make*. Complete these reported statements of how Mike set up his business, using a suitable phrase from the ones below.

make an impression	make a profit	make a success of
make a start	make use of	

a   Mike said that he had .... in a small way while still at school.

b   He admitted that he had .... the school computer in his lunch breaks.

c   He explained that he had .... on some cheap flights.

d   He said that he had .... the business from the start.

e   He complained that the careers teachers at school had not .... on him.

6   Below are some short descriptions of the first jobs some famous people had. See if you can work out which job was done by each person.

7   In the extracts there are several words commonly found in letters of application, which will be dealt with in the next Writing folder. Underline any words you think may be useful. Check their meaning in an English-English dictionary and look for further examples of their use.

A
His parents divorced when he was 12 and his mother was left to bring up four children single-handed. All four kids had jobs – his three sisters worked for different local restaurants, while he cut grass and did a paper round. It probably took him a year to earn what he can now make in a single day.

B
He inherited the family sculpting business but showed little interest in it. He had no talent for stonework whatsoever and so, not surprisingly, the business went downhill fast. Instead, it was his determination to solve the twin mysteries of life and death that led him to be considered the wisest man alive.

C
On leaving school at 17, the only jobs available were in the local fish factory. The smell was appalling and working on the filleting machine made her constantly want to throw up. She escaped to London in the end and found employment as a waitress.

D
He became an apprentice on a cargo ship at the age of 17 and his very first experience was gained on a voyage to Rio de Janeiro. Altogether he spent five years at sea. He devoted his spare time to his hobby, which was ultimately to become a full-time career, but only once he was 35.

E
She worked long hours at a hamburger restaurant and was so poor that she had to search through the dustbins after work for any thrown-out food. She also sold ice-cream and was a coat-check girl at the *Russian Tea Rooms* in New York.

F
Initially, she took a position as an unpaid assistant in a chemist's shop, and later qualified in pharmacy. Her duties gave her a sound knowledge of poisons, that would subsequently be extremely relevant.

Reporting

1 Look at quotes a–c and explain why the tenses underlined have been used in reporting them.

  a 'I can't remember much about my first school; my mother will, though.'
    Greg claimed that he <u>couldn't</u> remember much about his first school, but thought that his mother <u>would</u>.
  b 'When Jack moved to secondary school he became less motivated.'
    His mother said that Jack <u>had become</u> less motivated when he <u>had moved</u> to secondary school.
  c 'Girls are now doing better than boys at school.'
    The expert said girls <u>are</u> now doing better than boys at school.

G ⋯⟩ page 203

2 There are a number of reporting verbs in English, many of which have already been used in this unit. If you can use a variety of them in your writing, you will impress the examiner!

  Decide which structures can be used after the following reporting verbs, giving examples. Two are done for you.

  accuse *She accused him of cheating.*
  admit   *He admitted (to) being wrong.*
          He admitted (that) he was wrong.

  apologise ....
  argue   ....
  claim   ....
  deny   ....
  explain   ....
  insist   ....
  promise   ....
  refuse   ....
  say   ....
  suggest   ....
  urge   ....
  warn   ....

3 Match the quotes a–e with the reported statements 1–5.

  a 'I visited my old school recently and it was much smaller than I remembered.'
  b 'Perhaps we should educate parents about how they can help their children.'
  c 'We belong to an anti-learning culture.'
  d 'I'll make more of an effort.'
  e 'Many factory jobs disappeared and there was no new employment.'

  1 She complained that society doesn't encourage education.
  2 He promised to work harder.
  3 The article claimed that the jobs which had gone had not been replaced.
  4 She explained that she had been back and had found it very different.
  5 He suggested showing parents what to do.

G ⋯⟩ page 203

Listening

4 🎧 You are going to hear some extracts from a radio phone-in, in which members of the public give their views about the current educational performance of boys and girls in Britain.

  Listen to the first caller. Then complete these statements.

  a The first caller said he .... to make two points.
  b He claimed that there .... too many women teachers in British schools and that boys .... men as role models.
  c He suggested boys .... more by broken marriages than girls.

5 🎧 Listen to the four remaining extracts and note down the main points each caller makes. Then summarise each person's views by writing statements similar to the ones about the first caller. Try to use different reporting verbs, choosing from the ones given in 2.

6 🎧 As you listen again, listen out for words or phrases that mean the same as a–h. The number of the extract is given in brackets.

    a are usually (1)
    b make good progress (2)
    c misbehaving (2)
    d earners (3)
    e dealt with (3)
    f referring to (4)
    g make longer (4)
    h applaud (5)   /praise, (not (clapping))

7 Discuss the following questions:

- Are girls doing better at school than boys in your country? Why?/Why not?
- How should the problem of underachievement be tackled?

ⒼGrammar extra

Reported questions usually involve changes in word order. Look at the questions below and how they have been reported. Then report questions a–e.

What's the answer to number 14?

He asked what the answer to number 14 was.

Where are the cassette boxes?

He asked where the cassette boxes were.

When did this term start?

She asked when this term had started.

Are there enough books to go round?

He asked if there were enough books to go round.

Should I repeat the question?

She asked whether she should repeat the question.

a Why are girls gaining more university places?
    He asked ....
b In what ways was the situation different twenty years ago?
    He asked ....
c Will things get better in the future?
    He asked ....
d Should British children spend more time at nursery?
    He asked ....
e Why haven't we faced up to this problem?
    He asked ....

---

8 Complete the second sentence so that it has a similar meaning to the first sentence, using the word given. Don't change the word given. You must use between two and five words, including the word given.

1 'You put that frog on my chair, didn't you, Charlie?' said Sally.
    of
    Sally ....
    that frog on her chair.

2 'Stop misbehaving or you'll be sent to the head,' the teacher said to Johnny.
    warned
    The teacher ....
    or he would be sent to the head.

3 At the interview, Kate was asked how well she had done in her exams.
    did
    The interviewer asked Kate, 'How well
    ....
    in your exams?'

4 'Please try to stay awake during the lesson,' the teacher told them.
    urged
    The teacher ....
    asleep during the lesson.

5 Susan denied wasting her time at school when she was younger.
    said
    Susan ....
    her time at school when she was younger.

6 'Have you tidied up in the science lab?' the headmaster asked them.
    tidied
    The headmaster wanted to know
    ....
    in the science lab.

7 'I'm sorry, I've forgotten my homework,' Nicholas said.
    apologised
    Nicholas ....
    his homework.

8 Stephen told me he would see me the next day at the lecture.
    see
    'I ....
    at the lecture,' Stephen said.

Exam folder 7

Paper 4 Part 2 Sentence completion / note-taking

Advice

- You must write down the actual words that you hear. Do not spend time trying to say things 'in a different way'. If you do that you will probably miss the next answer.
- If you cannot do one question it is very important not to worry; you will, after all, hear the piece twice. Leave the difficult question and come back to it later.
- You will only need to write very little – one, two, or three words. Do not try to answer in a sentence or write too much – you don't have the time or the space.
- Minor spelling mistakes are accepted. However, you should check your spelling before transferring your answers to the answer sheet.
- Always try to write something, even if you're not sure that it's the correct answer.

In this part of the Listening paper you hear either a monologue or a conversation. The task will be to complete a sentence or to fill in notes. Sometimes you are given, as in the example below, a mixture of the two.

1   In this example question, the first section is note-taking, and the second section is sentence completion.

Before you listen, read through the question paper and try to predict what the answers are going to be. Together with a partner, try to do this now, and then see how many of the answers you predicted correctly at the end of the exercise. These clues may help you.

1   Other words for occupation are:

....

....

Try to think of as many as possible.
2   What type of skills should a person doing this job have?
3   Probably another type of …?
4   A hotel name.
5   What does 'attend' collocate with?
6   What does a secretary spend time doing?
7   Where might you have lunch? Listen carefully to this one as you may hear more than one place.
8   Another way of saying 'cope with'?
9   What sort of things do you try to resist?
10   The name of another job?

2 You will hear part of a radio interview with a woman called Christine Whitelaw. For Questions 1–10, fill in the missing information.

Name: Christine Whitelaw

Occupation: [_____ 1]

Skills:

• Good memory
• Confident phone manner

• [_____ 2]

Training: One year [_____ 3]

One year secretarial college

First job: At the [_____ 4] Hotel

Christine had to attend [_____ 5] in order to

get her present position with Patrick Millar.

In the afternoon, Christine is busy with

correspondence and [_____ 6]

Working lunches take place in the [_____ 7]

Christine's previous job taught her how

to cope with [_____ 8]

Christine finds it hard to resist all the [_____ 9]

Christine says she wouldn't want to change her job

and be a [_____ 10]

1 Identify the jobs in the photos and say what skills are important in each one. Which job would you prefer and why?

2 Check you know the meaning of these words and then choose three to complete the quotes below.

| calculating | concerned | insecure | flexible |
| self-motivated | academic | redundant | |

a A career used to be for life. Once you had left school, you found a job and worked your way up the career ladder. Today, the job market is far more .... , and no one knows what tomorrow may bring.

b You have to be ready to accept change, in short be .... , if you are going to stay in the job market. There's a positive side to this – instead of feeling that you have to stay in the job you've been trained to do, you have more freedom to move around and try different things.

c Women are more willing to take career risks, partly because they are less .... with status, but also because they like to experiment. It's just a question of saying: I think I can do this. And then giving it a go.

3 Do you view these trends in the job market positively or negatively? In what other ways has the job market changed?

4 You are going to read a magazine article about five women who have recently changed careers. For Questions 1–15, choose from the women (A–E). They may be chosen more than once. There is an example at the beginning (0).

Which of the women

used to own a company?		**0**	E
studied while working?	**1**	**2**	
expects to earn more eventually?		**3**	
gets by on less money?		**4**	
took voluntary redundancy?		**5**	
travelled in her original job?		**6**	
like meeting people in her work?	**7**	**8**	
enjoys her new lack of routine?		**9**	
took some time to get on top of her work?		**10**	
now work from home?	**11**	**12**	D
used to work in government?		**13**	D
found their previous job stressful?	**14**	**15**	

5 Now answer these questions about the women.

a Why do you think Amanda felt increasingly *discontented* in her old job?

b How might Linda become *demotivated*?

c In what context does Sue describe her salary as *unimaginable*?

d How might Petra's new life seem *uncertain* and *insecure* to some people?

e Why did the fact that Helen had had her own business make her seem *unemployable*?

f Why would an *immature* applicant be *unsuitable* for Helen's job as a registrar?

6 Choose suitable negative prefixes for these words.

| practical | capable | organised | dependent |
| successful | honest | loyal | patient |

Meet five women who have changed careers

A — Amanda, 39

I had been working in sales for twelve years when I suffered an ankle injury that was to change my whole life. Someone suggested alternative medicine and I was so impressed by the treatment that I began evening classes out of interest. I had reached a point in my life where things had to change. In many ways I had it all: a company car, foreign business trips, my own house, job security. But at 33, I felt increasingly discontented. So I persuaded my boss to let me work a four-day week and did homeopathy classes on the remaining day. It ... difficult years to qualify, as I was studying 25 hours a week on top of my job. Al... income has reduced by a third, my overheads are lower too. As for the BMW, I d... at all!

B — Linda, 34

I'd always wanted to have my own business, but something had held me back. I did various jobs in marketing, including four years in the cosmetics industry. When I was made redundant last year, I knew the time was right. I'd had my own colours done and I'd found it fascinating, so I used my redundancy money to buy a 'House of Colour' franchise. My work is very sociable and the best thing of all is that I answer to no one but myself. Everything is based here in the house, so I have to be incredibly organised and self-motivated. I'm nothing like as tense ... despite giving it my all. The only downside is the money, although in all ser... reckon the takings will have overtaken my previous salary by next year. I hope s...

C — Sue, 34

I'd never seen myself as academic. Hairdressing seemed glamorous and I wanted a car, so I went to work in a salon as an apprentice. It paid very little, but I had fun. Then my husband announced that he was moving to London. That was the catalyst I'd been waiting for. I stayed put and took English and Law at night school. I was spending 45 hours a week in the salon and working for exams as well. I lost ten kilos in weight, but for all the stress of studying, I knew I was doing the right thing. After leaving college I went into market research. My confidence has always been low and it was three years before I felt I'd cracked the job. My present earnings would have been unimaginable back in the salon.

D — Petra, 45

I worked for three cabinet ministers, earning £60,000 a year, but at the cost of having to work a 65-hour week. When I turned 35, it hit me: I've worked here for nearly 15 years and I've probably got 25 to go. If I'd added up the hours they ...

[note overlay:]
EXTENSION
Speaking Activity

① Job Interview Questions
   – Greatest Strength
   – Greatest weakness
   – Career Goals
   – A time you handled stress
   – Made a decision.

...ormal working ..., and then get ...e. Choosing to ...ties. I've set up ...ently editing a ...ing I'd always ... and structure ...n all, I feel I've ...

dropped. By 1994 it was hopeless and I went into voluntary liquidation. My friends said I would be unemployable, not just because of my age but because I'd run my own business. However, I've been working as a registrar* for the past three years. The original advert sought a mature, understanding person to deal with people from all walks of life, which was tailor-made for me! Although I miss my business, I've experienced two different careers, and it's marvellous to have another job which needs genuine commitment.

*a person who keeps official records of births, marriages and deaths

NOT CORRECTED.

G rammar extra

There are a number of expressions with *all* in the article. Say how *all* is used in a–h.

a I had it all (A)
b I don't miss it at all! (A)
c the best thing of all (B)
d giving it my all (B)
e in all seriousness (B)
f for all the stress (C)
g all in all (D)
h all walks of life (E)

Sometimes, *all* is confused with *whole*. In this example, it is not possible to use *all*.

... an ankle injury that was to change my whole life.

Now complete these sentences using *all* or *whole*. Where it is possible to use either, write both alternatives. Add any words necessary.

a The firm acknowledged .... 279 applications the same day.
b The recession had affected .... car industry, causing many redundancies.
c Microsoft is a household name throughout .... world.
d Accountants have a powerful voice in .... companies.
e We had been staring at figures on screen .... day and .... us were fed up.
f There are disadvantages to .... jobs.

What rules can you make about the use of *all* and *whole* on the basis of these examples?

G ⋯⫶ page 203

Perfect tenses

1 Explain the differences in meaning in these sentences and identify the tenses used.

   a I have never sent an e-mail.
   b I never sent an e-mail in my last job.
   c I had never sent an e-mail until I started working here.
   d I will have sent over 500 e-mails by the end of this week!

2 Now look at these examples of perfect tenses from 14.1. Identify their uses, choosing from 1–7.

   a I had been working in sales for twelve years.
   b My income has reduced by a third.
   c I'd always wanted to have my own business.
   d The takings will have overtaken my previous salary by next year.
   e That was the catalyst I'd been waiting for.
   f My confidence has always been low.
   g If I'd added up the hours …
   h I've set up the spare room as an office.
   i I've been working as a registrar for the past three years.
   j I've experienced two different careers.

   1 talking about a recent event or situation
   2 talking about an event or situation which started in the past but is still true
   3 emphasising the duration of a recent event or situation
   4 talking about an event or situation that happened earlier than the past time being described
   5 emphasising the duration of an event or situation which took place earlier than the past time being described
   6 used in a conditional structure
   7 talking about an event that will happen within a specified future time

   Which perfect tense has not been exemplified in a–j? Give an example of this tense.

   G⋯⟶ page 203

From: sally@purple.co.uk
Date: 19/8/99

Jamie

Extension

Question - making in all 4 tenses.

ing
of

n voted

/ has
nds.
been
working in the department for exactly a year.

   e The end of year results were not as bad as the directors *had feared / have feared*.
   f By May, eight new designs *have been launched / will have been launched*, increasing our sales potential.
   g Our sales director *has made / made* some appalling decisions and frankly, we'd be better off without him!
   h They *were waiting / had been waiting* for the fax all day but when it came through the final page was missing.

Listening

4 🎧 You are going to hear five people talking about relevant experience for particular jobs. Note down skills and qualities mentioned by each person.

   Speaker 1: office administrator
   Speaker 2: interpreter
   Speaker 3: shop assistant
   Speaker 4: first-aid worker
   Speaker 5: cook

   What other skills and qualifications would be useful in each job?

5 Now read the role play instructions for Student A or B.

Student A

You are about to attend an interview for a job which you really want, working at an international sports event in Australia, next summer. The job will be one of the five described in Listening 4 on page 92, but you don't know exactly which one yet! Spend a few minutes thinking about relevant experience and qualifications.

Remember to be enthusiastic at the interview and explain why you think you would be suitable.

Student B

You are going to interview someone for a job at a major international sports event in Australia. Tell the interviewee what the job involves (choose one of the five described in Listening 4 on page 92). Then ask the interviewee about relevant experience (including knowledge of English), qualifications, general commitment, and suitability for the job you have in mind.

Then decide on a scale of 0–5 (5 being the most positive) how your interviewee has performed, according to these criteria:

Experience   Qualifications   Commitment   Inter-personal skills
Enthusiasm

6 Skim the article below to decide who it is aimed at. Then put the verbs in brackets into the correct perfect tense.

How to survive in business today

By the early 1990s, the stripping away of management layers and large-scale staff redundancies **(1)** .... (shrink) companies radically. In some ways, this harsh new reality **(2)** .... (bring) bosses and workers closer together. At the same time, there **(3)** .... (never, be) so many small businesses starting up, with the result that, since the mid-1990s, a staggering 60 per cent of the working population **(4)** .... (work) in small groups, usually of five or less. Alongside these trends, the need to apply psychology in the workplace **(5)** .... (grow) constantly. 'Jobs for life' **(6)** .... (cease) to exist, and in contrast, survival skills at work **(7)** .... (become) absolutely essential. A group of streetwise employees **(8)** .... (tell) us their top tips on how to survive in the office.

- Fax or e-mail people at night – it will look as though you **(9)** .... (put in) extra hours.

- Never stay later than the boss – it's too obvious and it **(10)** .... (know) to cause widespread office discontent.

- Try to remember people's names – recent studies **(11)** .... (show) that this simple gesture makes people think more highly of you.

- Spend money on good clothes – a survey by Hays Personnel Services **(12)** .... (find) that 42% of men and 52% of women think well-dressed people have a career advantage.

- Become known as a safe pair of hands rather than a high-flying genius – in ten years' time, you **(13)** .... (give) the top job while your flashy colleagues **(14)** .... (claim) unemployment benefit for five years at least.

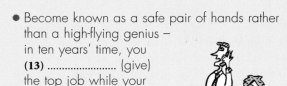

- Be concise in meetings – if you **(15)** .... (ramble on) at length, the chances are that you won't have got your message across.

Writing folder 7

Applications 1

1 Give the adjectives related to these nouns, using your dictionary if necessary.

motivation ....
commitment ....
determination ....
cheerfulness ....
enthusiasm ....
energy ....
organisation ....
talent ....
skill ....
confidence ....

2 Read this advertisement. Decide which skills would be essential for the job, choosing from the nouns above and adding ideas of your own.

WANTED

– friendly, English-speaking people to work as restaurant and bar staff on our Mediterranean cruise ships.

Tell us about
◆ why you would like to work for us
◆ any relevant experience you may have
◆ personal qualities that would be useful on board.

Contact ZY Cruises, PO Box 500, Southampton SO4 5TR, quoting reference PM44.

---

3 Now read these two letters of application. Has each applicant covered all the necessary points? Who would stand a better chance of getting the job?

A

Dear Sir or Madam

I have just seen your advertisement for jobs on board your cruise ships (reference PM44) and I would like to apply. I am a 20-year-old Swede with determination and commitment. I have often thought of spending time at sea and your job seems the perfect opportunity.

Although I have no on board experience, I have been working as a waiter in a local restaurant for the last 18 months and I have also had some experience of bar work. My knowledge of English is quite good, as I have been attending classes for the last six years. I would like to add that I have visited many parts of the Mediterranean myself and could talk to guests confidently during the voyage.

As for other personal qualities which might be useful on board a ship, I am an organised and easy-going person, so sharing a cabin with other crew members would not be a problem.

I am sure I would make a success of this job and I hope you will consider my application.

Yours faithfully
Pernilla Axelsson

B

Dear Mr or Mrs

I saw the job you advertised and I want to give it a go. I love the idea of going on a cruise and I'm just the person you need. I never thought of working on a ship but it sounds fine.

By the way, I've worked in a bar, though I didn't enjoy it that much. I wouldn't mind being a waiter on your ship though. Do the staff eat the same food as the guests? I've heard it's very good.

You ask about me. Well, I tell good jokes. I'm always cheerful and I think you would have to be, stuck on a ship for so long.

Write to me soon.

Harry

4 Make improvements to the second letter, rewriting it according to these guidelines.

a Change the open and close. Make sure the style is formal throughout.

b Rewrite the first sentence to make it clear which job is being applied for. Remember to use the present perfect!

c Edit the first and second paragraphs to make them sound more positive. Build up the information about previous experience, including some reference to learning English.

d Write a new third paragraph on personal qualities, using some of the adjectives and nouns in 3.

e Try to write around 180 words in all.

Exam spot

If you choose to write a letter of application in Part 2 of Paper 2, you do not need to write any addresses. Remember to cover all the points in the question and try to sound positive about yourself. You should use a formal style, with an appropriate open and close.

5 Now look at this exam question. Underline the parts of the task that you need to cover. Remember to plan your answer before you start writing.

You see the following advertisement in an international magazine.

> ## Can you answer YES to these questions?
>
> ▼ *Do you speak English confidently?*
> ▼ *Do you enjoy visiting new places?*
> ▼ *Do you get on well with people?*
>
> If so, we would be interested in hearing from you! We are looking for energetic and cheerful guides to lead our 15-day coach tours round Europe. Tell us why you would be suitable.
>
> **Apply to: Europewide Coach Tours, PO Box 23, London W1X 6TY, stating where you saw our advertisement.**

Write a **letter of application** in 120–180 words.
Do not include any postal addresses.

UNIT 15 Too many people?

1 Have you ever visited a place that is famous for being beautiful or interesting and been disappointed when you arrived? Think of some of the problems that people cause, like litter, for example.

What do you think should be done to stop places being spoiled?

Is there somewhere in your country that you think needs to be protected?

Listening

2 🎧 You are going to hear a woman talking about some of the problems faced by the Grand Canyon National Park Service. Complete the notes. Some answers are one word only, others are longer, but you do not need to write more than five words.

Grand Canyon Fact File

Location: [_____1_____] part of Arizona

Depth: [_____2_____]

Opened in: [_____3_____]

Number of visitors today: [_____4_____] a year

Main problems in park:

- too many [_____5_____]
- [_____6_____] from elsewhere
- lack of [_____7_____]

Colorado river

Problems caused by Glen Canyon Dam:

- Temperature of water 7 degrees [_____8_____]
- Some kinds of fish no longer exist
- [_____9_____] are getting bigger

Conclusion

Park may soon no longer be one of the world's [_____10_____]

Vocabulary

3 In the listening you heard the following words that are connected with **water**.

> floods   dam   reservoir
> rapids   drought   river

Now sort out the following words into these categories:

a throw away   **b use again**

> re-cycle   litter   junk
> rubbish   bottle bank
> second-hand

🅥 ocabulary spot

Think of different meaning categories and write down all the words you know for each one. Compare your lists in groups, to check spelling and learn more words.

→ not done

4 How green are you?

   a What do you do with the rubbish in your household?

   b Are you economical about using water and electricity? Why?/Why not?

   c How would you feel if you had to walk or cycle everywhere?

   d What do you think about being a vegetarian?

   e What's your opinion of people who wear real fur coats?

5 Make nouns, verbs and adverbs from these adjectives.

longest weakest deepest
strongest widest shortest

Now complete this text, using an appropriate form of the word in capitals.

Oil on beaches, vehicle exhaust fumes, litter and many other waste (1) .... **PRODUCE** are called pollutants, because they pollute our environment. Pollutants can affect our health and harm animals and plants. We pollute our (2) .... **SURROUND** with all kinds of (3) .... **CHEMIST** waste from factories and power stations. These substances are the (4) .... **WANT** results of modern living. Pollution itself is not new – a hundred years ago factories sent out great clouds of (5) .... **POISON** smoke.

(6) .... **FORTUNATE**, pollution has spread to the land, air, and water of every corner on Earth. (7) .... **SCIENCE** have much to learn about pollution, but we do know more about how to control it. We can also reduce pollution by recycling waste and using biodegradable materials which (8) .... **EVENTUAL** break down in the soil and (9) .... **APPEAR**.

Pronunciation

6 🎧 Listen again to the woman talking about the Grand Canyon. Write down all the numbers that she mentions.

7 🎧 Now practise saying these numbers and then listen to the tape to check your pronunciation.

Measurement
13km
30cm
0.5km
2.5m
153 kilos
1m 53cm
$\frac{1}{2}$
$\frac{1}{4}$
$\frac{2}{3}$

Dates
1st May 1899
3rd August 2000
12th February 2004
25th December 1990
the 15th century
4/5/45

Money
10p
£1.45
$50

'0'
'0' can be pronounced in different ways in English.
Telephone number – 012-323-66778
Football score – 3–0
Tennis score – 40–0
Science and temperature – 0 degrees Celsius

Telephone numbers
01256-311399
00-44-324-667012

Maths
$2 + 6 = 8$
$3 - 2 = 1$
$4 \times 4 = 16$
$10 \div 2 = 5$
20%
3°
$\sqrt{16}$

8 Now answer the following questions. Then get into teams and make up your own questions about numbers.

   a What's your date of birth?

   b What's your telephone number?

   c What's your address?

   d How tall are you?

   e How much do you weigh? (You don't have to be honest.)

   f When did man first walk on the moon?

   g What's the average temperature in summer in your country? In winter?

   h What's the population of your country?

   i How many people are there in a football team?

Countable and uncountable nouns

1 Decide which words in the following pairs are countable.

a	land	country
b	spaghetti	meal
c	recommendation	advice
d	travel	journey
e	job	work
f	money	coin
g	lightning	storm
h	weather	temperature
i	English	verb
j	vehicle	traffic
k	seat	furniture
l	hair	hairstyle
m	luggage	suitcase
n	mountain	scenery
o	information	note

Which four words can be both
countable and uncountable?
What is the difference in meaning?

2

Plural countables or uncountables e.g. coins or money
plenty of, a lot of, lots of

Uncountables e.g. money
much, little
a great/good deal of, a large/small amount of

Plural countables e.g. coins
many, (a) few, several
a great/good/small number of

All verbs, determiners and pronouns referring to uncountable
nouns are singular:

*A **great deal** of research **has been done** into the pollution produced
by cars in cities. Unfortunately, very **little** of **it is taken** seriously by
politicians.*

Use this information to correct the following sentences where
necessary.

a How much of the tourists actually realises the problems they
cause?

b Little of the soils can be used for cultivation now the trees have
been cut down.

c A large number of equipment are needed to camp at the
bottom of the Canyon.

d Few luggages can be carried on the back of a donkey down the
dirt tracks.

e A large number of rainforests is being cut down every year.

f The amount of traffic are causing too many congestions in
major cities.

g Much governments believes that nuclear power are the key to
future energy problems.

h The Park Ranger gave me several good advices about camping
in the national park.

i Little people nowadays wear fur coats.

⤳ + p 116 - 7

3 Both these pairs of sentences are correct, but there is a difference in meaning. What is it?

I make few mistakes with English grammar.
I make a few mistakes with English grammar.

I have little time to watch the TV at the weekend.
I have a little time to watch the TV at the weekend.

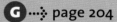rammar extra

some and *any* and *no*

Look at the following sentences and decide what the rule is for using *some* and *any* and *no*.

a At lunchtime the Prime Minister announced some of the government's plans for reducing congestion in cities.
b I haven't been able to see any stars in the sky recently because of light pollution.
c Would you like me to give you some information on ways you can cut down on using water?
d Have you any idea of the amount of food that is wasted each day in the developed world?
e No amount of persuasion will make some people use public transport rather than private cars.
f Have you got any/some change for the phone?

G ⤍⁝ page 204

Vocabulary

4 Expressions like *a piece of* or *a bit of* are often used to limit an uncountable noun. However, these words aren't very precise and it is better to use the right expression.

EXAMPLE: *in a shop you ask for <u>a loaf of</u> bread*
         at home you ask for <u>a slice of</u> bread

Which of the words on the left are used with the uncountable nouns on the right?

shower	clothing
slice	lightning
item	rain
glass	cake
clap	string
pane	people
ball	glass
flash	chocolate
crowd	water
bar	thunder

5 Using the information in this unit, complete the following sentences.

a Would you like .... chocolate to take on your trip? – Yes, could you put in a couple of ....
b Did you have .... bad weather over the weekend? – Yes – heavy rain and enormous .... of lightning.
c .... of the football hooligans spent Saturday night smashing all the .... of glass in my local school.
d I used to have short .... , but I've decided to grow it.
e Could you give me .... about travelling in India?
f My bank always refuses to change .... that I bring back from abroad.
g Even though .... vehicles use unleaded petrol nowadays, it doesn't make it any pleasanter to sit in heavy ....

G ⁝ page 203

6 For Questions 1–15, think of the word which best fits each space. Use only **one** word in each space. There is an example at the beginning(0).

The Pyramids

On **(0)** ..the.. great rocky plain of Giza in Egypt, stand **(1)** .... of the world's most remarkable buildings – three pyramids. There are quite a **(2)** .... other pyramids in Egypt, but these three are the largest and most famous. They were erected more than 4,000 years **(3)** .... and, while other great monuments have fallen **(4)** .... ruins, these pyramids have stood the test of time.

As the Egyptians believed **(5)** .... life after death, each ruler had a great **(6)** .... of his treasure buried with him. **(7)** .... the pyramids are enormous, the rooms inside are very small, because the pyramids themselves consist chiefly of solid stone. The largest, the Great Pyramid at Giza, was built by King Khufu in about 2500 BC **(8)** .... is still mostly intact. Its original height was almost 147 metres, and it weighed more **(9)** .... seven billion kilograms.

The pyramids were made **(10)** .... huge blocks of stone **(11)** .... were quarried, trimmed to a fairly regular shape, transported to the construction site and then piled on top of **(12)** .... another with astonishing precision. It **(13)** .... to be believed that over 100,000 men **(14)** .... been needed to build the pyramids, but now the scientists think the true figure **(15)** .... nearer 10,000.

Paper 4 Part 3 Multiple matching

In this part of the Listening paper you hear five short extracts, usually monologues, which are all related to each other in some way. It may be that they are all speaking about the same subject or experiences. Another possible link may be function or feeling or job. You need to match each extract to one of six options. You hear the extracts twice, and it is very important that you take the opportunity to check your answers carefully during the second listening. One mistake could affect two answers.

1 🎧 You are going to hear the first speaker talking about his experience of education. Look at the statements A–F and decide which one is true for the first speaker.

A I really enjoyed meeting new people.

B My attitude to studying had been wrong.

C It taught me how to cope with money.

D I'm not sure what I want to do now.

E I realised I worked better in a freer environment.

F I had to work harder than I expected.

The answer for Speaker One is B. Now look at the tapescript. The part containing the answer is underlined.

Advice

- Don't sit looking out of the window while you're waiting for the tape to start. Read the questions carefully.
- Try to predict what each person might say.

Tapescript

Speaker 1:

When I started my last year at school, I didn't take it seriously enough. <u>I should've chosen subjects which were useful rather than ones I liked or that sounded easy.</u> By the time exams came I'd given up and I did very badly. I knew I'd have to work hard but I wasn't able to catch up with my friends. Because I failed at science I can't be a teacher, which is what I really want to do. I'm doing a part-time job in order to make ends meet and next year I'll be starting evening classes to get better qualifications.

Look carefully at the options.

A I really enjoyed meeting new people. – *He doesn't mention new friends.*

B My attitude to studying was wrong. – *Right answer.*

C It taught me how to cope with money. – *Money is mentioned (to make ends meet) but nothing is said about learning what to do with money.*

D I'm not sure what I want to do now. – *He's going to study so this isn't the answer.*

E I realised I worked better in a freer environment. – *This isn't mentioned at all.*

F I had to work harder than I expected. – *This isn't the answer as he knew he had to work hard.*

King's College, Cambridge

2 🎧 Listen to the other speakers and for Questions 2–5, choose from the list A–F which each speaker states. (Remember that B has already been used.) Use each letter only once. There is one extra letter which you do not need to use.

Speaker 2   [2]
Speaker 3   [3]
Speaker 4   [4]
Speaker 5   [5]

3 Now look at the tapescript for Speakers 2–5 and underline the parts which give you the answers.

Tapescript

Speaker 2:
I left school and moved to a college to take my final exams. It was the best decision I could have made. At the college nobody seemed to care about homework and this really motivated me. I had to plan my work myself – there was no one to make you do it and no one to check up on what you'd done. I was still dependent on my parents for money – but that was OK. I learned a lot about real life there – things like getting on with people and organising your time – which has been really useful now I'm working.

Speaker 3:
When I left school I didn't have a particular career in mind so I decided to do Environmental Studies at university, mainly because I'd enjoyed geography at school. I didn't really like the course at university and I did think about leaving, but instead I changed courses, which was easier than I expected. I think university was useful in that I learnt how to live alone and how to budget, and as I'm an underpaid teacher now, that really helps.

Speaker 4:
I had no difficulty choosing what I was going to do – my parents are both doctors and ever since I was small I also wanted to do that. They really encouraged me and I did well at school and got into a good medical school fairly easily. It was surprisingly tough at medical school, but I had some good friends and we pulled through together. I think the doubts only began to set in when I graduated and got my first job in a hospital. I began to wonder if I'd missed out because I'd been so focused on becoming a doctor. So now I'm doing some voluntary work in Africa which I'm really enjoying.

Speaker 5:
I decided to take a year off after doing my last year at school. I'd had enough of revising and sitting in a library so I decided to go off to Australia for nine months and earn a bit of money. I've got relatives there who put me up when I first arrived and found me a job. It wasn't doing anything particularly interesting, but the great part was that I was getting to know people who were completely different to the ones I'd known back home. I really recommend taking a year out, but you need to have a firm plan or it could end up a waste of time.

Akiko (Japan)

Breakfast	Lunch	Dinner

Kunu (Alaska)

Breakfast	Lunch	Dinner

Gayle (USA)

Breakfast	Lunch	Dinner

1 Make a list of what you normally eat in a day. Compare your list with a partner.

2 What do you think someone in the following countries eats?

- Japan • Alaska • USA

3 🎧 Now you are going to hear three women talking about the food they normally have. Listen and make brief notes about what they eat.

Which person's diet would you like to try?

4 You are going to read an article from a newspaper, talking about a new food product that is aimed at children. Seven sentences have been removed from the article. Fill each gap (1–6) with the sentence which you think fits best from the list A–H. There is one extra sentence, which you do not need to use. There is an example at the beginning (0).

Tasty Vegetables for Kids

Flavoured frozen vegetables – including chocolate-tasting carrots – went on sale yesterday. 0 | H |. This is in response to a plea from Gordon McVie, director general of the Cancer Research Campaign charity, for a solution to unhealthy eating habits among young people.

1 | | It found that many mothers had all but abandoned the struggle to get their children to eat vegetables.

'We know that a third of all cancers are diet related and potentially preventable,' said McVie, who has lent his name to the new range of vegetables. 2 | |.

The idea for the 'wacky' vegetable grew out of an impromptu discussion in January between Professor McVie and Malcolm Walker, chairman of Iceland Frozen Foods. They talked about why frozen vegetables could not incorporate some of the flavours used to market packets of crisps. 3 | |.

4 | |. Interestingly, the majority rejected a number of potential lines, including bubble gum broccoli, prawn cocktail cauliflower and toffee apple

5 Look back at the article and, using your dictionary to help you, find the words that mean:

   a given a special taste
   b what you eat
   c natural and artificial chemicals
   d helpings
   e covering

In English we often use the expression *off*. What other word can you use in these phrases? There is an example first to help you.

EXAMPLE: *The milk was off. – sour*

   a The waitress told us the spaghetti was off today.
   b The meat was off.
   c The waiter was a bit off with us.
   d I'm off cakes at the moment, I'm on a diet.

6 In groups discuss these questions.

   a What do you think of the idea of flavouring fruit and vegetables? Would it be popular in your country? Why?/Why not?
   b What is your favourite food?
   c Do you think you have a healthy diet?
   d Are you or could you become a vegetarian?
   e What are the typical national dishes in your country?
   f Is there anything you can't stand or aren't allowed to eat?
   g When you were a child did you eat the same things as your parents? Why?/Why not?

sweetcorn. The company declined to comment on the flavouring process, except to say it had made use of 'natural' additives and had not altered the vegetables' underlying taste or nutritional value. 'In fact, there has been no genetic meddling and our market research shows that children and parents are very keen,' said Barbara Crampton, an Iceland spokeswoman.

Professor McVie said the recommendations of specialists for a healthy life were that children and adults should eat five portions of fruit and vegetables a day. The study came up with an amazing result. [5   ].

The big supermarkets, responding to increasing public awareness of the problem of children not wanting to eat their 'greens' have started to repackage fresh produce to appeal more directly to children. [6   ]. Both the Tesco and Sainsbury chains are also developing vegetables with sauces and coatings aimed at children.

Professor McVie said he hoped the flavoured vegetables might encourage children to move on to more traditional forms of vegetables, in the same way that fish fingers encouraged children to try fish.

A These have always proved popular with children.

B A study for the charity was carried out among working class families last year.

C Safeway, for example, recently introduced a children's range of miniature fruit and vegetables with softer flesh and skin.

D Researchers are experimenting with 'super-vegetables' which contain more vitamins.

E It found that for most children this was achieved on only one day a year – Christmas Day.

F The products were extensively market-tested on children aged 7 to 10.

G He believes that unless the British public understands this, there will be potentially serious health implications for the future.

H Also available are baked-bean-flavoured peas, cheese and onion cauliflower, and pizza sweetcorn.

The article

1 Look at these nouns from the listening in 16.1:

waiter	noodles	fish	cheese	lunch

Which of these nouns are
- singular countable?
- plural countable?
- uncountable?

Which of them take
- *a/an* (the indefinite article)?
- *the* (the definite article)?
- nothing?

2 Link the sentence in A with the rule in B. Some rules can be used more than once.

A
1 He's a waiter.
2 The Earth is egg-shaped.
3 The United States exports wheat.
4 The British love curry.
5 He's the best chef in Bangkok.
6 I usually go to a restaurant that overlooks the River Thames.
7 I had some great meals when I went skiing in the Rocky Mountains.
8 I hate fast food.
9 There's a restaurant on the corner – it's the restaurant with a red sign.
10 I get very hungry after playing football.

B
a *the* is used with rivers/oceans/seas/mountain ranges
b *no article* is used with most streets/villages/ towns/cities/countries/lakes/single mountains
c *the* is used with national groups
d *a/an* is used with jobs
e *no article* is used with sports
f *the* is used when there is only one of something
g *the* is used for countries in the plural e.g. The Netherlands
h *the* is used with superlatives
i *no article* is used when a noun is used generally
j *a/an* is used when something is mentioned for the first time
k *the* is used when a noun has already been mentioned

3 Read through this article and decide whether to use *a/an*, *the* or nothing in the spaces. Some spaces can have more than one answer.

'I'll have what he's having.' That's what (1) .... diners sometimes tell (2) .... waiters when another customer is served (3) .... meal that looks delicious. Wouldn't it be simpler if you cou see every dish on (4) .... menu before making up your mind? In (5) .... Japan, that's exactly what diners can do. There, (6) .... restaurant displays of real-looking fake food, called *sanpuru*, serve as (7) .... three-dimensional menu.

At one time, restaurants in Japan used to display real foo to advertise (8) .... restaurant's specialities, and to allow customers to 'preview' their meal. (9) .... displays also meant that (10) .... foreigners unak to read (11) .... Japanese menu could figure out (12) .... best thing to order. In the 1930s (13) .... first fake foods were made from (14) .... wax. Eventually such fake foods replace (15) .... real foods. Today *sanpuru* are made from vinyl, (16) .... kind of plastic.

4 Decide whether you need to use an article or not in these sentences.

a I went to .... hospital to see a friend who was ill.
b I went to .... hospital when I was knocked off my bike.
c I go to .... library once a week.
d She always goes to .... bed early.
e I often get hay fever in .... summer.
f The shops in my town always close for .... lunch.
g My father used to go to work by .... bike.
h When are you going on .... holiday?
i Tom never gets to .... work on time.
j He earns £800 .... week.
k I'll visit you in .... October.
l I can't play .... football very well.

m Ronald Reagan once held .... office of president.

n My uncle goes to .... prison to teach the prisoners computer skills.

o I've played .... flute ever since I was a child.

G ⋯⟶ page 204

Possession

1 When we are talking about people we use 's or s':
my sister's boyfriend, the visitors' cars
In the first example there is only one sister so the apostrophe is before the *s*. In the second example the apostrophe is after the *s* because there is more than one visitor.

2 's is also used when we are talking about time or distance:
a month's holiday, a kilometre's walk

3 We usually use *of* when we are talking about objects or position:
the back of the room, the film of the book
Also for when a container has something in it:
a bottle of milk

4 Quite often we use a noun to describe another noun when it describes either the kind, use or place:
a pear tree, a coffee cup, a shop window

5 Correct the following sentences where necessary.

a The father of my husband works in an Italian restaurant.

b I looked through the restaurant's window but couldn't see anyone.

c He was sitting at the front of the terrace.

d I bought a magazine of cooking.

e I'm sure we all always look forward to pay day.

f Most waiters get tips to help supplement their day's pay.

g Can I have a coffee cup and a piece of that delicious cake, please?

h The boss of my company is having a big party to celebrate his birthday.

Grammar extra
Prepositions of time

When we talk about time we usually have to use a specific preposition. In the article in 16.1 there was the example of *in January*. The preposition *in* is used with months of the year. Fill in the spaces in the sentences below using a suitable preposition from the box. (More than one answer is sometimes possible.)

in	at	on	for	during	since
from	to	by	over	until/till	

a I was born .... Monday 8th December .... 1973 .... 7.30 .... the morning.

b What are you doing .... the weekend?

c I find it really difficult to sleep .... night .... summer.

d I have .... Friday to make my decision.

e .... Christmas Day we usually eat turkey.

f I'm going .... holiday .... the end of May.

g The film lasted .... 6.30 .... 9.00.

h I've known him .... June.

i .... the summer holidays I spent some time in Italy.

j I've lived in this house .... twelve years.

k I'll have finished decorating the house .... next week.

Listening

6 🎧 Listen to a man talking about how to make his favourite dish.
The first time you listen write down the ingredients you hear.
The second time you listen write down the method of making the dish.
Now, using the basic vocabulary from the listening, tell your partner how to prepare your favourite dish. Notice you need to use the imperative – *do, put, cut,* etc. Remember to use articles correctly.

Writing folder 8

Transactional letters 2

This question is compulsory – all exam candidates have to answer it. 'Transactional' means that the letter will require further action by its reader, usually in the form of a written response. The letter must be based on the information given in the question.

1 When you write a letter it is important that you keep in the same style all the way through. Read through this letter and, with a partner, decide which is the best alternative, a or b, in 1–10 below. The first one has been done for you.

> Dear Pete,
> (1) ......Thanks a lot...... for coming along
> (2) .... plans for the new student café on campus. I really think we all
> (3) .... and I hope that we can
> (4) .... some ideas for interesting menus. (5) .... asking your friend Marco Brown, the TV chef, to open the café on Saturday.
> (6) .... when we open, and I think the café will (7) .... with the students. Anyway, (8) ....
> (9) ....
> (10) ....
> George

1 a I am writing to thank you
  b Thanks a lot *(circled)*
2 a to discuss the
  b to talk about
3 a found it very useful
  b thought it was extremely productive
4 a come up with
  b propose
5 a We all appreciate your
  b Thanks a million for
6 a I feel sure everyone will have an enjoyable time
  b It's certain to be a great night

7 a go down well
  b prove very popular
8 a that's all for now
  b I will contact you again at some point
9 a See you soon
  b I look forward to seeing you in the near future
10 a Yours faithfully
  b Best wishes

2 Look at this exam question.

Below is an invitation and map you have received from your friend Anna. You want to go to her party but you need to find out some information. Read the invitation and map, and look at the notes you have made. Then write your reply.

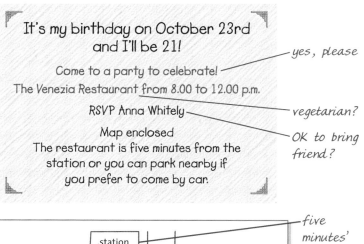

> It's my birthday on October 23rd and I'll be 21!
>
> Come to a party to celebrate! — *yes, please*
> The Venezia Restaurant from 8.00 to 12.00 p.m.
>
> RSVP Anna Whitely — *vegetarian?*
>
> Map enclosed — *OK to bring friend?*
> The restaurant is five minutes from the station or you can park nearby if you prefer to come by car.

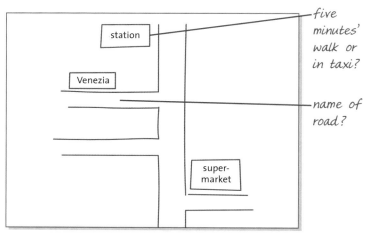

five minutes' walk or in taxi?

name of road?

3 This is the letter that Anna received. It would receive very low marks in the exam. Discuss with a partner what the main problems with the answer are. Then work together and rewrite it in a more appropriate way.

Dear Anna,
I'm writing with reference to the invitation you sent me on September 4th. I'm really grateful you asked to me and I'm really pleased to come.
I am extremely grateful if you could tell me name of road restaurant is in and also if possible take a taxi from station?
As you know, I am vegetarian eating and insist on that.
I will have friend staying with me. She is nice. I bring her.
I look forward to see you in the near future.

4 Look at this exam question.

You saw this advertisement in your local paper, and you wrote some notes after ringing up to find out more information. You know two friends of yours want to go with you, but you need someone else to go too.

Now read through the advertisement and the notes carefully. Then write a letter to a friend, persuading your friend to come with you and your other friends on the weekend.

Write a **letter** of between 120 and 180 words in an appropriate style. Do not include any postal addresses.

Remember, you want your friend to go with you so you need to be persuasive. Make sure you read both the advertisement and your notes carefully. Make sure any negative points are countered with positive ones. You need to sound enthusiastic and make this friend feel he/she is really wanted on this holiday.

EXAMPLE: *I know you really like swimming and that's one of the reasons I think you would enjoy this holiday. However, as it's spring the lakes might be too cold to go swimming in. The advertisement does say that there's a heated indoor swimming pool in the nearby town, so perhaps we could go there instead.*

1 Here are two pairs of photographs showing various hobbies. Look at the first pair with another student. Decide who will be Student A and who Student B. Then read your instructions. Student A can also refer to the notes below.

2 Look at the second pair of photographs and change roles. Student A should listen carefully to what Student B says. Remember to keep talking for up to a minute.

Student A

Compare and contrast the pictures, describing the possible benefits and problems of collecting the things shown.

Fossils – very old! Books and equipment needed (hammer, etc.) to find your own. Dangerous? Travel to good places. Educational?

Football items – lots available. Expensive! Takes up a lot of space? What would friends think of this hobby?

Student B

When Student A has finished, say which hobby you would find more interesting, and why.

Student B

Compare and contrast the pictures, describing the main differences between these two hobbies. (about 1 minute)

Student A

Say which hobby appeals to you more, and why. (20 seconds)

Exam spot

In Part 2 of Paper 5, each candidate has to take a 'long' turn, speaking for about a minute. Listen carefully while the other candidate is speaking, as you will have to make a brief comment afterwards.

Now carry out the speaking task. Student A should try to keep talking for about a minute and then Student B should talk for a maximum of 20 seconds. Time yourselves.

Did Student B manage to talk for a full minute? Suggest other ideas if necessary.

3 How many hobbies can you think of which involve collecting or making something? Work in two teams: the collectors and the creators. See who can produce the longer list! Then, in pairs, decide on the four most interesting hobbies from the two lists, giving your reasons why. You can agree to disagree!

Listening

4 🎧 You are going to hear eight short extracts to do with hobbies. For Questions 1–8 choose the best answer, A, B or C. You will hear each extract twice. Compare your answers with another student.

1 You hear a man giving a talk about his hobby. Where does he find his best fossils?

A at shops   B on beaches   C up cliffs

2 You overhear this conversation in a café. What sort of postcards is the woman keen to collect?

A ones that are in good condition
B ones from the 1930s
C ones with a printed message

3 You hear a woman talking on the radio. Why were the wooden objects she describes unusual?

A They were painted with beautiful designs.
B They were made from different types of wood.
C They were carved from a single piece.

4 You hear this radio interview. Who suggested the boy took up slot-car racing?

A his father   B his friend   C his cousin

5 You hear part of a radio programme. Which kind of beads does the girl have most of?

A glass   B wooden   C plastic

6 You overhear a man talking on the phone. Who is he talking to?

A an assistant at a shop selling kits
B a journalist working for a magazine
C a member of staff at a factory

7 You hear part of a radio interview. Which opinion does the interviewer express about Jenny's pictures?

A They are well-researched.
B They are carefully chosen.   pebbles Yes, paintings no
C They are extremely detailed.

8 You will hear a man talking on the radio. How does he spend his weekends?

A pretending to be a soldier
B studying a history course
C producing different plays

5 In pairs, decide which of these hobbies would interest you **least**, explaining why. Report your views to the class.

6 In listening extracts 3, 4 and 6, *look* was used as in a–e below. Four more uses are given in f–i. Check their meanings before answering questions 1–9 below.

a look at
b look for
c on the lookout
d the look of
e look after
f Now look here!
g look into
h Look out!
i look up to

1 Who might **look at**
A teeth   B a passport   C a burst pipe?

2 What are you planning to do if you are **looking for**
A a needle   B a saucepan   C a dictionary?

3 Who might be **on the lookout** for
A a missing yacht   B murder clues
C tax savings?

4 Describe **the look of**
A leather   B thick mud   C concrete.

5 Who **looks after**
A patients   B rose bushes   C local residents?

6 Continue the statement **Now look here** …, as if you are arguing with
A a bank manager   B a young child
C a journalist.

7 What might you discover if you **looked into**
A a kitchen cupboard   B your friend's eyes
C deep space (with a telescope!)

8 Why might someone shout **Look out!** at you, if you were
A driving   B swimming in the sea
C walking under a ladder?

9 Who might these people **look up to**?
A a six-year-old boy   B a first-year student
C a trainee cook

Relative clauses

1 Look at the pair of sentences a and b, then answer questions 1 and 2 for each of them.

   a The children who were tired went straight to bed.
   b The children, who were tired, went straight to bed.

   1 Were all the children tired?
   2 Did all the children go to bed?

Which sentence contains a defining relative clause? Which has a non-defining clause in it?

G ⋯⟶ page 204

Explain the difference in meaning between c and d.

   c It was getting late, so we decided to stay at the first hotel which had a pool.
   d It was getting late, so we decided to stay at the first hotel, which had a pool.

2 Here are two examples of relative clauses from the listening extracts. Which is a defining relative clause and which is a non-defining one?

   a Jamie Eagle, who is the outright winner of today's slot-car racing, is with me now.
   b I'm on the lookout for older ones that have text on the picture.

Identify the relative clause in each of these examples, underline the relative pronoun used, and decide whether the clause is defining (D) or non-defining (N).

   c Looking at the stamps, they're older than you say, which is brilliant.
   d I knew someone once who had an absolute passion for making things out of wood.
   e It was my cousin who's to blame.
   f Jenny Braintree, whose bedroom I'm sitting in right now, has a rather unusual hobby.
   g I'm trying to paint a scene from every country in the world, most of which I haven't been to.
   h The group that puts on these events was only formed about four months ago.

3 What relative pronoun has been left out in this example? Insert it in the correct place.

> *Here are those cards I bought for you in Oxford.*

Omission of the relative pronoun is quite common in spoken English, but can only be done when it is the object of a defining relative clause. So, for example, you could not leave out the word *that* in example *h*.

Decide what relative pronouns have been left out of these sentences and underline the defining clause in each.

   a The picture I wanted to buy had already been sold.
   b She was the teacher I really looked up to.
   c The thing I can't stand about Harry is his odd socks!
   d That boy you met at John's party plays tennis.
   e The hotel we stayed at had luxurious bathrooms.

4 The last example could be rewritten like this:

The hotel <u>where</u> we stayed had luxurious bathrooms.

You can use *where*, *when* and *why* in defining relative clauses after nouns to do with place, time and reason. Again, in spoken English, *when* and *why* are sometimes omitted. Here are two examples from 17.1.

1987 was the year I found the most.
That's not the reason she's mad at me though.

In non-defining clauses, these words cannot be omitted.

Insert *where*, *when* or another relative pronoun into these non-defining clauses.

   a The writer Iain Banks was born in Fife, Scotland, ... he still lives.
   b The earthquake happened shortly before dawn, ... most people were asleep.
   c Aidan, ... lives in our road, plays the double bass.
   d They sent an information booklet, ... was really helpful.
   e I went to the Body Shop, ... they had that make-up, but they had sold out.

5 Read this text. If a line has a word that should not be there, write the word at the end of the line. If a line is correct, put a tick (✓) next to it. There are two examples (0 and 00).

A PASSION FOR BOTTLES

0	The problem with hobbies is that they can so easily to take over, and	...to...
00	I mean that in every sense. They either monopolise your life, making	...✓...
1	too many demands on your time, or, worse than, they physically	....
2	invade your living space. One friend of mine is haunted by the desire	....
3	to collect bottles. This passion, which it started quite by chance five	....
4	years ago, has now reached an absurd stage, where he has literally	....
5	had to rebuild his house to accommodate with the 3,429 (at the last	....
6	count) assorted exhibits. Some of his bottles are indeed worth having,	....
7	including and an example of the very first Coca Cola design, a hand-	....
8	painted wine bottle from the 1920s, and some rather so attractive	....
9	milk bottles, which carry brightly-coloured images of the advertising.	....
10	However, that the overwhelming majority are plain ordinary and	....
11	should have been taken away to a bottle bank since years ago. The	....
12	reason he has hung on to them for all of this time is far away from	....
13	clear, though I suppose that's being true of all hobbies. Once they	....
14	have taken you over, you become a mere slave to the obsession.	....
15	If only my friend had chosen bottle tops – such a collection would fill three drawers at most!	....

Pronunciation *Contrastive stress*

6 🎧 In two of the listening extracts in 17.1, where a person was being interviewed, there are examples of contrastive stress. In each case, the interviewer makes a factual error, which the interviewee corrects. Listen to the stress patterns used by the interviewee in these examples.

Interviewer Did he know what he was doing when he persuaded you to take up such a time-consuming hobby?

Jamie Er, actually, it was <u>me</u> who persuaded <u>him</u> – he's only been racing this year.

Interviewer Jenny, you took up this hobby four years ago and …

Jenny Er … it was four <u>months</u> ago, in fact.

7 🎧 Now listen to these short exchanges. In pairs, underline the words that are stressed by each second speaker. Read the dialogue again with your partner, who should check whether you have stressed the right words.

a Would you like a coffee?
  No, thanks – it stops me sleeping. I wouldn't mind a cold drink though.
b I'm going to wear my red dress to the interview.
  Oh no, red's much too bright. I'd wear your blue one – with the grey jacket.

c Hello, Jan? Listen, I've been waiting outside the cinema but no one's turned up.
  The others said they'd meet you inside, didn't they?
d Why is it always my turn to empty the dishwasher?
  It isn't. I did it yesterday – and I cleaned the cooker, too.

8 In pairs, read these short exchanges aloud, taking turns to respond to each suggestion with an alternative plan. Stress any word in bold and your new idea each time.

a Let's go and play tennis – it's not too cold, is it?
  It's **freezing**! I think we should …
b Why not stay in and do your homework this evening?
  Not **again**! I'd much rather …
c Paint your room yellow – it would look really good.
  Ugh! Yellow's too …
d You know, you could have that magazine sent to you every month.
  But it's so **expensive**. I think I'll just …
e Brian's the one who's interested in model cars.
  No he isn't, that's …
f Here's the CD I bought in town. It was only £12.99.
  £12.99? I've seen it for …

Exam folder 9

Paper 4 Part 4
Choosing from two or three answers

In this part of the Listening paper there are seven questions. You may have two alternatives (Yes/No, True/False), or three. If you have three it may take the form of a three-option multiple choice or a 'Who said what?', where the conversation has two or three people expressing opinions or feelings. It is also possible to have questions which ask, for example, in a discussion comparing three cars, 'Which car offers what?' or, in a discussion about restaurants, 'Which restaurant is famous for what?' The questions follow the order of the information in the conversation.

Advice

- Read the questions carefully and try to predict what you might hear.
- You can write notes on the question paper as you listen the first time.
- Remember to put your answers on your answer sheet after the second listening!
- Always write down an answer even if you are unsure that it is correct.

You will hear an interview with two people, Rebecca Laing and Philip Lawson, who live on an island. There are seven questions but instead of all seven being of the same type as in the examination, here there are two True/False, three Multiple choice and two Who said what? questions. This is to give you practice in the kinds of questions you may have in the examination.

True/False

1 The island is following the population pattern of many Scottish islands. [1]

2 Philip's social life is better than it was in London. [2]

Multiple choice

3 Rebecca says the kind of people who want to live there [3]

A enjoy their independence.
B are prepared to accept disadvantages.
C don't have children.

4 Philip believes the island needs to [4]

A attract more industry.
B encourage more people to live there.
C be cautious about any new plans.

5 Rebecca thinks that the island [5]

A suffers from traditional thinking.
B should attract more tourists.
C should put people before wildlife.

Who said what?

R = Rebecca
P = Philip
N = Neither

6 It's best to keep your opinions to yourself. [6]

7 People respect your need for privacy. [7]

1 Look at the illustration and decide what it represents. Whereabouts in the world might this be?

2 You are going to read an extract from *The Old Man and the Sea* by Ernest Hemingway. First, read these brief reviews of the book. What do you learn about the book from them?

Not only the finest short story that Hemingway has ever written, but one of the finest written by anyone.

Every word is meaningful and there is not a word too many.

The writing is as tight, and at the same time as cleverly played out, as the line on which the old man plays the fish.

Ⓔxam spot

The text in Part 2 of Paper 1 is sometimes an extract from a novel. There may well be words which you don't know, but these are unlikely to be tested, so don't panic!

3 Now skim the text below quickly, to get an idea of the scene that is being described.

The old man rubbed the cramped hand against his trousers and tried to ease the fingers. But the hand would not open. Maybe it will open with the sun, he thought. He looked across the sea and knew how alone he was now. The clouds were building up for the trade wind and he looked ahead and saw a flight of wild ducks against the sky over the water, and he knew that no man was ever alone on the sea.

He thought of how some men feared being out of sight of land in a small boat and knew they were right in months of sudden bad weather. But now they were in hurricane months and, when there are no hurricanes, the weather of these months is the best of all the year. If there is a hurricane you always see the signs of it in the sky for days ahead, if you are at sea. They do not see it ashore because they do not know what to look for, he thought. But we have no hurricane coming now. He looked at the sky and saw the white cumulus clouds built like friendly piles of ice cream and high above were the thin feathers of the cirrus against the high September sky. 'Better weather for me than for you, fish,' he said.

His left hand was still cramped, but he was unknotting it slowly. I hate a cramp, he thought. It is a treachery of one's own body and it humiliates oneself especially when one is alone. If the boy were here he could rub it for me and loosen it down from the forearm, he thought. But it will loosen up. Then, with his right hand he felt the difference in the pull of the line. As he leaned against the line and slapped his left hand hard and fast against his thigh he saw **it** slanting slowly upward. 'He's coming up,' he said. 'Come on hand. Please come on.'

The line rose slowly and steadily and then the surface of the ocean bulged ahead of the boat and the fish came out. He came out unendingly and water poured from his sides. He was bright in the sun and his head and back were dark purple and in the sun the stripes on his sides showed wide and a light lavender. His sword was as long as a baseball bat and he rose full-length from the water and then re-entered it, smoothly, like a diver and the old man saw the great blade of his tail go under and the line started to race out.

He is a great fish and I must convince him, he thought. I must never let him learn his strength nor what he could do if he made his run. If I were him I would put in everything now and go until something broke. But, thank God, they are not as intelligent as we who kill them; although they are more noble and more able.

The old man had seen many great fish. He had seen many that weighed more than a thousand pounds and he had caught two of that size in his life, but never alone. Now alone, and out of sight of land, he was fast to the biggest fish he had ever seen and bigger than he had ever heard of, and his left hand was still as tight as the gripped claws of an eagle.

It will uncramp though, he thought. Surely it will uncramp to help my right hand. There are three things that are brothers: the fish and my two hands. It must uncramp. It is unworthy of it to be cramped. The fish had slowed again and was going at his usual pace.

I wonder why he jumped, the old man thought. He jumped almost as though to show me how big he was. I know now, anyway, he thought. I wish I could show him what sort of man I am. But then he would see my cramped hand. Let him think I am more man than I am and I will be so.

4 Read through the questions below and then read the text through again, more carefully this time. Then, in pairs, identify the parts of the text that relate to each question. Work out the correct answers together and decide why the other options are wrong.

1 How did the old man feel about being out at sea?
  A He enjoyed it because he had time to himself.
  B He didn't mind as there were creatures around him.
  C He realised how dangerous his work was.
  D He wasn't happy at being out of sight of land.

2 Why was he sure the weather would stay fair?
  A It was not the right time of year for hurricanes.
  B Bad weather had not been forecast ashore.
  C He could see no trace of an approaching hurricane.
  D There are more fish during good weather.

3 What does 'it' refer to in line 20?
  A his boat   **C** his hand
  B the line   **D** the fish

4 What does the old man worry about after seeing the fish?
  A The fish is too powerful for his boat.
  B He isn't as clever as the fish.
  C He doesn't have enough line.
  D The fish could escape if it swam fast.

5 What does the writer mean when he says the old man was 'fast to the biggest fish he had ever seen' in line 35?
  A He was joined to the fish by his line.
  B He was attracted by such a big fish.

C He was chasing the fish in his boat.
D He was surprised to see the fish's size.

6 The old man didn't want the fish to see that he was
  A alone in the boat.
  B so small.
  C too tired.
  D in some difficulty.

5 The extract described the fish *coming up* and *going under*. Can *come* and *go* both be combined with the following particles? Make phrasal verbs and use these in a suitable form in the sentences below.

	after
come	in for
go	out
	through
	without

a The novelist has .... a lot of criticism on his latest book.
b I don't mind .... most things, but I do need coffee.
c Let's .... the passage together to check on any difficult vocabulary.
d The dog .... the burglars but wasn't fast enough to catch them.
e We .... a major problem when we moved – the sofa was too wide and it wouldn't .... the new doorway.
f Those yellow roses have .... very early this year.
g I don't usually .... detective novels, but this one's really good.
h After all you've .... , you must be exhausted!
i When the tide .... , we did a guided reef walk and saw some wonderful shells and starfish.
j My blood went cold, as I noticed a dark figure with a hunched back, who was .... the fog towards us.

6 Finish this paragraph about the extract you have just read by giving some description of the old man's left hand.

In this part of the book, the writer keeps referring to the old man's left hand, which won't move. He mentions the hand so often in order to make sure the reader understands the serious difficulty the old man is up against. I imagine the hand looks like ...

enough, too, very, so, such

1 Identify the books shown, choosing from these types.

> science fiction biography
> short stories thriller non-fiction
> historical novel play western

2 🎧 You will hear five people talking about books they have enjoyed. Match the books in the picture to the five speakers. There is one extra which you do not need.

Speaker 1 ☐ 1
Speaker 2 ☐ 2
Speaker 3 ☐ 3
Speaker 4 ☐ 4
Speaker 5 ☐ 5

3 Read this article about the role of the book today, ignoring the missing words. Does the writer believe that the book has a future? Why?/Why not?

Fill in spaces 1–15 with one suitable word. There is an example at the beginning (0).

The book in the 21st century

How many times in (0) ..the.. last hundred years or so have people talked of the imminent death of the book? Films (1) .... an early threat, because they were so effective at telling stories in a visual way. Next there was radio, (2) .... swept into the mid-twentieth century and provided such alternatives to books (3) .... drama, documentaries and discussions. When television arrived, many people believed that it (4) .... finish the book off. Nowadays, (5) .... the threat by TV, the book is thought to be endangered by computers and the Internet, and by other technological attractions (6) .... the CD and the video game, too.

Surely there are now enough reasons (7) .... the book ought to be dead, (8) .... at least very badly injured. If so, why does it not show proper respect for these reportedly (9) .... literate times and die out? There is clearly more than a (10) .... answer to this question. Firstly, we have more leisure time than we (11) .... to, and people are generally living longer, which means there is more time to do more (including reading books). As (12) .... as this, there is the strength of the book as a tradition. We are all too dismissive of traditions in our modern world, but they can have a very strong pull (13) .... us. Added to this, the book is such a practical tool: it doesn't cost too (14) ...., it is usually small enough to carry around, and it can easily (15) .... revisited. We will never go without books, because they have served us so well for so long.

4 Find all the examples of the following words in the article and study the ways in which they are used. There are 11 examples in all. Then match the examples to the statements a–k. There is one extra statement which you do not need.

enough

a used before an uncountable noun or a countable noun in its plural form to say that there is as much of something as is needed

b used after an adjective or adverb to say that someone or something has as much of a quality as is needed

c used after an adverb in certain expressions for emphasis

too

d used in front of an adjective or adverb to say that there is more of something than is acceptable or desirable

e used after a piece of information, to emphasise its importance

very

f used to give emphasis to an adjective or adverb

so

g used to emphasise an adjective or adverb

h used to indicate that an amount is approximate

i used in a conditional clause

such

j used to give an example of something

k used to emphasise an adjective in a noun group

Now compare some of these examples. What are the differences in usage between the two words in brackets?

b and d (enough/too)
d and f (too/very)
f and g (very/so)
g and k (so/such)

ⓖ⋯⟶ page 205

5 Insert *enough* into each of these sentences in the correct place.

a Surely you've had time to finish the exercise?

b The room wasn't large to hold everyone.

c There weren't books to go round, so we had to share.

d I had had of other people's problems, so I left work early.

e The course was cancelled as not people enrolled for it.

f 'How much money do you have on you?' – 'I've got to pay for the cinema and buy us supper after.'

g 'But that's quite about me! What about you?'

h 'Funnily, I'm reading one of his books at the moment too.'

6 Complete the second sentence so that it has a similar meaning to the first sentence, using the word given. Do not change the word given. You must use between two and five words, including the word given.

1 The weather was too cold for us to go out.
   such
   It was .... didn't go out.

2 I'm sorry there's not enough time to explain.
   too
   I'm sorry there's .... you an explanation.

3 Why not turn professional, as you are such a good swimmer.
   so
   You swim .... turn professional.

4 Barry really knows how to get other people involved.
   very
   Barry .... other people involved.

5 I make all my clothes by hand so it's very time-consuming.
   such
   It .... time because my clothes are all hand-made.

6 Provided this is the case, your money will be refunded.
   so
   If .... will be given.

Writing folder 9

The set book

1 Read this composition and correct the twenty spelling and punctuation errors.

2 Does the composition answer the following question? How could it be improved?

How true to life is the book you have read?

Write a **composition**, explaining your views with reference to the book or one of the short stories you have read.

3 Now think about the same question in relation to *The Old Man and the Sea*. Look again at the extract on page 114 and think about how it could be used to illustrate this answer. Then read the notes. What else could you mention from the extract to support the view that this book is very true to life? Think about where the scene takes place and what is described apart from the old man.

The book 'Marcovaldo', by Italo Calvino, is actually a series of twenty short storys, all conteining the same charakter, Marcovaldo. He lives with his large family in an unamed city in Northern Italy. Each story is set, in a diffrent season: there are five stories about living in the city in summer, and so on.

Many aspects of modern life are described, such as advertiseing and pollution of the enviroment, but the book is not completly true to life. This is perhaps it's greatest strength. It has a unique mixtur of realistic events and bizare ones, which often take the reader by suprise. One particluar story features the publicity campains of rival soap powder manufacturers. Marcovaldos' children and their frends collect hundreds of free cartons of washing powder, which they hope to sell to people in the neigbourhood. In the end, they have to get rid of everything quickly and so throw the cartons into the River. The story closes with a memmorable description of soap bubbles being blown over the city, their whiteness competing with the black factory smoke. Black wins.

Introduce book briefly and give my opinion on how true to life it is (= very!)

Mention part where old man gets fish on his line (mustn't describe story in detail here)

Discuss character of old man – believable – strong, has great determination in spite of age, but has physical problems (mention writer's focus on hand in this scene)

Add something else here?

Include a conclusion

4 The notes talk about the old man's *determination*. Here are some other nouns that are useful to the set book question. Sort them into the two basic categories below, using a dictionary if necessary. Do any apply to both characters and events?

personality	atmosphere	mood
incident	qualities	defects	adventure
reputation	episode	temper	risk
attitude	climate	sympathy	impact
humiliation	determination	surroundings

Characters	Events

5 Say which nouns in exercise 4 collocate with the adjectives below. For example, you can talk about *great determination* but not *small determination*.

important	serious	great	enormous
deep	small	minor	unimportant
narrow	shallow	good	positive
interesting	strong	attractive	bad
weak	negative	difficult	dangerous
final	concluding	closing	last

6 When answering the set book question, you should begin your answer by stating which book you have read, as in the opening paragraph for question A below. Notice how the question has been addressed early on in this first paragraph.

A How likeable is the main character in the book you have read?
Write a **composition**, answering this question with reference to the book you have read.

> In 'The Old Man and the Sea', the old man, who is the main character, shows great determination. Although he is old and suffers a lot of physical pain, he is mentally strong. For this reason, he is extremely likeable and the reader has deep sympathy with him from the start. When he goes through the final humiliation of seeing the fish he has successfully caught being torn apart by sharks, we feel enormous sadness for him.

7 Now write a similar opening paragraph for question B, using the extract in Unit 18 as the part of the book you will refer to. Include some of the adjective-noun collocations in your answer.

B Which part of the book do you remember best and why?
Write a **composition**, giving your opinions.

8 Choose which question you will answer, A or B. Finish the composition in 120–180 words.

UNITS 13–18 Revision

Topic review

1 Together with a partner read these sentences and discuss which are true for you, giving more details. Try to use as much of the vocabulary and language from the units you have just studied as you can.

   a Although I like to read at night, sometimes I'm just too tired to stay awake.

   b I have never considered being a vegetarian.

   c I don't do enough to save the planet.

   d I'd rather have an interesting job than a large salary.

   e There was one teacher that I had at school who I just couldn't stand.

   f My cooking is so bad that no one will eat it.

   g My teachers told me that I would never do well after I left school.

   h I think that more men have hobbies than women.

   i I don't have enough time to read books.

   j I admit that I could have worked harder at school.

Vocabulary

2 For Questions 1–15, read the text below and decide which answer **A, B, C** or **D**, best fits each space. There is an example at the beginning (0).

Example:

0   **A** made   **B** done   **C** got   **D** had

0	A	B	C	D

KITCHEN STAR

Peter White has (**0**) .... such a great success of his new restaurant 'Tastes' that he has just received a second star. The fourteen-table restaurant is (**1**) .... booked every evening this year, and two receptionists are on full-time duty to ensure the business (**2**) .... smoothly. Not only is he fulfilling a lifelong ambition, he is also (**3**) .... more than he ever dreamt possible – he's just bought a new Ferrari to add to his (**4**) ....

However, life hasn't always been so easy for Peter. He (**5**) .... in Northern Ireland, in a family which, although poor, always (**6**) .... on eating well and they never went (**7**) .... After doing a (**8**) .... at catering college, and (**9**) .... his exams with distinction, he moved to London to work in one of the city's (**10**) .... restaurants. On his first day Peter remembers two things – the smell of (**11**) .... bread and the chef throwing a pan of sauce at him because he hadn't (**12**) .... it enough! Peter (**13**) .... that he doesn't treat his own (**14**) .... in such a manner, (**15**) .... he does admit to regular shouting and bursts of anger!

1 **A** totally	**B** fully	**C** absolutely	**D** entirely
2 **A** runs	**B** happens	**C** flows	**D** moves
3 **A** taking	**B** gaining	**C** winning	**D** earning
4 **A** collection	**B** store	**C** set	**D** group
5 **A** brought up	**B** put up	**C** grew up	**D** showed up
6 **A** promised	**B** insisted	**C** accepted	**D** maintained
7 **A** without	**B** after	**C** over	**D** under
8 **A** training	**B** work	**C** course	**D** lecture
9 **A** passing	**B** succeeding	**C** graduating	**D** qualifying
10 **A** head	**B** peak	**C** top	**D** lead
11 **A** roasting	**B** grilling	**C** baking	**D** cooking
12 **A** stirred	**B** chopped	**C** grated	**D** turned
13 **A** tells	**B** claims	**C** denies	**D** speaks
14 **A** crew	**B** troop	**C** staff	**D** band
15 **A** despite	**B** because	**C** even	**D** although

Grammar

3 Correct the following sentences.

 a There are too much traffic in our town.
 b I have so a lot of the work to do, I don't know where to start.
 c The United States and the Switzerland have high levels of the productivity.
 d Her house, which roof is thatched, is twelfth century.
 e John plays piano and the football, whereas his brother prefers playing the chess.
 f Let me give you an advice – don't go on a travel without checking whether you need any visa or not.
 g That shop has been standing on that corner for ten years.
 h There's a man over there which has been watching us for about half an hour.
 i I lived in Las Vegas for ten years and I am still finding it exciting.
 j By this time next year I will taught since twenty years.
 k He asked me where was the police station.
 l I saw a bit of lightning when I was out in the garden.
 m Have you got information enough to object about the factory noise?
 n He's the one to whom I gave the book to.
 o My eldest son who lives in Paris is a physicist.

4 Complete the sentence beginnings in A with suitable endings in B.

EXAMPLE: 1 *He apologised + e for overcooking the meat.*

A
 1 He apologised
 2 She denied
 3 The chef claimed
 4 The customer insisted
 5 My neighbour warned
 6 Next time you come I promise
 7 The waiter urged

B
 a me that the restaurant was expensive.
 b to make you a cake.
 c overcharging them for the coffee.
 d on seeing the kitchen.
 e for overcooking the meat.
 f them to try the chocolate ice-cream.
 g he hadn't forgotten to order the eggs.

Phrasal verbs

5 Complete the following crossword using ordinary verbs to replace the phrasal verbs in bold. There is an example to help you.

Across
 1 *I've been **looking for** my new pen everywhere.* (9)
 2 The Titanic **went down** in 1912. (4)
 3 I've never been able to **add up** very well. (5)
 4 It's hard to **put by** any money if you're on a low salary. (4)
 5 I need to **draw up** a timetable for revision before I do an exam. (7)
 6 I've **hung on** to all my old toys, and not given them away. (4)
 7 Mr Jones **brought up** the question of parking at the meeting. (6)
 8 People's hobbies **take over** their lives. (7)

Down
 9 I need to **sort out** my desk, it's a bit of a mess. (8)
 10 I think you need to **look into** the deal carefully before buying a second-hand car. (7)
 11 A role model is someone you **look up to**. (7)
 12 **Chop up** the onion into small pieces. (3)
 13 What sort of hobby should I **take up**? (5)
 14 **Face up to** the fact that your work is poor. (8)
 15 The police **went after** the bank robbers. (6)
 16 The rollercoaster ride made him **throw up**. (5)
 17 I need to **come up with** some holiday ideas. (7)

UNIT 19 An apple a day ...

Modals 3: Advice and suggestion

1 How healthy are you? Read through this questionnaire and decide which is the best answer for you.

1 **How often do you get a good 8 hours' sleep?**
  ✓ **A** Every night – and I prefer 9 or 10 hours.
  B Not often – I don't need much sleep.
  C I find it hard to sleep.

2 **How often do you do any exercise?**
  A once a week
  ✓ **B** every day
  C hardly ever

3 **What do you usually have for lunch?**
  A a large meal
  B salad or sandwiches
  C nothing

4 **When did you last have a cold?**
  A I usually have one or two a year.
  B I can't remember.
  C I get them all the time.

5 **How many cups of tea or coffee do you drink a day?**
  ✓ **A** No more than 3
  B I don't drink anything with caffeine in it
  C 4–14

6 **You have had a few headaches recently. Do you**
  A go straight to the doctor?
  B take an aspirin or paracetamol?
  ✓ **C** hope they will go away?

7 **Do you think it's necessary to add salt to your food?**
  ✓ **A** sometimes
  B never
  C always

8 **Which is true for you?**
  A I've given up smoking.
  B I've never smoked.
  C I smoke about 5 cigarettes or more a day.

9 **Which is true for you?**
  A I think I'm really fit and healthy.
  B I think illness is all in the mind.
  C I worry about my health

How did you score?

Mostly As
You are fairly healthy and have a good attitude to life. You should try to watch what you eat a little more and if I were you I'd try to do a little more exercise. Too much work and not enough play isn't good for you! I think it's about time you thought about your diet.

Mostly Bs
You are obviously in the peak of condition! I recommend you relax, as you ought to get some rest even if you don't need much sleep. Overdoing things can lead to illness! Why don't you try doing more reading, or go on holiday – or have you ever thought of playing a musical instrument?

Mostly Cs
Oh dear! It's time you took a good look at your lifestyle. Missing meals and not getting enough sleep and exercise are very bad for you. My advice to you is to start right away – you'd better book a place in the gym. I also suggest cutting down on coffee and drinking more water and fruit juice. Too much caffeine will keep you awake!

Do you agree with what is said about you? Compare your answers with a partner.

2 Reread the 'How did you score?' section and underline the verbs and phrases in which are used to express advice and suggestion. One has been done for you in A – *You should try* is an example of advice. Make a special note of the construction which follows the verb or expression.

EXAMPLE: *'should' + infinitive without 'to'*

Look at the following problems and, with a partner, take it in turns to give appropriate advice and make suggestions. Try to vary the verbs and phrases you use.

EXAMPLE: *I can't stop sneezing.*
ADVICE: *If I were you, I'd take a cold shower. How about putting your head over a bowl of hot water?*

a I can't stop hiccuping.
b I woke up covered in spots this morning.
c I can't sleep at night.
d I worry about my health all the time.
e I think I've broken my wrist.
f I'm going on holiday to a tropical country.
g I'm going to faint.
h I keep getting bitten by mosquitoes.
i I've put on so much weight recently.
j I've burnt my hand.

3   The expressions *It's time …*, *It's about time …*, and *It's high time …* are used to express strong feelings about something that hasn't been done or about something that should happen very soon.

*I think it's about time **you thought** about your diet a bit more.*
*It's time **you took** a good look at your lifestyle.*
*It's high time **you ate** less chocolate.*

Notice that after these phrases you must use the past simple. When you are talking generally it is possible to use the infinitive, but only after *It's time* and *It's about time*, not after *It's high time*.

It's time to go home now. (All of us including the speaker)
It's time you/he/she/we/I/they/Peter went home now. (Referring to specific people)

What would you say to a friend in these situations?

EXAMPLE: *Your friend's hair is too long.*
            It's about time you went to the hairdresser's.
            It's time you had a haircut.

a   He smokes 40 a day.
b   She drives everywhere.
c   She watches TV for 6 hours a day.
d   He lost his job six months ago.
e   He likes eating chips.
f   He's been living with his parents for 30 years.
g   Her coat has holes in it.
h   He never buys you a drink.
i   She's always borrowing the newspaper from you.
j   He's always late for work.
k   Her car is always breaking down.

G ⋯⋮ page 205

4   **Can you name the parts of the body the arrows are pointing to?**

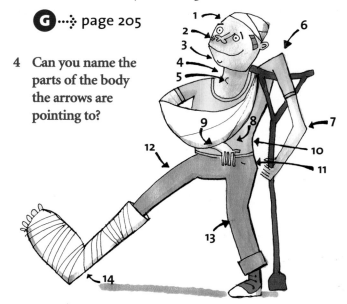

5   Which of the items in B would you do if the following in A happened to you?

EXAMPLE: *If I broke my arm, I'd wear a sling.*

A	B
If I	**I'd**
broke my leg	take an aspirin
had a headache	have stitches
cut my knee badly	go to bed
grazed my elbow	take some syrup/mixture
sprained my ankle	put a bandage on it
had flu	get an elastoplast/a plaster/
had a cough	a Band-Aid
	have it put in plaster

Phrases with *on*

6   In the questionnaire on health, the phrase *on holiday* was used. Look at the following expressions with *on* and then complete the sentences with a suitable expression.

on sale	on purpose	on duty	on time
on business	on foot	on fire	
on the whole	on holiday		

EXAMPLE: Unfortunately, I was in Paris *on business* rather than *on holiday*.

a   As my gym is quite near to where I live, I always go there ……………… .
b   When I opened the oven I saw, to my horror, that the cakes were ……………… .
c   Honestly, the way my boss talks anybody would think I broke my leg ………………
d   Joe can't come to the party as he has to be ……………… at the hospital.
e   Why is it you can never be ……………… for anything?
f   ……………… I prefer jogging to cycling.
g   There was a wonderful new exercise bike ……………… at my local sports shop.

Listening

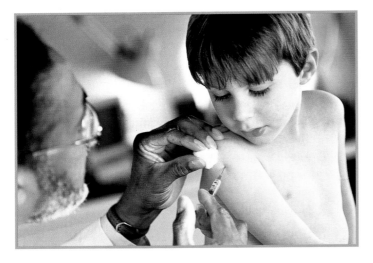

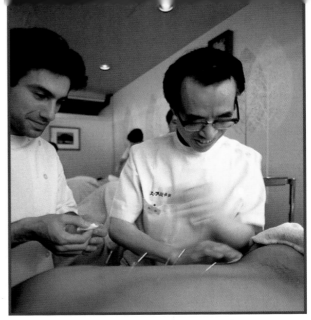

1 How do you think the patients in the photos feel at this moment? What differences do you think there are in the types of treatment being given?

2 Acupuncture is used in Chinese medicine. It consists of needles made of steel being inserted into the skin. Have you ever tried it?

3 Would you ever try a different type of medicine to the one you normally have?

4 🎧 You are going to hear part of a radio programme about health matters. A doctor is being interviewed about acupuncture. Look at Questions 1–7 and choose the correct answer from A, B or C.

1 What do we find out about Dr Carpenter's time in Hong Kong?
   A She was there to study acupuncture.
   B She practised acupuncture while she was there.
   C She enjoyed seeing a different approach to medicine.

2 Patients who she recommends for acupuncture
   A go to the local hospital.
   B choose who they want to see.
   C need to go on a waiting list.

3 What does she say happens if you have a problem with backache?
   A You spend some time answering questions.
   B You have a needle inserted into the area which hurts.
   C You are given advice about changing your lifestyle.

4 What does she say happens after a treatment?
   A You usually feel better.
   B You might feel tired.
   C You have to go to bed.

5 She says people who have acupuncture complain of pain when the needle
   A is put in.   C is taken out.
   B is in position.

6 What does Dr Carpenter say about acupuncture?
   A It works whether you believe in it or not.
   B It's best to keep an open mind.
   C A negative attitude will stop it working.

7 In 1971 acupuncture received a great deal of publicity because an American reporter
   A went to China to investigate its use there.
   B was given some acupuncture treatment in China.
   C talked to patients who'd had operations without anaesthetic.

G rammar extra

'to have their chests X-rayed'
'to have a blood test done'

What do you think the difference is between
a to do a blood test
b to have a blood test done

You have a blood test done in a hospital.
You can also say 'to get a blood test done'.

Why do you go to the following places?

a a dry cleaner's
b a hairdresser's
c a garage
d a dressmaker
e a tailor
f a manicurist
g a jeweller
h a painter and decorator's
i a furniture maker

G ⋯❖ page 205

Pronunciation

5 🎧 Listen to these words from the interview.

limb	though	knee	wrist

In small groups discuss what these words have in common.

Can you add two or three more words, where the same letters are silent, to each of the words below?

a knowledge
b climb
c wrinkle
d whistle
e foreign
f although
g walk
h enough

ⓥocabulary spot

List words with silent letters in your vocabulary notebook and look at them again before the Paper 5 Speaking test.

6 Look at the picture. Have you ever tried yoga? Why?/Why not? Read through the text below and then look at the questions. Decide which of the answers A, B, C or D best fits each space. There is an example at the beginning (0).

Example:

0 **A** taken   **B** lasted   **C** spent   **D** passed

0	A	B	C	D

7 Look at the sentences, or parts of sentences, below. They are all from the interview. Change the word in capitals into the right part of speech. Make sure you spell the word correctly.

a You're a great .... (BELIEF) in Chinese medicine, aren't you?

b We referred patients to .... (SPECIALISE) at the local hospital for .... (TREAT).

c When I was a .... (MEDICINE) student, …

d I saw how .... (EFFECT) acupuncture could be.

e Insert needles in .... (VARY) parts of your body.

f Some areas are more .... (SENSE) than others.

g Acupuncture has been used .... (SUCCEED) on cats.

h He felt no pain during or after the .... (OPERATE).

Yoga

Yoga is one of the most ancient forms of exercise, originating in India 5000 years ago. Yoga has **(0)** ..... several years to become recognised world-wide, **(1)** ..... recently, much more attention has been **(2)** ..... to it because of the ways in which it can benefit health. Yoga can be practised by anyone, at any age, **(3)** ..... any physical condition, **(4)** ..... on physical needs. For example, athletes and dancers can practise it to **(5)** ..... their energy and to improve stamina; executives to give a much needed **(6)** ..... to their overworked minds; children to improve their memory and concentration.

It's a good idea to **(7)** ..... with a doctor first if you've suffered from any type of **(8)** ..... . None of the exercises should **(9)** ..... you any pain, but it's best to start slowly at first. The best **(10)** ..... to practise is either in the morning or in the evening. Beginners **(11)** ..... it easier in the evening **(12)** ..... the body is more supple.

Contrary to what many people believe, you do not **(13)** ..... to practise an hour of yoga **(14)** ..... day. Just taking ten to fifteen minutes out of your schedule can **(15)** ..... to be extremely helpful.

	A	B	C	D
1	although	whereas	if	unless
2	put	paid	allowed	provided
3	at	in	of	on
4	according	matching	fitting	depending
5	restore	return	realise	receive
6	pause	break	interval	interruption
7	see	check	control	call
8	hurt	ache	injury	scratch
9	make	do	result	cause
10	hour	season	time	stage
11	find	discover	notice	recognise
12	though	when	until	despite
13	insist	require	need	want
14	each	all	either	several
15	demonstrate	prove	show	turn

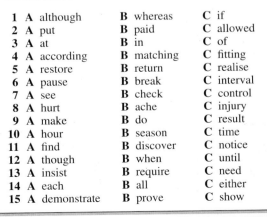

Exam folder 10

Paper 1 Part 1 Multiple matching

In this part of the Reading paper you are given a text divided into paragraphs. Your task is to identify the main idea in each paragraph. (The paragraphs may have more than one idea in them.) You are then asked to match the paragraph with the most suitable heading or summary sentence. There is one extra heading or summary sentence that you do not need to use.

You are going to read a magazine article about a husband and wife who started a world famous series of guidebooks. Choose the most suitable summary sentence from the list A–I for each part (1–7) of the article. There is one extra heading which you do not need to use. There is an example at the beginning (0).

You will see that the words that give you the answer in the example paragraph have been underlined. Now you do the same with the other paragraphs.

Advice

- Read the title and any information you are given in the instructions or in the 'blurb', if there is any.
- Skim the text to get a general idea about what it is about. Don't worry about difficult words at this stage. ALWAYS READ THE EXAMPLE AS THIS WILL HELP YOU.
- Read through the headings or summary sentences and think carefully about what they are about.
- Match a heading or summary sentence with a paragraph, underlining the part of the text which gives you the answer.
- Double check the answers you are unsure of, but make sure you write down an answer.

A The Wheelers have profited from the success of the *Lonely Planet* guidebooks.

B Getting a guidebook like the *Lonely Planet* right can be a tricky business.

C There are disadvantages to following the advice given in the *Lonely Planet* guidebooks.

D The Wheelers are still very actively involved in the *Lonely Planet* guidebooks.

E The Wheelers believe that the *Lonely Planet* guidebooks have always benefited from criticism.

F The *Lonely Planet* guidebooks have been successful from the outset.

G The passing years have changed the Wheelers' outlook on life.

H The Wheelers have strong views on the benefits of travel.

I The *Lonely Planet* guidebooks have changed for the better since the Wheelers first introduced them.

Guide to the Planet

It all began with their account of a van journey to Australia in 1972. Now there are Lonely Planet guidebooks to some 200 destinations worldwide, and founders Tony and Maureen Wheeler are multi-millionaires.

0 | I

Tony Wheeler is the man behind the *Lonely Planet* guidebooks, books which are loved and hated in equal measure. It's hard to pin down why they provoke such violent emotion; once it was simply because they lied – you'd turn up for the weekly Wednesday ferry to find that actually it goes on Tuesdays. <u>Nowadays they are carefully researched, the information is generally true, and the maps are accurate.</u>

1 | C

[handwritten margin: he downside LP.]

No, it's something about the way they take you over – you become a slave to the guidebook. Arrive in a place and out comes the book: Places to Stay, Things to See, Getting Around, Places to Eat – all of which is undeniably useful, but you end up living a life dictated by Wheeler, and that life might not be right for you. On top of that, everyone else has got one too, so instead of being the independent traveller you thought you were, you end up being just another tourist.

2 | F

[handwritten margin: beginning the first publication]

It's not entirely fair to blame only Tony. His wife Maureen, who runs the company with him, is equally to blame. It all started in 1972 when, bored with Britain, they set off for Australia. They arrived in Sydney three months later with 27 cents between them. Tony sold his camera, then sat down and wrote about the trip. They put the pages together and took it around the local bookshops and one of the bookshops sold thousands of copies.

3 | A

[handwritten margin: success for LP]

Twenty-five years on, *Lonely Planet*, has quite literally, taken over the world. Their 200-odd guidebooks cover nearly everywhere and there are phrasebooks, atlases, walking guides. They sell more than three million books a year and employ around 200 people. The *Lonely Planet* website is visited a million times a day and the Wheelers have replaced the van with a red Ferrari.

4 | G

[handwritten margin top: Wheelers don't match preconceptions.]

I met them for lunch. Tony, now 52, is small with glasses – more like a geography teacher than a traveller. Maureen admits they don't rough it like they once did. 'I don't want to spend all night on a train in India. I've been there and done that, I don't need to keep doing it.'

5 | H

[handwritten margin: Travel is a growth experience]

So what do they think about travel in general? 'My children have travelled all over the world so they're aware of a lot of things,' says Maureen and Tony agrees. 'It helps you grow up a lot, just knowing how other people live and what happens in their countries. Secondly, being on your own, having to make your way from one place to the next and work out how you do that, gives you a self-sufficiency that I think is very important.'

6 | E

[handwritten margin: Controversy boosts sales]

There has been controversy surrounding the guidebooks. There are the people who say that by encouraging people to go places they're destroying them – an accusation they both deny, claiming that people would go there anyway. They admit that none of this is bad for business. 'All the publicity has sold our books.'

7 | D

[handwritten margin: Life today for the Wheelers]

After lunch, Maureen is flying back to Australia to do a bit of business and Tony is off for a bit of travelling. He's bought himself maps, guidebooks, a new one-man tent, and he's going to walk across Corsica, on his own.

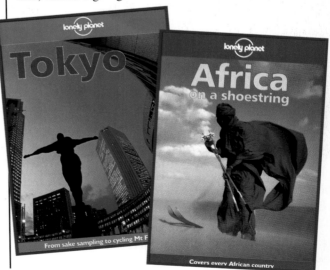

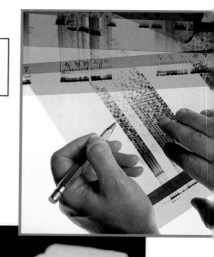

E **xam spot**

Part 3 of Paper 5 is a 'shared task', where you must have a discussion with the other candidate and decide together on a solution to the task. Remember to allow your partner time to give his/her opinion. Don't keep interrupting with your ideas.

1 Read and complete the task below.

Look at the five photographs of clues in a police case. Discuss which two clues are the most reliable, giving reasons for your choice. You have about three minutes to do this. It is not necessary to agree with each other, but make sure you have completed the task and not spent too much time on one point.

2 In Part 4 of Paper 5, you are encouraged to broaden and discuss further the topic introduced in Part 3. Discuss the following questions together.

a What do you think are the causes of crime? (e.g. unemployment)

b Do videos and TV help to cause more crime? Why?/Why not?

c Should life imprisonment mean 'life'?

d Is prison really the answer to crime?

3 Look at the vocabulary below. These are all words and phrases that you will see in the article you are going to read. Fill the gaps in the sentences with the word or phrase which fits best. (You may have to change the form of the verb.) Remember to use your English-English dictionary to help you.

to cover your tracks	a forensic scientist
the suspect	genetic code
to prove	evidence
guilty	to take someone to court
to be caught red-handed	

a My sister studied to be a doctor but then decided she wanted to change careers and become .... working alongside the police.

b It's up to the prosecution .... you committed a crime.

c The shoplifter was .... with the CD under her coat.

d Psychologists believe you can tell if someone is .... by their body language.

e Everyone has a completely different .... unless they are identical twins.

f When the police have enough .... they will arrest ....

g It is virtually impossible nowadays .... completely when you've committed a crime – there is always something that will give you away.

h If you are caught drinking and driving you will be .... and fined.

4 You are going to read an article about detecting crime. Choose the most suitable summary sentence from the list A–H for each part (1–6) of the article. There is one extra sentence that you do not need to use. There is an example at the beginning (0).

5 The following pronouns are in bold in the article. What do they refer to?

a Paragraph 0 line 5 – they
b Paragraph 1 line 13 – they
c Paragraph 2 line 23 – it
d Paragraph 3 line 29 – it

A The police and forensic scientists are still happy to use tried and trusted methods.

B More scientists are needed to find new and better ways of tracking down criminals.

C Scientists are both introducing and updating ideas all the time in the war against crime.

D Forensic scientists were quick to see the potential of a new technique.

E Scientists can now give police very firm evidence of a suspect being at the scene of a crime.

F Scientists have a technique which enables them to search large areas effectively.

G Scientists cannot always prove someone's guilt from some tests they do.

H Certain scientists specialise in gathering evidence from the scene of the crime.

The Professionals

0 — H

Scientists believe that it is impossible for someone to commit a crime without leaving something behind or taking something away with them. If these traces of evidence can be found, they may provide the proof needed to bring the
5 criminal to justice. **They** may take the form of fingerprints, hairs, fibres from clothing, tiny traces of chemicals, documents, bullets or fragments of glass. This evidence is collected and studied by forensic scientists.

1 — C

Science is applied to crime-fighting now more than ever
10 before. As people find new ways to cover their tracks, scientists develop new techniques for linking suspects with their crimes and proving their guilt. Old techniques are constantly being improved so that **they** can be applied to smaller and smaller traces of materials. In the past, there
15 was no way of identifying a criminal unless he or she was caught red-handed – that is, actually committing the crime. Nowadays the story is very different.

2 — G

Not all evidence, however, carries the same weight of proof. A fingerprint offers definite identification of a person's
20 presence at the scene of a crime, whereas a footprint may only suggest that someone was there. Nonetheless, all evidence is worth analysing. Even if an item does not offer enough proof to stand up in a court of law, **it** can still assist the police in focusing their enquiries in a certain direction.

3 — A

25 Fingerprints have been used to help identify criminals for almost 100 years. In that time, many new scientific research

methods have been developed, although the traditional way of dusting surfaces for fingerprints is still used most of the time. In most cases **it** works very well, but sometimes, different methods are needed.
30

4 — E

Forensic scientists can now use a small portable laser to look for fingerprints. The scientist 'paints' the scene of the crime with the laser beam. As the beam sweeps across doors, walls and furniture, any fingerprints present glow because they are fluorescent.
35

5 — D

An even more recent technique is called DNA profiling. The human body is composed of millions of microscopic cells. Each cell contains a unique code, the genetic code that determines what we look like and how we develop. The code takes the form of long strings of molecules called DNA, and
40
no two people have identical DNA unless they are identical twins. A technique for reading genetic codes was developed in the 1980s. DNA profiling or genetic fingerprinting was rapidly taken up by the police and forensic scientists as a way of linking suspected criminals with their crimes.
45

6 — E

The process of making a DNA profile may begin with a scrap of stained clothing found at the scene of the crime. A tuft of hair or spots of blood or saliva can be used too. With a good sample that is rich in DNA, the chance of two people producing the same genetic fingerprint is only one in 2.7
50
million, which is good enough for a court of law.

Gerunds and infinitives 2

Listening

1 🎧 Before you listen to the tape, read through the questions and make sure you understand them. You are going to hear a man talking about a daring escape from Alcatraz, the prison in the United States, which had a notorious reputation. Take notes while you are listening and then in pairs discuss the answers to the questions. What do you think happened to the men eventually?

a What happened at 9.30 pm?
b How long was Morris in jail for?
c What did some men prefer to do in the evenings?
d What did Morris do when he heard about the missing fan motor?
e Why did he buy an accordion?
f Why did they need a vacuum cleaner?
g How were they going to leave the island?
h What did they remember on the roof of the jail?
i What did the guard do?
j What happened in the end?

2 Look at the extracts from the story.

a Everyone had to stop talking.
b He stopped to listen.

c He tried picking at the concrete.
d ... others [liked] to try to learn to play a musical instrument.

What's the difference in meaning between *stop* and *try* + gerund, and *stop* and *try* + infinitive?

3 In Unit 7 you looked at which verb or expression took a gerund and which took an infinitive. However, there are some verbs that can take both.

1 No change in meaning start, begin, continue	
2 A slight change in meaning like, prefer, hate, love	
3 A change in meaning try, stop, regret, remember, forget, mean, go on	

Complete these sentences with the right form of the verb.

a The householder tried .... (fit) a burglar alarm to the house to deter thieves.

b I remember .... (read) about that kidnapping case in the papers some years ago.

c I regret .... (inform) you that your car tax has expired.

d Selling my car will mean .... (walk) home in the dark every night.

e I'm sure Peter didn't mean .... (hurt) the little girl – he only pushed her.

f I wasn't shoplifting – I just forgot .... (pay) for the scarf.

g I regret not .... (tell) the police about my suspicions.

h Although he'd been arrested for drunk driving he continued .... (drink and drive) just the same.

i I like .... (keep) an eye on my neighbours' houses when they are away.

j The policeman talked about robbery in general and then he went on .... (talk) about sentencing.

k I was mugged as I stopped .... (do up) my shoelace.

l Susan tried .... (run) after the pickpocket but she couldn't catch him.

4 This exercise revises the work done on Gerunds and Infinitives in this unit and Unit 7. Complete the leaflet with the correct form of the verb in brackets.

Personal Possessions

A thief only needs a moment (1) .... (make off) with your valuables. Your coat hung up in a restaurant, your briefcase beside your chair, even your cheque book and cheque card left on the table while you pay the bill … all are vulnerable if you look away for a second. So try (2) .... (be) careful at all times. Carry your wallet in an inside pocket, preferably one it is possible (3) .... (fasten), not your back pocket. If someone bumps into you in a crowd, it's worth (4) .... (check) (5) .... (see) that you still have your purse. Try (6) .... (avoid) (7) .... (carry) large amounts of cash. When on holiday abroad remember (8) .... (take) travellers' cheques. If your credit card is stolen, tell the Card Company immediately. If you delay (9) .... (report) the loss, it could (10) .... (lead) to a crime being committed in your name. Never let anyone (11) .... (know) your PIN number and remember (12) .... (sign) any new plastic cards you receive. In a car, keep your handbag or briefcase out of sight. If you have the windows open a thief may reach in when you stop (13) .... (turn) at a junction. Remember that the best way to minimise any risk is by (14) .... (take) sensible precautions.

G ···→ page 206

Writing folder 10

Stories 2

In Writing folder 3 you saw how to approach the short story question in Part 2 of Paper 2. Remember to include the sentence you are given which either begins or ends the story.

1 Look at this question and the sample answer that follows. Discuss with a partner which of the endings A, B or C would have the best chance of winning the competition and say why.

You have decided to enter a short story competition. The rules say that the story must begin with the following sentence:

I couldn't believe my eyes when I opened the front door.

Write your **story**.

I couldn't believe my eyes when I opened the front door. When I had left home that morning the house had been clean and tidy. Now, everything was lying on the floor in a terrible mess. There were books on the carpet and all the drawers in my desk had been opened and the papers scattered round the room. I realised at once that I had been burgled. I rushed to the telephone to call the police. They told me to keep calm and not to touch anything.
I decided to take a look round to see what had been stolen. The TV was still there and so was the video. I went into my bedroom and that seemed to be completely untouched. The mess was only in the sitting room. I couldn't understand why, especially as nothing was missing.

A

Suddenly, the telephone rang. I picked it up. A voice said, 'Let this be a warning to you!' It was a woman's voice, and it made my blood run cold. I was now really scared. I didn't know what she could be talking about. I tried to dial the police again, but my hand was shaking so much I wasn't able to. Just then there was a ring at the front door.

B

I decided to make a cup of coffee while I was waiting for the police to arrive. Then they rang the doorbell and came in. They spent half an hour looking at the mess and told me that there had been a lot of burglaries in the neighbourhood recently. I felt very unhappy.

C

Suddenly, there was a knock on the door and my sister was standing there with her little boy, Tom. 'Oh, dear,' she exclaimed. 'Yes,' I said, 'isn't it terrible? I've called the police and they are on their way.' Tom suddenly threw himself into my arms. 'I'm sorry,' he said. 'It was me, it was me!'

2 It is very important when you are writing a story to keep in the right tense. Look at the following story and make the necessary changes to the verbs in brackets. This story has to end with the sentence:

For Joe, life at the office would never seem stressful again!

'I can't believe this (1) .... (happen) to me,' Joe thought. He (2) .... (arrive) at the tiny island only hours before and now he (3) .... (find) himself lying on the deck of a small fishing boat. 'What I (4) .... (go) to do,' he (5) .... (think). He (6) .... (look) forward to coming to the island for months. Anne, his cousin, (7) .... (come) the year before and (8) .... (tell) him how wonderful it (9) .... (be). 'It (10) .... (have) got everything you (11) .... (need) for a complete rest, away from the stresses of everyday life,' she (12) .... (say).
At this moment Joe (13) .... (want) to strangle her. 'Why I (14) .... (decide) to follow her advice?' he asked himself. He (15) .... (know) no one on the island and (16) .... (have) no idea why he (17) .... (kidnap). Then he (18) .... (hear) footsteps coming. It (19) .... (be) a man, about fifty years old with short, black hair and a beard. He (20) .... (wear) a sort of uniform – brown shorts, a blue shirt and tie.
'We (21) .... (decide) to let you go,' the man (22) .... (say). 'A case of mistaken identity,' he (23) .... (continue). 'We (24) .... (be) sorry and (25) .... (hope) you (26) .... (enjoy) the rest of your holiday.' With that, he (27) .... (untie) me and pushed me off the boat. Luckily, I (28) .... (not have) far to swim to the shore. For Joe, life at the office would never seem stressful again!

3 Now discuss with a partner how you could change the parts of the story that are in the different colours.

the place
the person
the ending

Try to think of interesting alternatives and then tell the rest of the class what you have written.

4 Now do this writing task.

You have been asked to write a short story for your college magazine. The story must end with the following sentence:

Pat could hear no one following him, and realised that he was safe at last.

Write your **story** in 120–180 words.

With a partner, think of some ideas for the story.

a The people in the story – how will you describe them?
b The place where the story happens – what is it like?
c The action – how will you describe what happens?

Advice

- Remember to check the spelling, punctuation and grammar.
- Count the number of words you have written.
- Try to keep within 20 words of the upper limit.
- Get used to judging how many lines of your handwriting will make 180 words.

UNIT 21 To have and have not

1 Look at the pictures above. Which things do you see as necessities – things you couldn't live without – and which as optional luxuries? Explain your reasons to another student.

2 What things do you like to treat yourself to every week? Do you ever buy something you don't really need on impulse?

Listening

3 🎧 You are going to hear five speakers talking about small luxuries they regularly pay for. Decide what each speaker values most about the thing they spend their money on, choosing from A–F. There is one extra letter which you do not need to use.

A the personal convenience of it

B the improvement to his/her surroundings   Speaker 1 [1]

C the feeling of privacy it gives   Speaker 2 [2]

D the entertainment it provides him/her   Speaker 3 [3]

E the professional care involved   Speaker 4 [4]

F the benefit to him/her physically   Speaker 5 [5]

4 🎧 Listen again to check your answers. Do you consider all five things as luxuries? Why?/Why not?

Phrasal verbs with *cut*

5 Look at these phrasal verbs with *cut* and read the examples from the recordings.

cut across   cut back (on)   cut down (on)
cut in   cut off   cut out

I wouldn't dream of cutting back on this …
I cut down on what I ate – and cut out cigarettes entirely.

What are the differences in meaning here, if any? Do these phrasal verbs have any other meanings?

In what contexts could the three other phrasal verbs with *cut* be used?

Choose the most suitable phrasal verbs with *cut* to complete the sentences below.

a After James announced his resignation, the department .... him .... of all their meetings.

b Let's .... the fields – it's much quicker than the road.

c You'll have to .... your composition – it's double the word limit!

d The interviewer tried to ask another question, but the angry politician .... again.

e Serious flooding has .... several villages, although the Red Cross is planning to drop emergency supplies by helicopter.

f The second engine .... and the plane began to lose height.

g I've had real problems with the phone today – that's twice now I've been .... !

h Despite record company profits, the research budget has been .... by 50%.

Vocabulary

6 🎧 In the listening extracts there are various words and phrases to do with money. Listen again and note them down under the headings below. The number in brackets tells you how many phrases there are. There are two examples.

Phrases to describe good value (3)

a small price to pay

Words/phrases about having money (4)

steady income

Nouns to do with cost (5)

Adjectives to describe being badly-off (4)

7 The example in 6 talks of a *steady* income. You can also say a *steady* job or describe 'progress' in this way, but you cannot use *steady* to describe some other things. So, for example, you would not say a 'steady river', because the words do not collocate.

Which noun in each set below does **not** collocate with the adjective given in italics?

a	account	charge	increase	path	*steep*
b	fit	road	schedule	spot	*tight*
c	cash	key	thought	time	*spare*
d	air	break	ideas	start	*fresh*
e	belt	hands	place	side	*safe*
f	film	girl	square	wasp	*delightful*
g	flavour	mood	report	swing	*full*
h	belief	confusion	horror	lack	*utter*

8 Now use some of these phrases to complete the story below.

Would you have done the same? Why?/Why not?

Last month I went to Italy on business. Despite being on a **(1)** .... during the trip, I had a little bit of **(2)** .... on the final afternoon, so I decided to have a walk and get some **(3)** .... Even though the sun was shining, I took an umbrella, to be on the **(4)** .... I strolled through some quiet streets and then walked up a **(5)** .... This eventually came out on a **(6)** .... , where a flower market was in **(7)** .... I decided to buy some roses to take home and took out my last 100,000 lire note. To my **(8)** .... , a sudden gust of wind blew the money out of my hand. I watched it flutter across the square and saw roughly where it landed. I rushed over, and, looking down, I could see that the note had fallen through an iron grill in the gutter. Fortunately, I had my umbrella and managed to push its spike through the grill, although it was a very **(9)** ....! At the third attempt, I speared my much-needed lire note. Putting it in a very **(10)** .... (my inside pocket), I went straight back to the hotel, got my luggage and found a taxi to take me to the airport, so I never did buy those roses.

Clauses

When you are writing in English, don't use too many short, simple sentences. Instead, make longer sentences which contain more than one clause and are connected by well-chosen linking words. This shows an advanced level of writing and also avoids repetition. Earlier in this course you have practised conditional clauses (Unit 6) and relative clauses (Unit 17). Here are some more types of clause.

Concessive clauses

1 Look at these examples from 21.1 and explain the function of the underlined words in the sentences.

   a He was always carrying an armful of flowers, <u>even though</u> sometimes he'd only been away for a couple of days.
   b We can usually decide on our order quite quickly, <u>even if</u> we still argue over some things!
   c <u>Despite</u> being hard-up, I would still try to buy flowers.
   d <u>While</u> not exactly loaded, I can afford it.

What is the difference between examples a and b and examples c and d?

Could the word *although* be used instead of the underlined words, without changing the meaning? If so, would you need to make any grammatical changes?

Several other words in English are used in clauses of this type.

G ⋯⟶ page 206

2 Correct any errors in these sentences.

   a I always forget something when I go to the supermarket, despite of making a list.
   b Even department stores claim to sell most things, I prefer using specialist shops whenever possible.
   c Sainsbury's has gone into in-store banking, whereas that Iceland, the frozen food store, is developing its home delivery service.
   d In spite of they want increased sales, some shops refuse to open on Sundays.
   e I'm usually happy with the clothes I bring home, even they have been bought on impulse.
   f The supermarket chain Tesco has found that more men are buying babycare products, although they usually picking up beer at the same time.

3 Look at these jumbled questions a journalist asked a student called Faye. What do you think happened to her? Skim the article to see if you have guessed correctly.

   A What was this final figure?
   B Hadn't the bank noticed by this time?
   C Would you do the same again?
   D Were they pleased at your honesty?
   E Were you surprised they did nothing?
   F How much was in there?
   G Was that the end of the story?
   H What happened next?
   I Was finding all that cash a shock?

4 Choose the most suitable heading from the list A–I for each part (1–7) of the article. There is one extra heading which you do not need to use. There is an example at the beginning (0).

When Faye Pattison, a penniless 21-year-old student, checked her bank account recently, she was surprised to find a very healthy balance …

0 | **I**

You bet. I'm a typical student, struggling on a part-time job at Woolworth's. It was two weeks before my next statement was due to be sent out from the bank. I was checking my balance at the cashpoint machine, just in case my wages had already been paid in. Then up came all these zeros. My first reaction was panic – I thought it was an overdraft – although I soon realised my account was actually in credit by a massive amount.

1 |

The balance the first time was £34,000. As I stood there staring at the screen, visions of touring Australia flashed through my mind. But I knew it wasn't mine so I went into the bank and told them they made a mistake.

2 |

I thought they would be, but they just sat me in a corner and ignored me for half an hour. They took it back in the end, explaining it was from another bank. One number was keyed wrongly so the money ended up in my account.

3 |

Two weeks later I again checked my balance, so as to be sure they'd sorted it out. Up popped £500,000! I felt like a lottery winner, though without the ticket. When I told the bank this time, they said that because

5 With a partner, discuss whether you would have behaved differently from Faye if this had happened to you. Think about her action at each stage and say what you would have done.

Purpose, reason and result clauses

6 In the article about Faye there are a number of these clauses. For example:

I was checking my balance at the cashpoint machine, *just in case my wages had been paid in.* (Purpose)

They said that *because their computers were down,* I would have to leave it with them. (Reason)

One number was keyed wrongly *so the money ended up in my account.* (Result)

Find other clauses like this in the article. Which other words like *just in case, because* and *so* are used?

…eir computers were down …would have to leave it with …em. I did, but within the …eek, the sum had doubled!

| 4 |

…ver a million! I was falling …bout laughing at the …ashpoint; the people behind …e must have thought I was …n drugs or something. It …as brilliant looking down at …ose figures and imagining it …as really mine.

| 5 |

…pparently not. Since my …oyfriend John works for …nother bank, he knows how …anks operate. He couldn't …elieve what had happened. …fter a few weeks, my friends …tarted saying I should move …e money abroad and take …ff! Even my dad, who's a …tired policeman, said I …ould start withdrawing …300 a day – that's the

interest, so I wouldn't have been touching the capital.

| 6 |

I was, and annoyed as well. I gave up on my local branch and contacted head office, in order to sort it out once and for all. But in spite of phoning them numerous times, it still took a while before anyone would deal with the matter. And even then, their attitude was amazing. They seemed very ungrateful considering all the hassle they caused me.

| 7 |

Not quite! The day after the £1m was finally debited from my account, £300 appeared. It was part of the interest earned. I know £300 isn't a fortune to some people but for me it was a lot. I did tell the bank about it but eventually they said I could keep it. I'm spending it on a trip to Turkey.

---

7 Join the following sentences together using the words in brackets, making any other changes necessary.

a Supermarkets give their customers loyalty cards. They want more information about what people buy. (so as to)

b There weren't many stalls at the market yesterday. Yesterday was a public holiday. (because)

c Some daily newspapers cut their prices. They want a bigger circulation. (in order to)

d I like filling the house with flowers. I buy a lot of flowers. (since)

e Harrods can charge a lot. Harrods is seen as a very exclusive shop. (so)

f I went to London. I bought a special present for Ellen. (to)

g It's always worth trying clothes on before you buy them. Clothes can be too tight. (in case)

h Some supermarkets create the smell of freshly-baked bread. This is to make a good impression on customers. (so that)

8 Complete the second sentence so that it has a similar meaning to the first sentence, using the word given. **Do not change the word given.** You must use between two and five words, including the word given.

1 Although it was cold last weekend, the store reported record sales of garden equipment.
despite
The store reported record sales of garden equipment .... last weekend.

2 Keep the receipt as it mightn't fit you.
case
Keep the receipt just .... fit you.

3 You usually find what you need in a smaller shop, although you pay more than at a supermarket.
if
Smaller shops usually have what you need, ...
more than a supermarket does.

4 Supermarkets have chocolate on sale at check-outs, because impulse buying of it is common.
since
Chocolate is sold at supermarket check-outs .... bought on impulse.

5 Saunas are popular in Sweden but not in Britain.
whereas
Many Swedish people enjoy Saunas .... not.

Exam folder 11

Paper 1 Part 2 Multiple choice

In this part of the Reading paper you are tested on a detailed understanding of the text. There might also be the following type of questions:

- a question which tests global understanding – What is a suitable title for the text?
- a question which tests the meaning of a word or phrase from the context – What does the writer mean by x in line z?
- a question which tests reference – What does 'it' refer to in line q?

Advice

- Skim the text to get a general idea of what it is about.
- All the questions, except for the global one, are in order so you can concentrate on each part of the text at a time. The global question will come at the end, but you need to make sure you take **the whole text** into account when you answer it.
- Some of the choices may be true but do not answer the question. Other choices may seem very plausible and even contain elements of the same vocabulary, but do not answer the question correctly.
- The reference question may refer either forwards or backwards so check carefully on either side of the pronoun to see what it refers to.
- As you read, underline the part of the text which you think contains the answer.

You are going to read an extract from a newspaper article about a woman's hobby. For Questions 1–7, choose the answer (A, B, C or D) which you think fits best according to the text.

1 What is the problem the writer has at the beginning of her holiday?
   A The weather is not good enough for painting.
   B She's brought the wrong materials with her.
   C There are no animals to paint.
   D She can't reproduce the exact colours. ✓

2 The writer hid her work because
   A she believed Royale paints better. ✓
   B it wasn't good enough to sell.
   C she thought it would disappoint Royale. ✓
   D it was only a quick sketch.

3 What does the writer mean by the phrase 'what I am up to' in line 38?
   A What I am painting. ✓
   B What I will give him.
   C What I can teach him.
   D What I might do.

4 What does the writer say about her previous holiday?
   A She preferred the teacher she had had then.
   B She was more familiar with the landscape. ✓
   C Her painting technique improved much faster.
   D She wasn't happy in Zimbabwe.

5 The writer says that Susan Scott-Thomas
   A looks at things in a different way from her.
   B is a very capable person. ✓
   C is not as good at cooking as her.
   D was a solicitor before going to Africa.

6 What does 'it' refer to in line 82?
   A The holiday
   B The country
   C The colour and shape
   D The finished painting ✓

7 What is a suitable title for the article?
   A An unsuccessful holiday
   B An artist in the bush ✓
   C Learning to paint
   D Travelling in a different country

BY THE MIDDLE OF THE SECOND DAY I KNOW I'M IN TROUBLE. In front of me the land stretches up and away towards a distant hill, and into the space, between that summit and me, is crowded one of the most vivid concentrations of colour I have ever seen. It starts with the trees. The wet season is only a few weeks off and, almost as if they can smell the coming rains, they have put out their leaves. They are no ordinary green and the dry grasses beneath them are ablaze with golds, browns and reds. I want to recreate this scene with watercolours. Although I can make a try at it with words, trying to paint it in my sketch book is another matter altogether. I've already made one attempt: a series of zigzags in orange and red, with bluish trees placed across them, which now lies face down in the grass beside me.

I've put it there because the last thing I want right now is for someone else to come along and look at it. A young man called Royale walks up the hill. Royale is a sculptor, and, with several other local men, produces pieces of work in the local stone. Recently, and quite suddenly, this work, and that of several other local co-operatives, has acquired an international reputation. I certainly don't want a man capable of such things looking at my own awful brushstrokes. So I put my foot, as casually as I can, on the finished painting beside me and we resume the conversation started earlier in the day.

I want to talk to Royale about his life here. He, however, is only interested in what I am up to. To begin with, it seems that he considers me a fellow artist, and for a moment I find myself staring into the depths of embarrassment. But when he asks me, 'What is painting like?' I realise that this professional artist has never painted anything in his life before. He just wants a go with my colours.

When I signed up for this holiday, I was hoping for an experience like the one I had had four years earlier in Wales. That was my first painting holiday, and I loved it. Two things made it great. First was the teacher, a man called Robin, who showed me that what is important about drawing and painting is not the finished article but the process of completing it. The second element of that week was the place. I grew up in places like that, and I connected with it immediately. But it was stupid of me to think that I could reproduce the experience down here, deep in the Southern Hemisphere. Zimbabwe is not a part of me, nor I of it. Trying to draw it for the first time, from a standing start, is like trying to start a conversation in Swahili.

There were compensations. The holiday was wonderfully organised by a friend of mine – Susan Scott-Thomas. Admittedly, there are some rather large differences between us – she's extremely wealthy and she inherited a farm in Africa when she was in her mid-twenties, and instead of taking the easy option of becoming a solicitor and staying in London, she came out to reclaim the land and rebuild the decaying farmhouse. In the process, she learnt how to lay foundations and make clay bricks. All of which she did while I was just about mastering making sauce for pasta.

Even my disastrous painting didn't detract from enjoying the holiday. Painting really forces you to look at things, to consider their shape and colour. And even if **it** is a disaster, that process of looking and thinking and transferring those thoughts into movements of your hand leaves an imprint of what you have seen. By the end of the week I have still not produced anything to hang on my walls, although there is a drawing of a local schoolboy of which I am rather fond, not because it is much good, but because it was so challenging to do.

Speaking

1 Look at these two pictures and discuss their similarities and differences.

2 🎧 Now listen to the recording, which is an example of Paper 5, Part 2. One student will talk about the pictures for about a minute. Then another student will talk briefly at the end. How do their views differ?

3 🎧 Listen to the recording again and tick any vocabulary you hear in the sets below.

Perform	Performers	Performance
play	musician	concert
take part	band	recital
improvise	orchestra	gig
participate	pianist	festival
join in	conductor	rehearsal
sing a solo	choir	show

Explain the differences in meaning of the words in the 'Performance' column.

4 Do you prefer to listen to music or to take part? What types of music do you enjoy? What do you dislike?

5 This article about a piano recital appeared in the *English Language Bangkok Post*. Skim the skeleton text and paragraph H, to get an idea of what the article is about. What do you think Myron Kropp did before he was taken away by the police?

6 Now go through the article again, underlining words and phrases that may help you to predict the content of each gap. Look out for any possible links too. Time yourself as you do this.

A RATHER STICKY CONCERT

The recital by American pianist Myron Kropp, which took place yesterday evening in the chamber music room of the Erawan Hotel, can only be described as one of the most interesting experiences in a very long time. It was Mr Kropp's first appearance in Bangkok.

0	H

It is appropriate to say at this point that Mr Kropp, like many pianists, is not happy about this form of seating. Due to the screw-type design, pianists often find themselves turning sideways during the most expressive parts of a performance.

1	

Although a fine instrument, the Baldwin Concert Grand needs constant attention, particularly in a climate such as Bangkok's. In the humidity, the felts which separate the white keys from the black ones tend to swell, causing keys to stick occasionally.

2	

However, by the time the 'storm' was past and he was into the Prelude and Fugue in D major, in which the second octave D plays a major role, Mr Kropp's patience was wearing thin.

3	

The stool itself had more than enough grease on it. During one passage, in which the music and

'lyrics' were both particularly violent, Mr Kropp was turned completely around. This meant that, whereas before his remarks had been aimed largely at the piano, to his surprise and that of those in the room he found himself swearing at the audience.

4	

Nevertheless, he bravely swivelled himself back into position facing the piano and, leaving the D major Fugue unfinished, went on to the Fantasia and Fugue in G Minor.

5	

It was with a sigh of relief therefore that the audience saw Mr Kropp slowly rise from his stool and leave the stage. A few men in the back of the room began clapping and when Mr Kropp returned to the stage a moment later, it seemed he was responding to this applause. Apparently, however, he had left to fetch a red-handled fire axe which was hung back stage in case of fire, for that was what was in his hand.

6	

It took six people, including the hotel manager and a passing policeman, to disarm Mr Kropp, and he was eventually dragged off the stage.

7   You will now need to scan paragraphs A–G (remember, H is the example and fits gap 0). What happens in paragraph A? Where must it go in the text, as a result?

Now decide where the other paragraphs fit. When you have finished, check that the extra paragraph cannot make sense anywhere in the text.

8   Explain the meaning of these words and phrases from the article. The ones in a–d appear in this order in the main text.

a   during the most <u>expressive parts</u>
b   needs <u>constant attention</u>
c   Mr Kropp's patience was <u>wearing thin</u>
d   to <u>disarm</u> Mr Kropp
e   the <u>awkward</u> D key (paragraph B)
f   deserves to be <u>severely reprimanded</u> (paragraph D)
g   regained its <u>composure</u> (paragraph D)
h   to <u>weather the storm</u> (paragraph E)
i   Having <u>settled himself</u> as best he could (paragraph G)
j   Deceptively <u>frail-looking</u> (paragraph H)

A   Mr Kropp began to chop at the left leg of the piano with it. At first it seemed that he was merely trying to make it tilt at the same angle as the right one. However, when both legs collapsed altogether with a great crash – and Mr Kropp continued to chop – it became obvious that he had no intention of going on with the concert.

B   Several concert-goers later questioned whether the awkward D key justified some of what was heard coming from the stage during softer passages of the Fugue. One member of the audience, who had sent his children out of the room because of the bad language, suggested that the workman who had greased the music stool might have done better to use some of the grease on the second octave D.

C   This is doubly true when the instrument is as old as the one provided in the Erawan Hotel yesterday, where the D in the second octave proved particularly troublesome. During the 'aging storm' section of the D-minor Toccata and Fugue, Mr Kropp must be praised for putting up with it.

D   The person who began to laugh at this point deserves to be severely reprimanded for his behaviour. Unfortunately, laughter is contagious, and many people joined in. By the time the audience had regained its composure, Mr Kropp appeared somewhat shaken.

E   As he was a true professional, Mr Kropp managed to conceal the mistakes, and carried on with the piece, apparently unmoved by the whole event. However, the audience began to doubt his ability to weather the storm.

F   Why the G key in the third octave chose that particular moment to start sticking is a mystery. Mr Kropp did not help matters when he began using his feet to kick the lower half of the piano, causing the right front leg of the piano to buckle slightly inward, and leaving the entire instrument leaning at an angle. A gasp went up from the audience, for if the piano had actually fallen, several of Mr Kropp's toes would surely have been broken.

G   There was a slight delay for this reason, as Mr Kropp left the stage, apparently in search of a bench. Sadly, he returned without one. Having settled himself as best he could, the performance got under way.

H   The room went quiet as he entered, dressed in formal black evening-wear. Deceptively frail-looking, with thin, sandy hair and a yellowish complexion, the man who has repopularised Johann Sebastian Bach approached the Baldwin Concert Grand Piano, bowed to the audience and placed himself upon the stool.

Complex sentences

1 To make his writing more interesting and to improve its cohesion, the writer of the article in 22.1 started sentences in various different ways. Look at these examples a–h and match them to descriptions 1–8.

   a Deceptively frail-looking, with thin, sandy hair and a yellowish complexion, …
   b It is appropriate to say at this point that …
   c Due to the screw-type design, …
   d Having settled himself as best he could, …
   e Although a fine instrument, the Baldwin Concert Grand …
   f This is doubly true when …
   g As he was a true professional, …
   h Why the G key in the third octave chose that particular moment to start sticking …

   1 linking to previous sentence
   2 prepositional phrase
   3 adjectival phrase
   4 concessive clause
   5 reason clause
   6 -ing clause
   7 rhetorical question
   8 emphasising new information

2 Now rewrite the following sentences a–h in a similar way, using the patterns 1–8 in exercise 1 and producing a single complex sentence. The first word of each sentence and the pattern required is given in brackets.

   EXAMPLE: *I don't know who it was that started a slow hand-clap. Immediately everyone joined in. (Who 7)*
   Who it was that started a slow hand-clap I don't know, but immediately, everyone joined in.

   a It was late. We decided not to stay for the final band. (As 5)
   b The cello, which has been beautifully made by hand and is reddish brown in colour, has an excellent sound. (Beautifully 3)
   c Ellen learnt the recorder for three years. Then she went on to the flute. (Having 6)
   d The trumpeter is technically brilliant. However, his playing has no feeling. (Despite 4)
   e The conductor made a mistake. The soloist had to miss out a whole verse. (Due 2)
   f (Previous sentence: Mick Jagger often sings flat.) You notice that he sings flat especially in recordings of live concerts. (This 1)
   g The Squier is a low-priced guitar. It sounds very similar to a proper Stratocaster. (Although 4)
   h Telemann composed a vast number of pieces. I should add that he lived to the age of 86! (It 8)

3 Expand these notes into complex sentences, using the linkers given and adding puctuation and any other words necessary. An example is given.

   EXAMPLE: *What/rubber chicken/doing/stage/ mystery/gig started/although/realised later/Zappa hurled/drummer*
   What a rubber chicken was doing on the stage was a mystery before the gig started, although we realised later, when Zappa hurled it at the drummer!

   a Due/delay/band's arrival/insisted/refund/tickets
   b Since/last train/eleven thirty/sadly/miss/ performance
   c Despite/unwell/singer/decided/cancel/although/ shortened
   d Instead/what/printed/programme/pianist improvised/over 40 mins
   e An oboe/suitable tone/even if/underused/jazz instrument
   f As/violinist/stage fright/rarely/performances/ large audiences

4 Sentences a–d all belong in the paragraph opposite. Which sentence should come at the very beginning of this paragraph?

Insert the three remaining sentences into the text, to make one cohesive paragraph.

a During the first half there were few problems, with only an occasional beep being heard.

b Although for the wrong reason, the Chicago Symphony Orchestra's Centennial concert in 1991 was a memorable event.

c Once the laughter had died down, they were instructed to take their gifts outside to the lobby.

d There were some 400 of these, each paying at least $500 for the privilege of attending.

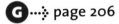 **G** ⋯⊰ page 206

Three of its most famous music directors participated: Solti, Barenboim and Kubelik. Immediately before the concert, a celebration dinner was held for special donors. At an event like this, it is customary to give diners a small gift, so each person was presented with an attractive alarm clock, gift-wrapped. Why some of the clocks were put in their boxes with the alarm switched on is a mystery, but this was the case. It is appropriate to remind the reader that the dinner guests went straight on to the concert, armed with these ticking timebombs! However, after the interval more and more alarms were going off, so the concert had to be temporarily stopped and an announcement made. As the clocks were inside boxes and gift-wrapped, nobody in the audience had realised what the problem was. The rest of the evening then proceeded without incident.

5 Read the text below. If a line has a word that should not be there, write the word at the end of the line. If a line is correct, put a tick (✓) next to it. There are two examples (0 and 00).

GEORGE GERSHWIN

0	George Gershwin, who was born for 100 years ago,	*for*
00	lived and worked in the perfect era for his unique	✓
1	crossover talent to develop. It was with a time when	
2	the Jazz Age coincided with composers such like	
3	Berg, as well as the first Broadway musicals. No one	
4	has been able to match his ability to write the original	
5	music that crosses off the boundaries of jazz, opera	
6	and classical. Gershwin's influence on modern music	
7	has been enormous. It is too appropriate to add that	
8	he has made the American composer a respectable	
9	figure around all the world, at a time when very few	
10	American compositions they were being performed.	
11	Although a gifted pianist, he had only basic reading	
12	skills in music, but due to that his regular attendance	
13	at concerts, he increased his own repertoire. He was	
14	admired by some of the most greatest composers,	
15	including to Ravel and Bartók. Sadly, Gershwin died	
	at the early age of 38.	

Writing folder 11

Reports 2

1 Before you read the following exam question and its answer, look back at Writing folder 6. This covered organisation and layout, as well as style. Consider the points made there when improving the answer as requested below.

  a What would you add in the two places indicated?

  b Where you see the symbol §, use a conjunction to join the two sentences together, making any other changes necessary.

  c Why are the underlined parts of the answer inappropriate to a report? How could you improve them?

Every year, you help at a local music festival, which takes place outdoors over one weekend. The organisers want to improve the festival and have asked you to write a short report. You should comment on the facilities that were available at this year's festival and make recommendations for next year.

Write your **report**.

Dear Organisers

Here is my report ....

The place in town where you hold the festival

The site this year was disappointing, mainly because it wasn't large enough. There was some car parking. § Many people had to park over two kilometres away.

Eating

There was some choice of catering at the site. § Very little vegetarian food was offered. However, my friends and I had to go to one end of the field for food and then we ran over to the opposite end for a drink. This drove us nuts!

The programme

People seemed to enjoy the performances. § Each band should be allowed more time on stage.

The cost

Several members of the audience thought the tickets were unusually cheap. § The price could be raised next year. This would help us, wouldn't it?

Recommendations

You need a bigger site and better-organised catering – some changes to the timing of the event too. ....

....

151 words

2 You could be asked to write a report about shopping facilities in your town. If so, you should think carefully about the group of 'shoppers' you are writing the report for. This is different from the target reader of the report, who will be specified – for example, the festival organisers in the last question, or your boss at the tourist office.

For each target group below, decide which types of shopping it would be suitable to focus on, choosing from a–j. Some will be used more than once. Remember to consider the advantages or disadvantages given in brackets and to recommend things that are realistic in the time allowed.

TARGET GROUP
1 American exchange students on a limited budget
2 Elderly tourists visiting as a group one weekend
3 Business people spending a free hour after their appointments
4 Families camping outside the town for a week

a an exclusive gift shop (in the main square)
b a large toyshop (limited parking)
c a central stationery shop (open late)
d the Saturday crafts market (very colourful)
e a discount computer warehouse (plenty of parking)
f a sports equipment store (good value)
g a supermarket on the edge of town (massive)
h a music store (very noisy)
i the university bookshop (discounts available)
j an art gallery (includes a coffee shop)

3 Now read this exam question.

Some British students are on an exchange programme at your college for a month. The college has asked you to write a report on local shopping facilities for the teacher who is in charge of the group. You should give advice on best value for money, including areas such as food, study materials and souvenirs.

Write your **report**.

Plan what you are going to write, starting with the ideas in 2. Remember that you are writing to the teacher, not the students, so your report should be fairly formal. Try to use some of the vocabulary on money and shopping from Unit 21.

UNIT 23 Unexpected events

1 In pairs, discuss the photographs. How does each photograph make you feel? Would you be more worried about one of the events than the others? Why?/Why not?

Which set of words goes with which photograph?

a a bolt, a storm, thunder, a flash   **c** lava, ash, an eruption, gases

b to be stranded, torrential rain   **d** a tremor, cracks, to tremble

Listening

2 🎧 You are going to hear an interview with a woman, Liz, who together with her friend, Dave, had a horrific experience when they were camping. For Questions 1–10, complete the sentences.

Dave thought at first that the cloud was the result of a	**1**
Liz says that what she saw was different from a	**2**
Liz thought it was odd because it was completely	**3**
The heat melted the coffee pot	**4**
Dave and Liz tried at first to reach	**5**
Dave and Liz had been protected in the hole by	**6**
Dave and Liz put their [**7**] round their heads to help them to breathe.	
It was hard to walk because of the depth of the	**8**
There was an awful smell similar to	**9**
Liz now regrets not having a [**10**] with them.	

Pronunciation

3 🎧 Listen again to part of the interview.

Interviewer: I expect you were very frightened by then, weren't you?

Liz: Frightened! I was absolutely petrified, and so was Dave.

Notice how Liz's voice rises on 'frightened' and falls on 'petrified'.
Now you do the same.

EXAMPLE:

Student A: *I expect the weather was very cold, wasn't it?*
Student B: *Cold! It was absolutely freezing!*

a weather – cold/freezing   **f** salary – large/enormous
b water – hot/boiling   **g** sister – clever/brilliant
c film – bad/awful   **h** TV play – long/never-endin
d food – good/delicious   **i** book – interesting/fascinati
e hotel room – small/tiny   **j** you – angry/furious

Phrasal Verbs with *off*

4 Match these phrasal verbs you heard in the interview with their meaning.

1 It gave off a terrible smell.   removed
2 We took off our shirts.   began the journey
3 When we set off it was   produced
  difficult to breathe.

Now complete the following sentences, choosing a phrasal verb that means the same as the word or words in brackets. Make sure you use the correct tense.

pay off	come off	break off	call off
put off	put off	wear off	drop off
write off	run off		

EXAMPLE: *Don't (postpone) what you have to do today until tomorrow.*

ANSWER: *Don't put off what you have to do today until tomorrow.*

a He (end suddenly) what he was saying in order to open the door.
b The Prime Minister's visit to Australia has been (cancelled) because of the floods at home.
c Anne decided to (request by letter) for the information pack advertised on the TV.
d The gold coating on the medal eventually (disappeared) with time.

e If I won the lottery, the first thing I would do is to (settle) my debts.
f I hope you won't be (discouraged from) seeing the film just because I didn't enjoy it.
g Mr Roberts asked his secretary to (duplicate) a copy of the invoice for me.
h The play was so boring it was all I could do to stop myself from (falling asleep).
i I hope the plans for the new dam to prevent future floods (succeed).

5 Read through this article about volcanoes and think of a word which best fits each space. Use only **one** word in each space.

An Unchanging Planet?

If you think of Earth (1) ………. a stable and unchanging planet, think again. Nearly five billion years (2) ………. it was first formed, the Earth is still developing – (3) ………. alarming ways. Unlike earthquakes that strike (4) ………. warning, volcanoes build up (5) ………. months and are usually easier to predict. But their spectacular climax is no (6) ………. devastating. A volcano can erupt in many different ways (7) ………. it can spill out a variety of materials. Mild eruptions spurt gas, steam and hot water and are (8) ………. geysers. Larger volcanoes shoot out ash and large chunks of hot rock into (9) ………. atmosphere, and enormous fountains of glowing red hot lava that flow (10) ………. the sides the volcano. This liquid lava quickly thickens into a steaming sticky carpet (11) ………. can travel 150 km before it stops and turns solid. Lava floods (12) ………. fire to and destroy (13) ………. that stands in their way. Famously, in AD 79, the Roman city of Pompeii (14) ………. covered in lava and ash, preserving buildings and some of their contents to (15) ………. day.

I wish / If only

1 Look at these examples from 23.1. Both *a* and *b* are wishes for the present and *c* is a wish for the past.

a … apart from wishing I were somewhere else!
b If only we could get in the tent, we'd be safe.
c I wish now we'd taken a radio with us.

• When talking about the present or the future you need to use a past tense after *wish* and *if only*.
• When referring to the past you must use the past perfect tense.

2 In the recording, Liz says that she wished she'd taken a radio. What other things do you think she wished for after the eruption? In groups, suggest five other things Liz might have said.

EXAMPLE: *I wish we had chosen a different place to camp.*

Tell your class about things that you regret doing or not doing in the past.

> *I wish I hadn't gone to that boring party.*

> *If only I had worked harder for the exam.*

3 When Liz says 'if only we could get in the tent, we'd be safe' and 'apart from wishing **I were somewhere else,**' she is saying what she felt at that **particular moment.**

Now write down ten things that you wish for right at this moment. Compare your sentences with a partner.

EXAMPLES:
I wish I was/were on a beach somewhere instead of in this classroom.
I wish I could give up smoking.

You can't say: *I wish I would/He wishes he would/They wish they would*, etc. This is because *wish … would* is usually used to express willingness, unwillingness, insistence and refusal.

4 After *wish* and *if only, would* can be used to complain about or criticise a person or situation.

EXAMPLES:
I wish it would stop raining. – It's raining at the moment and I want it to stop.
If only my neighbour would be quiet. – She's making a lot of noise at the moment.
I wish he would stop smoking. – The smoke is getting in my eyes.

Is there anything bothering you at the moment? Write down a few examples using *would*.

5 *Wish* is often confused with *hope*.

I hope I see you soon.
I wish I could see you soon.

Hope usually takes a present tense with a future meaning. When we use *hope* we usually don't know or can't tell the outcome, whereas with *wish* we do know the facts and they are the opposite of what we want.

Decide on the correct alternative in the following sentences.

a I hope / wish the rain stops soon.
b I hope / wish you can come to my party.
c I hope / wish I could speak Arabic.
d I hope / wish Peter would finish writing his book.
e I hope / wish I had remembered to bring the sleeping bags.

6 Here are some other expressions followed by the past tense.

a as *if / as though*
It wasn't like a smoke cloud, it was as if it were alive – it wasn't alive.
What is the difference between:
You talk as if / though you were an expert on disasters!
You talk as if / though you are an expert on disasters.

b *would rather* (Remember: don't confuse *had better* and *would rather*)
This takes an infinitive without 'to' or a past tense.
I'd rather you didn't ask me about the experience.
I'd rather not tell you what really happened.

Correct these sentences, if necessary.

a I wish I would have more money.
b John wished he hadn't sold his motorbike.
c If only he stopped smoking – I can hardly breathe.
d She wishes they were here at the party.
e I had rather you went now.
f Liz wishes she would go home now.
g I wish I learned the violin when I was at school.

7 For the following questions, complete the second sentence so that it has a similar meaning to the first sentence, using the word given. **Do not change the word given. You must use between two and five words, including the word given.**

1 I regret not listening to the park ranger's advice.
wish
I .... the park ranger's advice.

2 I think it's better for the children to stay inside in bad weather.
rather
I .... inside in bad weather.

3 What a pity we didn't see any wildlife on our trip.
only
If .... wildlife on our trip.

4 I don't like living in an earthquake zone.
wish
I .... somewhere else.

5 Don't walk so fast, I can't keep up with you!
wish
I .... so fast, I can't keep up with you!

6 I'd prefer you not to repeat what I've just told you.
rather
I .... repeat what I've just told you.

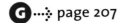 page 207

Vocabulary

8 Liz and Dave had to 'unroll' their trousers to empty out the ash that had collected in them.

What sort of things do you:

a untie
b unbutton
c undo
d unwrap
e uncover
f unearth
g unfasten
h untangle
i unwind

EXAMPLE: *unzip – your trousers, a dress*

9 Fill in the missing letters for these weather words.

a The Mid-West states of the USA suffer from T _ _ _ _ D _ _ _.
b Last winter we had huge S _ _ _ D _ _ _ T S and had to dig our way out of the house.
c The meteorological office have issued a G _ _ _ W _ _ _ _ _ G to all shipping.
d The weather F _ _ _ C _ _ _ for tomorrow is quite good.
e The sky's a bit O _ _ _ _ _ _ T this morning.
f I got caught in a S _ _ _ _ _ and got soaked to the skin.
g H _ _ _ _ _ _ _ _ S are usually found in the Caribbean.
h Global warming has led to D R _ _ _ _ T conditions in parts of the world.
i Britain is famous for being D _ _ _, while parts of India are often H _ _ _ _.

Paper 1 Part 3 Gapped Text

This part of the Reading paper requires you to read a text from which seven or eight sentences or paragraphs have been removed, and then choose the correct sentences or paragraphs to fill in the missing spaces. There is always one extra sentence or paragraph which you don't need.

Although there are fewer questions in this part than in Part 4, like Part 2, each question is 'double-weighted', that is, it is worth two marks instead of one. Part 3 is a difficult task and you must allow enough time for it.

Complete the exam task below using the steps in the Advice box. Try to keep to the suggested timings.

Advice

- Read the skeleton text and example (0) quickly, in order to get an idea of what the text is about.
  3 mins
- Underline key words in each paragraph, to predict what a gap might contain. Look for linking and reference words too.
  6 mins
- Scan the missing sentences or paragraphs for matching information and note down likely answers.
  6 mins
- Read through the whole text with your answers in place, to check that it all makes sense.
  3 mins
- Make sure that the extra sentence or paragraph does not fit anywhere.
  2 mins

You are going to read a magazine article about intelligence. Eight sentences have been removed from the article. Choose from the sentences A–I the one which fits each gap (1–7). There is one extra sentence which you do not need to use. There is an example at the beginning (0).

What makes intelligent?

The days when all you needed to make a living was sufficient physical strength to bring in the harvest are long gone. To survive today you need to be educated to rocket scientist level just to program a video recorder, make sense of a public transport timetable, or follow a complicated plot on TV. **0** **I**

But what exactly is intelligence? Are there ways of getting smarter, or are you stuck with what you were born with? There aren't any easy answers. Despite the progress that has been made in genetics and psychology, human intelligence has remained one of the most controversial areas of modern science. **1** **D**

Robert Plomin of the Institute of Psychiatry in London and his colleagues in the US have been looking into genetic make-up.

From their research, they have established that a slightly different gene is more common in those with a high IQ. Plomin analysed DNA from two groups of 51 children aged between six and 15. What he found was that the first group had an IQ of 136, putting them in the top 5% of the population, while the other group had an average IQ of 103. An analysis of their genes revealed that 32% of children in the higher group had the gene in question, while only 16% in the second group did.

2 **G** He suggests that there are probably many genes that contribute to intelligence, rather than just one.

If you were born with a full set of intelligence-enhancing genes, then you'd expect to be very clever indeed. But just how important are genes in intelligence? Most of the early research depended on measuring the IQs of identical twins who had grown up separately. The argument was that if intelligence was 100% inherited, both twins would have the same IQ, no matter how different their backgrounds. **3** **A**

someone

...nce it is difficult to find many who have been separated at ...rth, recent studies have concentrated on adopted children ...stead. One does suggest that adopted children become ...creasingly like their biological parents as they get older.

... the past, the idea that intelligence is mainly inherited ...ecame an excuse for prejudice and discrimination. The ...oncept of IQ itself was first developed a century ago by ...ench psychologist Alfred Binet. **4** [C] IQ measures ...omething called general intelligence, testing word and ...umber skills, as well as spatial ability.

...everal studies have shown a strong link between IQ and ...areer success, although some psychologists remain ...nconvinced about this. **5** [F] 'The people with the ...ghest IQs are not usually the ones who do best in their ...areers, but there's a big business out there with ...ccupational psychologists offering all kinds of selection ...sts for companies. They won't go away because there's ...lot of money to be made. But intelligence is not like ...mperature, and you cannot measure it in the same way. ...s much more complicated than that.'

...any psychologists now believe that when it comes to ...telligence, IQ isn't everything. Many alternative views ...ve been put forward recently. **6** [B] This offers a ...uch broader view than the IQ theory, including creativity ...d communication skills as relevant factors in intelligence.

...ny Buzan, brain expert and author of *Master your ...emory*, is enthusiastic about this belief, arguing that true ...eniuses do indeed appear to combine high levels of each ...pe of intelligence. **7** [E] At the same time, Buzan ...lieves that everyone can develop their intelligence, if only ...ey take the trouble to exercise their brain. Perhaps there's ...ope for us all!

A This may seem remote from everyday concerns, but does illustrate what the human brain is capable of.

B One example is the idea of 'multiple intelligences', which was developed in the 1980s by Harvard psychologist Howard Gardner.

C The tests were meant to select bright but socially-disadvantaged children, to ensure that they got a good education.

D Until now, that is, for the discovery of a gene linked to intelligence has made the experts think again.

E He lists Alexander the Great, Pablo Picasso and Albert Einstein as examples.

F Professor Michael Rowe, who has written a book called *Genius Explained*, is one of these.

G However, there is a lot more research to be done, and Plomin himself is cautious at this early stage.

H On the other hand, if differences in their IQs were found, this would point to background or environmental factors.

I In short, what you have in your head has never been more important.

1 Discuss the two paintings and decide which one you like best and why. If you were very rich, would you spend any money on works of art? Do you have a favourite artist or sculptor? Describe in detail a work of art you admire.

2 Read this title and opening paragraph. Decide what you think the article is going to be about.

A New Genius?

The artist had some difficulty pointing out the features of his 3-metre-wide painting, which had just been sold for $19,000 to an adoring crowd at the opening night in Beverly Hills – perhaps because he is only 1 m 40 cms tall.

3 Now read through the whole article and answer the questions which follow.

THE ART WORLD'S LATEST CHILD PRODIGY, ten-year-old Beso Kazaishvili from the Republic of Georgia, looked resplendent in traditional costume: a belted cream wool tunic with sewn-in gunpowder tubes and a sinister curved dagger. He was 'very
5 happy' about the sale but emphasised: 'Money is not everything.'

Beso has burst upon the art scene two years after the Romanian-born Alexandra Nechita was hailed as a genius at the age of ten. She has now made $10 million from her paintings. Her family has moved from a cramped bungalow by a Los Angeles freeway
10 to a $1 million mansion. Alexandra began in California and made a successful European tour. Beso began with some success in London, where his family stayed with the Georgian ambassador, and he is now touring the United States. His work is mostly in oils of human figures and faces, executed in a lively way in
15 bright, sometimes almost garish, colours. Many tell stories with symbolic themes of good and evil, death and time, and all are executed remarkably quickly. Ink drawings, which sold for £200 in London, are fetching up to $3,000 in Beverly Hills, where they are very highly thought of.

20 Beso and Alexandra are managed by the Californian art publisher Ben Valenty. Beso has signed a contract in the 'mid-six figures'. Mr Valenty always takes half but pays all expenses. It is good money for both sides – Beso's sales hit $30,000 in an hour in the USA. Cynics like myself may question a second genius
25 arriving so soon, but Mr Valenty argues that there are probably half a dozen or more in the world. He adds: 'No sooner had I

discovered Alexandra than parents from all over the world began sending me their kids' work. Yet none measured up to Beso, and I went to see him. Lightning can strike twice. Beso's work is deeper. After Alexandra the door is open. People believe a child's art is worthy of serious consideration, so Beso won't meet the earlier scepticism. I believe he's a genius, and I'm prepared for the verdict of time.'

Mr Valenty and his colleague Rick Lombardo, a television producer preparing a documentary on child prodigies, cheerfully admit that sales of the children's works are market driven. 'If Beso makes $19,000 in half an hour, it's because people want his work. Dozens of other youngsters haven't made that mark. Well, that's the market. Who knows what will happen next?'

Beso's parents, Badri an engineer, and Irma, a schoolteacher, believe their son's work was influenced by Georgia's civil war of 1993–1995. They were often without water and electricity, and food was scarce. Short of money to buy paper, Beso made a drawing on the blank side of a card from his mother's stockings packet. 'That one is priceless and not for sale,' said Mr Valenty, who acknowledges that Beso's 'story' helps sales. 'He's not like other kids,' Mr Lombardo says. 'He's structured. Sure, he'll watch television, play baseball, do his homework, but then start painting. He's never distracted from that. We're only just beginning to find out about these kids. Nobody studied **it** before. Who knows what Picasso was like at 11? We don't know.'

1 Beso and Alexandra both
   A come from the same country in Europe.
   B are American citizens now.
   C paint similar kinds of pictures.
   D have an unusual gift.

2 What do we find out about Beso's painting?
   A He enjoys doing portraits.
   B He spends time getting the details right.
   C He prefers using subtle colours.
   D He uses ideas from famous fairytales.

3 What does Mr Valenty say about child artists?
   A He knows at least six possible geniuses at the moment.
   B He wants to meet as many as possible.
   C He believes that their work will be easier to sell in the future.
   D Their work improves as they get older.

4 What do you think 'measured up to' means in line 28?
   A had the same height
   B was the same standard
   C was the same age
   D had the same experience

5 What does Mr Valenty say about the money that Beso earns?
   A Beso could earn a lot more when he is older.
   B It's hard to put a price on Beso's works.
   C Beso only earns what people are prepared to pay.
   D It's crazy for people to pay so much for a child's work.

6 What do we find out about Beso from the article?
   A His only interest is painting.
   B He's a good student.
   C He is surprised that he is making so much money.
   D He loves being in the USA.

7 What does 'it' in line 50 refer to?
   A the subject of young artists
   B the particular style of painting
   C the way Picasso painted when young
   D how history can affect young people

8 How do you think the writer feels about Beso and his paintings?
   A He was impressed by how good the paintings are.
   B He isn't sure that Beso is really as good as Alexandra.
   C He's not convinced about child geniuses.
   D He thinks that money is Beso's real motive.

4 What do you think about Beso and his new career? Is it possible to put a price on a work of art?

Vocabulary *Collocations*

5 Look at this example from the article.

She has now made $10 million from her paintings.

The collocation is 'to make money'.
Can you match each verb in A with a word or phrase in B? Some are used more than once.

A	B
break	a conversation
sit	a promise
get	20 kilometres to the litre
spend	a look
taste	an expression
keep	still
have	a fortune
do	awake
wear	funny
	a secret
	a week
	a holiday
	better

6 🎧 You will hear people talking in three different situations. For Questions 1–3, choose the best answer A, B or C.

1 You overhear a conversation in a café. What does the woman say about her trip?
   A It hadn't been worthwhile.
   B She got to see some good paintings.
   C She went too early in the morning.

2 You overhear this man talking on the phone. What is his opinion of what is happening at his workplace?
   A He is unhappy about the idea.
   B He feels people should think carefully about it.
   C He thinks his colleagues have chosen unwisely.

3 You overhear this woman speaking about the first night of an exhibition she recently attended. Why was the artist unhappy?
   A He hadn't sold enough paintings.
   B Few people attended the exhibition.
   C One of his favourite paintings had been bought.

Adverbs and word order

1

never   seldom   rarely   hardly   no sooner

These adverbs can be put in the normal adverbial position. However, if they are put at the beginning of a sentence, the word order must be changed – this is called 'inversion'. This is because the subject and verb are 'inverted', that is, the word order is changed so that it looks like a question. It is done to give greater emphasis.

No sooner had I discovered Alexandra than parents all over the world began sending me their kids' work.

I had no sooner discovered Alexandra, than parents all over the world began sending me their kids' work.

2 Below are sixteen sentences, fifteen of which show mistakes in word order made by students of English. Work with a partner to identify the errors and then rewrite the sentences correctly. You may need to add a word. One sentence is correct.

G ⋯▸ page 207

a I like very much Van Gogh.
b I yesterday visited a gallery in London.
c She would have never suggested buying it.
d He still is hoping to have an exhibition.
e I asked him to not stand in front of the painting.
f Always there is a queue for the Summer Exhibition.
g I go often to Los Angeles.
h The price is enough high, so don't bid any more.
i Never have I seen a painting like that.
j Can you tell me what is the price, please?
k I don't know what is it called.
l It was a such heavy frame that no one could carry it.
m The artist gave to my father the small portrait.
n How it is magnificent!
o He me described the photo.
p She drew quickly the sketch.

3 Read the following information about adverbs.

Adverbs are usually formed by adding *-ly* to an adjective. However, some words ending in *-ly* are adjectives and have no adverb.

friendly, lonely, lovely, ugly, silly

If you want to use these words as adverbs you need to add 'in a … way'.

He held out his hand in a friendly way.

- Some adverbs keep the same form as the adjective.
  She walks fast.
  She is a fast walker.
  He works hard.
  He is a hard worker.
- Some adverbs have two forms, with a difference in meaning.
  She works hard. (a great deal)
  She hardly does any work. (almost no work)
  I came home late yesterday. (not on time)
  Have you seen Peter lately? (recently)

Adverb or adjective? Complete these sentences by using a word or phrase based on the word in capitals. Some sentences do not need to be changed.

a He seemed to be a very SILLY person.
b He drives quite GOOD for someone with so little experience.
c The gallery owner shook my hand FRIENDLY.
d I think Picasso painted GOOD pictures than Braque.
e Don't paint so FAST, you'll make a mess of it.
f Women painters were often GOOD than men, it's just they are less GOOD known.
g She draws CAREFUL than anyone else in the class.
h If you painted a little INTERESTING, people might buy more of your paintings.
i A painter's life can be very LONELY.
j Luckily my art teacher's drawing was BAD than mine.
k I've eaten HARD any dinner.
l Your hem isn't very STRAIGHT.

Vocabulary *Confusable words*

Vocabulary spot

Some words in English are easily confused, either because they look or sound similar, or because they exist in another language with a different meaning. Take special care when learning these words.

4 The article about Beso talked about a work of art being 'priceless'. This means that you can't buy it because it is so valuable: it has no price.
In the following sentences there are two words or phrases which are often confused by students. Decide which one is correct, then write another sentence to show how the other word or phrase is used.

a My sister spent so long talking on the phone every day that *at the end / in the end* my parents bought her a mobile phone.

b My next door neighbour's help has been *invaluable / priceless* while my mother was in hospital.

c You don't see many people smoking *nowadays / actually*.

d Prices of impressionist paintings have *raised / risen* a great deal in the last few years.

e *Lie / lay* down on the bed and have a rest.

f *Tell / say* me the story about how you met Monet.

g My mother is an excellent *cook / cooker*.

h The bank in town was *stolen / robbed* this morning.

i I *damaged / injured* the piano when I tried to move it.

j The watch I got for my birthday was very *priceless / valuable*.

k My friend was very *sympathetic / friendly* when I broke my arm.

l Jean is so *sensible / sensitive* that she cries whenever she watches a sad film.

5 Read the text below. Use the word given in capitals at the end of each line to form a word that fits in the space in the same line. There is an example at the beginning (0).
Remember you need to spell the word correctly.

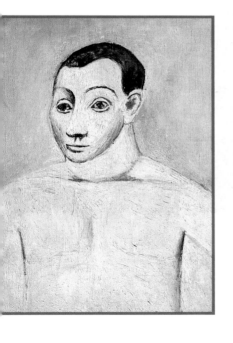

Pablo Picasso was born in Spain. As a child he was very **(0)** _talented._	**TALENT**
At the age of 19, he went to Paris and experimented with **(1)**	**DIFFER**
styles, from sad paintings in blue , to more **(2)** .... ones of circuses	**CHEER**
in reds and pinks. Picasso very quickly became **(3)** .... He was	**SUCCEED**
constantly looking for new **(4)**	**INSPIRE**
He became interested in **(5)** .... masks, which were being shown in	**AFRICA**
Europe for the first time. He particularly liked the simple but **(6)**	**EXPRESSION**
way they distorted the human face. He began to use **(7)**	**ANGLE**
shapes to build up an image – this was the **(8)** .... of cubism. Even	**BEGIN**
though his cubist pictures are **(9)** .... we still understand what	**REALISM**
they are supposed to be **(10)**	**SYMBOL**

Writing folder 12

Articles 2

In Part 2 of Paper 2 you might be asked to write a description of a place, a person or an object as part of the task.

1   Look at this exam question.

You see this notice in an international arts magazine and decide to write to them.

Write your **article**.

Look carefully at this painting and then read through a student's answer to the question.

My favourite painting is of a woman, a servant in a large house and it was painted about 1660 in Holland by Vermeer Van Delft. The young woman is a cook and is quite tall and I'd say fairly strong, probably as a result of having to carry heavy objects from an early age. I would say she is about 18 or 19 years old. She's wearing a white cap or scarf, which completely covers her hair, a yellow blouse, which buttons at the front, a blue apron and an orange floor-length skirt. This painting gives you a good idea of what ordinary working women wore in the seventeenth century.

The girl seems fairly happy and is concentrating very hard on what she is doing. I think she probably enjoys her job and her life, even though it is likely to be quite hard. Perhaps she already knows who her husband will be and is looking forward to getting married – the only option open to a young girl in those days. I find this an interesting painting because it isn't of someone rich or famous, but of an ordinary person going about her daily tasks. Although she isn't dressed in silks and lace she is, in her own way, rather beautiful.

Now think about what information the answer has given you about the cook and her life. Which of these titles would be best for this article?

A *Everyday life in the seventeenth century*

B *A painting is as good as a photograph*

C *Bringing the past to life*

2 Look again at the painting of the cook and complete this short paragraph which describes the room she is in. Join the words together – you must keep them in the same order. You may need to add some words.

EXAMPLE: *The room she / probably / kitchen / house. The room she is standing in is probably the kitchen of the house.*

The walls / bare / painted white. There / window / wall / basket / hanging / it. the window / there / table / basket / bread, / bowl / milk, / cakes. Jar / milk / bowl / make / brown pottery. There / blue and white tiles / wall / joins / floor. floor / box / containing / pot / handle.

3 Look at this exam question.

You see this competition in an international nature and science magazine and decide to enter it.

EARTH MATTERS MAGAZINE
✳ **Have you ever been caught in severe weather conditions?**
✳ **Write and tell us where you were and what you did.**
We will print the six best articles we receive and the writers will get a year's subscription to the magazine.

Write your **article**.

Advice

- Make a plan – Remember there are two parts to this question.
- Think of a title.
- Use your own experience, or what you have read or seen on TV or heard about.
- Think about what kind of person reads the magazine.
- Try not to repeat yourself, especially when you use adjectives.

4 How many synonyms can you think of for the following words? Use your dictionary to help you.

a big   e hot   i pretty
b small   f cold   j bad
c rich   g fat
d poor   h thin

Topic review

1 Answer these questions, giving your own opinions.

a What should someone do to lose weight?

b When should you tell someone it's time for them to leave a party?

c Even if someone has committed a crime, is prison the best form of punishment?

d Would you rather spend your money on entertainment or clothes?

e Is there a luxury you regret not having?

f Do you ever wish you were famous?

g What do you hope to do after you have passed FCE?

h What would you do if you were stranded in a storm?

i How often do you go to art exhibitions?

j Are modern painters and sculptors exceptionally talented professionals or totally worthless con-artists?

Vocabulary

2 Read the statements or questions and choose the best option, A, B or C.

1 You have been out in the wind and your hair looks a mess. Should you
A untie it? B unwind it? C untangle it?

2 If you give away your friend's secret even though you agreed not to, have you
A broken a promise? B kept your word?
C spent a fortune?

3 Which performer would you not see at a classical recital?
A a violinist B a cellist C a bass guitarist

4 You are driving in torrential rain and a tree falls across the road 200 metres in front of you. Are you in danger of being
A cut down? B cut off? C cut out?

5 While a photograph is being taken of you, should you keep
A quiet? B calm? C still?

6 If you have a steady income but enjoy paying everyone's expenses, are you likely to be
A tight? B broke? C loaded?

7 What should you do about a large debt?
A pay it off B break it off C call it off

8 It's about time you found a glass of water. Are you
A fainting? B hiccuping? C sneezing?

3 The twenty words below have all appeared in Units 19–24. Decide what they are with the help of the information given and then use one from each set to complete the sentences a–e.

● two verbs to do with illness or injury:

1 _ P _ A _ _

2 C _ _ _ H

● three words to do with volcanoes:

3 _ _ U _ _

4 _ _ H

5 L _ _ _

● four musical instruments:

6 O _ _ _

7 _ I _ _ O

8 _ U I _ _ _

9 _ L _ _ _

● five serious crimes:

10 _ A _ _

11 F _ _ _ _

12 _ _ G G _ _ _

13 _ _ S _ _

14 _ I J _ _ _ _ _ _

● six adjectives to describe works of art:

15 W _ _ _ _ _ E _ _

16 _ X _ _ _ _ _ I V _

17 _ R _ _ _ _ _ _ S

18 _ _ L _ _ _ L _

19 G _ _ I S H

20 S Y _ _ O _ _ C

a She picked up the shiny silver .... and began to play her favourite piece.

b Molten .... moves at an extremely fast speed.

c If only that painting weren't so .... ! I would rather look at softer colours.

d It is very easy to .... your ankle when running to the back of the court for a difficult ball.

e Firemen found a half-full can of petrol near the incident, so .... seemed a certainty.

Grammar

4 Read the text below and think of the word which best fits each space. Use one word in each space. There is an example at the beginning (0).

How to make a small fortune

Have you ever wished you had some savings to fall back (0) ....on.......... ? Perhaps you already have something put aside for a rainy day, but if (1) ...., here are some unusual ways to make a pile (2) .... cash. If you are prepared to wait for your money, David Leach, (3) .... is a specialist in collecting, suggests keeping empty Spice Girls crisp packets: 'Most people throw them away, so (4) .... there are millions of them now, one day they (5) .... be extremely valuable.' Very (6) .... old toys remain in a condition that is good (7) .... for them to be sold, (8) .... that a pre-1950, well-looked-after teddy bear can be worth (9) .... to £2,000. Musical instruments can raise (10) .... large sum, sometimes unexpectedly. Hazel Morgan hadn't played her violin for more (11) .... forty years, so she decided to sell (12) .... To her surprise, the violin itself was valued (13) .... £1,500 and the bow, despite (14) .... in bad condition, was expected to fetch even more. Fine wines can also be highly profitable, and even (15) .... your investment doesn't prove as big an earner as you hoped, you can still enjoy drinking the wine!

1   Compare and contrast these two pictures, and talk about the advantages and disadvantages of living in each city area. You can use some of the words below to help you.

Neighbourhood:
peaceful, quiet, calm/noisy, polluted, dangerous
deprived, derelict, run-down/regenerated, improved

Buildings:
low-rise/high-rise spacious/cramped

Amenities:
entertainment centre, multiplex cinema, mall, pedestrian/shopping precinct, out-of-town shopping

Services:
litter/refuse collection, maintenance, street-lighting

Transport:
congestion, traffic jam, parking restrictions

Listening

2   🎧 You are going to listen to an extract from a radio programme called *Do they really know best?* In this programme, a member of the public is invited to challenge an expert about his/her field of work. First, listen to the programme host introducing the speakers and decide:
   • what profession the expert is in
   • what objections Gareth wants to raise.

How do you think the conversation might develop?

3   🎧 Now read the questions below. As you listen, decide who says what: write G for Gareth, J for Jennifer, or B for both of them.

1   Who argues that high-rise housing was an improvement for certain people? | 1 |
2   Who says they grew up in a deprived area? | 2 |
3   Who expects more mistakes in city planning to occur? | 3 |
4   Who criticises the development of suburbs? | 4 |
5   Who wants to live in the centre of London? | 5 |
6   Who believes that buildings should have more than one function? | 6 |
7   Who thinks that city people should be able to own cars? | 7 |

4 🎧 Compare your answers with another student. Then listen again to check, noting down any phrases that helped you to decide.

5 🎧 These words with *up* all occurred in the recording. Listen again and work out their meaning from context. Then match them to 1–5.

a uprooted	**1** maintenance
b upheld	**2** expensive
c upkeep	**3** made to leave
d upmarket	**4** improvement
e uplift	**5** supported

6 Explain what you think each speaker meant by the following statements. Do you agree with them?

a People have been uprooted and put in high-rise buildings against their will.
b Lack of consultation over new buildings is not an issue with the public.
c What I believe in is the regeneration of our cities' core.
d Living in the city has to become a healthier and more acceptable option.

Speaking

7 **Say whether the purpose of these turn-taking** moves is

i to involve someone in the discussion
ii to encourage someone to be quiet
iii to support what someone is saying

a You clearly know a lot about this, but let's move on.
b Would you say that this is true in your case?
c I believe your own view is slightly different?
d Come on, you're talking rubbish!
e Well, I have to admit you have a point.
f I'm going to say something here.
g What do you think?
h Absolutely, I couldn't agree more.

Do you consider any of these rude or offensive? In what other ways can a speaker or listener direct a conversation?

8 Now practise these turn-taking skills. Get into groups of four to discuss the following statements. For each statement, one person in the group should stay silent, and time how long each of the others speak for.

- There are both good and bad examples of modern architecture.
- Living conditions in our cities have got worse.
- City centres should be traffic-free.
- Urban sprawl is a serious threat to nature.

Mixed conditionals

1 Look at these two quotes from the recording in 25.1, which are examples of mixed conditionals. Explain what tenses are used and why.

If we were meant to live up in the sky, we would have been born with wings!
If 60s architecture hadn't happened, we would be making similar mistakes today.

In both examples, the second and third conditional forms are mixed.

2 You can use a mixed conditional to talk about a past action affecting a present situation, as in the second example above. Finish these mixed conditional sentences in a suitable way.

EXAMPLE: If we had bought that house, we *would be short of money now.*

a If people hadn't objected to the plans, the building …
b If Tom had remembered to book a table at the restaurant, we …
c If I hadn't seen that programme, I …
d If they had been paid less, the players …
e If she hadn't answered the advert, she …

3 You can also use mixed conditionals to talk about how a different present situation would have affected a past situation, as in this example:

If the city centre was traffic-free, the council wouldn't have needed to build all these car parks.

Finish these sentences in a similar way, using the ideas in brackets.

a If high-rise buildings were of better quality, more people (choose to live in them in the first place)
b If there weren't so many distractions, you (tidy up your bedroom by now)
c If the suburbs were smaller, local taxes (be so high for the last 20 years)
d If the supermarket was open 24 hours, I (go out at 3 am this morning to buy you some paracetamol)

(G) ⋯⋮ page 207

4 Imagine a city with no advantages to it whatsoever. Discuss the impact of these problems.

- no refuse collection
- no bus service
- no shops
- no police

EXAMPLE: *If there was no refuse collection service, rubbish would pile up on the streets and there might be rats.*

5 Read the article about the architect Sir Norman Foster. For Questions 1–15, decide which answer, A, B, C or D, best fits each space. There is an example at the beginning (0).

Example:

0 A chose **B** fixed **C** dealt **D** wished

0 | A | B | C | D

The grand designer

When asked to select his favourite building, Sir Norman Foster **(0)** ..... a Jumbo jet. His own buildings frequently **(1)** ..... materials and technology developed by the aerospace industry. Perhaps his most **(2)** ..... building is the Hongkong and Shanghai Bank, a massive construction of three linked towers 41 **(3)** ..... high. His most ambitious European **(4)** ..... has been the reconstruction of the Reichstag as the new German parliament building. He has also built a metro **(5)** ..... in Bilbao, and two space-age communications towers in Barcelona and Santiago de Compostela.

Foster **(6)** ..... in the vertical city, an architect's dream that began a hundred years ago and is still **(7)** ..... to be fully realised. He says that the city is in a continuous process of renewal; if buildings cannot **(8)** ..... to social or technological change, then unless they are outstanding, they should be replaced. It's all about **(9)** ..... the past and the future.

Foster's latest **(10)** ..... is to re-design part of central London. The World Squares For All team of **(11)** ....., which also includes transport planners, civic and landscape designers, and economists, is led by Foster himself. The aim is to **(12)** ..... pollution and improve safety, by re-routing cars away from key **(13)** ..... such as Trafalgar Square and Westminster Abbey. As part of this, Foster's company is currently researching pedestrian movement and traffic **(14)** ..... in the centre, and has undertaken more public **(15)** ..... than Londoners have seen for decades. The response so far is very positive.

1	**A** lend	**B** fetch	**C** borrow	**D** bring
2	**A** famous	**B** known	**C** understood	**D** common
3	**A** flights	**B** levels	**C** storeys	**D** stages
4	**A** activity	**B** project	**C** occupation	**D** post
5	**A** method	**B** plan	**C** routine	**D** system
6	**A** believes	**B** hopes	**C** relies	**D** depends
7	**A** standing	**B** expecting	**C** waiting	**D** resting
8	**A** alter	**B** adapt	**C** fit	**D** match
9	**A** steadying	**B** settling	**C** estimating	**D** balancing
10	**A** trial	**B** challenge	**C** question	**D** attempt
11	**A** masters	**B** authorities	**C** experts	**D** teachers
12	**A** reduce	**B** shorten	**C** dilute	**D** lower
13	**A** neighbourhoods	**B** districts	**C** grounds	**D** sites
14	**A** stream	**B** rush	**C** course	**D** flow
15	**A** consultation	**B** appointment	**C** conference	**D** dialogue

6 There are a number of words containing the prefix *re-* in the article, such as *renewal* and *re-routed*. Make new words from the ones below, using the same prefix. Sometimes, words with different parts of speech can be made. Use some of the words to complete sentences a–d.

consider	construct	generate
open	possess	write

a The old industrial city of Duisberg has been .... and now has new, cleaner industries right in its centre, alongside schools and housing.

b Following extensive fire damage, the timber framed buildings have now been fully .... in their original style.

c The city council's .... of the enquiry into noise pollution has been supported by local residents.

d Anyone who has left the city for the suburbs should .... their move, particularly in the light of how far rents have fallen in the centre.

Exam folder 13

Paper 1 Part 4 Multiple matching

This part of the Reading paper focuses on your ability to retrieve specific information from a text. You are given 13–15 questions and you must find the answers either in a group of texts or in one which has been divided into sections. In addition, there are sometimes two multiple choice questions on the text or texts as a whole.

Advice

- Look at the title and any information you are given about the text or texts. Skim the texts very quickly to find out what they are about. Do not worry about vocabulary that you aren't familiar with. For this particular passage see how quickly you can find out what Raquel, David, Martin and Dick do for a living.
- Read through the questions carefully.
- You are looking for specific information to answer the questions, so you need to scan the texts rather than read them in detail.
- When you find the answer in a text, underline it and put the question number next to it (a highlighting pen is quite useful for this).
- Don't spend too much time looking for the answer to a question. Leave it until the end and go on to the next question.
- When you've finished the easy questions, go back and have another go at the difficult ones. If you still don't know – guess. Never leave a blank on your answer sheet.
- If there are more than four texts you sometimes have more than one answer to find to a question. When this happens you can answer in any order.

Many of the questions ask you to locate words and phrases that mean the same as the ones used in the question. Sometimes more than one person talks about the same subject, and you need to decide which one really answers the question.

Now read the exam question. If you need any help, look at these clues:

0 'To cancel a meeting' means the same as 'can't make our appointment'.
1 The key word here is 'important'. Remember that as you look through the texts.
2 What examples of modern technology can you think of? Now the phrase is 'working with' which narrows down the text.
3 Two texts talk about money. What sort of words do they use? Which one talks of 'a drop'?
4 What do you think 'at a moment's notice' means?
5 All of the people in the texts have done other jobs before. However, only one person did two jobs 'at the same time'. Which one?
6 Another way of saying 'has a good relationship with'?
7 Find a phrasal verb that means 'freedom of choice'.
8 What does an 'aspect' mean here?
9 Are you an early riser?
10 In a play a 'role' means a 'part'. Here it means a 'job'.
11 Look back at Unit 5 if you don't know what 'claustrophobia' means.
12 Key word is 'hard'.
13 If you don't plan, then something happens by …
14 'Assistance' means …?
15 You need to find the word that means 'boring' in the text.

You are going to read a magazine article about people who have dream jobs. For Questions **1–15**, choose from the people **A–D**. There is an example at the beginning (**0**).

Which person

had to cancel a meeting?	0	A
says their job was more important than it appears?	1	
dislikes working with modern technology?	2	
took a drop in salary in order to do the job?	3	
often has to travel at a moment's notice?	4	
used to do two jobs simultaneously?	5	
has a good relationship with their employer?	6	
says they believe in freedom of choice?	7	

doesn't enjoy one aspect of the job?	8
says they aren't an early riser?	9
now has another role to play?	10
suffers from claustrophobia?	11
finds their job hard?	12
didn't plan to do this job?	13
needs assistance with their work?	14
has to do some very boring duties?	15

It's a tough job?

Chris Arnow asks people with dream jobs if they're as wonderful as they seem.

A Raquel Graham

Raquel Graham rings from the taxi taking her to the airport. She can't make our appointment tomorrow because her boss wants her to be in Los Angeles instead. When you're personal assistant to a pop star, you're expected to jet around the world at the drop of a hat. Raquel loves her job and gets on well with her boss.

There's just one minor problem – she can't stand flying. 'On a nine-hour trip to California I usually take sleeping tablets to help calm me down,' she admits. Her worst experience was being on Concorde. 'It seemed so shut in with those tiny windows.'

Offices in Manchester and London occupy her when she comes down to earth. There's some mundane paper work to get through – organising the diary, sitting in on meetings with solicitors and accountants, sorting out itineraries and making yet more travel arrangements.

She didn't train for the job. A chance meeting with the manager of a pop group led to the offer of work behind the scenes. Five years later she was in the right place at the right time when her boss needed a PA.

B David Brown

David Brown has been an accountant and a golf caddy, a man who carries a golfer's bags. On the whole, he preferred the golf. Well, so would you if golf was your passion. There were drawbacks however. A small flat fee is on offer, plus a percentage of the winnings. The average earnings are between £25,000 and £35,000 and much of that will go on travel and hotels.

He was 31 when he first caddied for the golfer, Greg Norman. 'You're not just carrying bags. You're offering advice, pitting your knowledge against the elements and trying to read the course.'

His accountancy skills were recently recognised by European Tour Productions when they made him statistical data administrator. From cards brought in by the caddies, he compiles and analyses the statistics of each day's play. The results are sought after by television commentators, golfing magazines, and the golfers themselves.

C Martin Fern

Martin Fern is the editor of the 'Food and Drink' pages of a daily newspaper and one of his less difficult tasks is to sample what's on offer in the finest restaurants. What does he think about restaurants that charge exorbitant prices? 'For those who can afford it, it's up to them,' he says. 'I'd rather spend £120 on a meal I'll remember for the rest of my life than buy a microwave.'

It was his talent as a cook that led to the offer of a food column from a friend who happened to edit a Saturday Review. For Martin, at the time creative director of an advertising agency, it was a useful secondary income. He was 42 when another newspaper rang to offer a full-time job. 'It meant a 50 per cent cut in guaranteed income,' he says. 'But it was a chance to convert my passion into a profession.'

He still does all the cooking at home and tries to keep his waistline under control by cycling a couple of miles to the nearest tube station.

D Dick Prince

'I started writing children's stories about twenty years ago,' says Dick Prince, one of Britain's most popular children's writers. 'Before that, I had always loved words and enjoyed using them, but my writing had mainly been verse. Then I had this idea for a story. I had been a farmer, and knew the problem of chickens being killed by a fox. So I wrote a kind of role reversal story called The Fox Busters, which became my first published children's story.'

Where do his ideas come from? 'Well, it's not easy, I have to work at them,' he says. 'That is what I usually do in the mornings. I'm not up with the dawn, I'm afraid. After lunch, I spend another couple of hours typing out the morning's scribbling – all of which I do with one finger on an old portable typewriter rather than on one of those awful word processors.

I get between fifty and a hundred letters a week and that is the part about being a writer that I enjoy the most. I do try to answer them all, but nowadays I have some secretarial help.'

UNIT 26 | Getting around

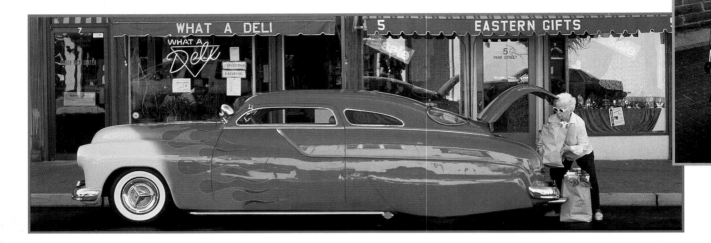

1 How important is the car to you? Could you live without one? Describe the role of the car in your way of life.

2 🎧 Listen to these short extracts, where five different people give their opinions on this subject.

Which speaker
- finds it necessary to use the car every day?
- would prefer not to travel by car at all?
- claims to be a car enthusiast?

3 You are going to read an article about traffic in the countryside. First, look at the headings A–I and discuss what information their paragraphs might contain.

A Pedestrians have rights too
B Harmful and wide-reaching effects
C Tailor-made suggestions
D Neighbourhood support is critical
E A problem requiring urgent attention
F The opinion of villagers
G Traffic experts share their views
H Part of the larger national picture
I Welcome plans for the countryside

4 Now choose the most suitable heading from the list A–I for each part (1–7) of the article. There is one extra heading which you do not need to use. There is an example at the beginning (0).

Rural traffic: getting it righ

0

A new way of looking at the car and other motor vehicles in the countryside was encouraged recently by this, the Countryside Commission's latest report: *Rural traffic: getting it right*. The report shows how solving the traffic problem in rural areas will require giving as much thought to people on foot or bicycles as to cars and lorries. However, it does also recognise that in many parts of the countryside the motor vehicle is a necessary means of transport in order to get around.

1

This report is perhaps long overdue, as we are all increasingly aware of the true price we pay for our continued use of the car. I trends continue over the next 25 years there could be three cars for every one there is now. Nowhere is increasing traffic more noticeable than in the countryside, whose pure air and green fields are now seriously under threat.

2

Attending the official launch of the report, a large group of local authority employees and specialists in this area were all keen to get the same message across. They say the time has come for us to change our view of traffic in the countryside and we won't get anywhere unless our dependence on the private car is reduced.

3

The report outlines the trouble that cars and lorries can cause in the countryside. As well as the obvious air pollution and noise, more traffic leads to changes in the character of quiet, rural areas, with more kerbs, signs and lighting. Visitors who come to the countryside to get away from it all are unpleasantly surprised, while residents face increased risks as pedestrians and cyclists. In addition, the more people use cars, the more they travel to distant towns to work and shop, so weakening the economy of country towns and villages.

5 In your country, is traffic a problem in the countryside? How do local residents there feel? What other means of transport besides cars are available for them?

4

Richard Simmons, who is chairman of the Commission, summarises the current position. 'The car is too dominant in our thinking. Some drivers even believe that if someone is crossing a road around a corner and an accident occurs, it will be the non-motorist's fault for being there. Transport has to become the servant, not the master. We must promote choice of transport, and that includes the right to walk safely.'

5

The key to solving rural traffic issues in the coming years is traffic demand management, in consultation with local residents. It is essential that the people for whom the plans are being developed are fully involved, so that they understand the reasons for suggested changes and are able to get behind them. These proposals must become part of their way of life and indeed improve it.

6

One of the Commission's current schemes is to create 'quiet roads', that is, keeping certain routes relatively free for use by cyclists, walkers and horse riders, and offering local people the chance to walk to school or to the shops. New, lower speed limits in villages and in the open countryside, improvements in public transport and new routes for cyclists are also raised in the report. The Commission's work with local government over the last four years has shown how these changes can easily be suited to local needs.

7

The Commission looks to the Government's forthcoming document on transport for support. One of the biggest questions in the short-term will be how to pay for the changes suggested. At the launch of the report, the Minister for Local Roads spoke encouragingly in this respect. So hopefully, the government, and all of us, will soon begin to get it right.

Vocabulary *get*

6 The title of the report included the phrase *getting it right*. Underline five more phrases with *get* in the article and then match them to their meanings, choosing from a–h. What are the *get* phrases for the other three meanings?

a escape
b criticise
c make no progress
d go to different places
e start
f communicate
g support
h finish something unpleasant

Grammar extra

Look at these examples. The first one is from the article.

Nowhere is increasing traffic more noticeable than in the countryside.

Not only did Matt fail to notice he was speeding, he also went through a red light!

What is the reason for starting sentences like this?
Rewrite the following sentences in the same way, using the words in bold first and paying attention to word order. In examples *c* and *f*, you have to add an extra word.

a There has **not only** been a huge increase in the number of private cars on the roads – more goods are now transported by lorry too.
b We can **no longer** depend on the unlimited use of our cars.
c Brendan **not only** rides a bike to work – in addition, he uses it to travel longer distances.
d The government should **in no way** weaken its transport policy.
e Members of the public are **seldom** willing to walk to work, especially if it's raining.
f Cars **not only** pollute the air but they endanger people's lives too.

G⋯⟶ page 207

Relative pronouns

1 First, reread the notes in the Grammar folder for Unit 17, which dealt with relative clauses.

   Now look at the examples 1–4 from the article in 26.1 and answer questions a and b about each one.

   a Is the information introduced by the relative pronoun essential or additional?
   b What does the relative pronoun refer to?

   Which of these relative pronouns does not always refer to people?

a Richard Simmons, who is chairman of the Commission, summarises the current position.
b Visitors who come to the countryside to get away from it all are unpleasantly surprised.
c It is essential that the people for whom the plans are being developed are fully involved.
d Nowhere is increasing traffic more noticeable than in the countryside, whose pure air and green fields are now seriously under threat.

who or whom?

2 In informal English, it is always safe to use *who* as both subject and object. However, in formal written English, *whom* is the object form, often used with a preposition, as in the example in 1.

   Rewrite the following sentences using *whom*, adding commas where necessary and making any other changes.

   EXAMPLE: The man they had given all their money to took a one-way flight to Rio.

   The man to *whom they had given all their money took a one-way flight to Rio.*

   a I went with Wetherby on several expeditions and he was always the perfect gentleman.
   Wetherby, with ....
   b The ranchers that cowboys worked for expected them to spend at least 12 hours a day on horseback.
   The ranchers for ....
   c The ancient Greeks believed in Apollo, who was supposed to ride a chariot of flame across the sky.
   Apollo, in ....
   d Rollerblading is seen as a quick way of getting around and teenagers often take unnecessary risks in traffic.
   Teenagers, to ....

whose

3 You use the relative pronoun *whose* to talk about something belonging to a person or thing, as in the example from the article.

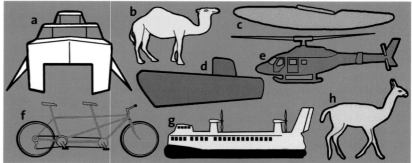

How many different means of transport do you know of? Identify what is being described in a–g, selecting the appropriate picture and giving the English word.

EXAMPLE: *A fast boat whose fins enable it to travel above the surface of the water.* hydrofoil

a A type of aircraft whose large blades rotate to allow it to hover in the air. ....
b A four-legged animal whose back has one or two humps. ....
c A narrow boat, usually for one person, whose hull is made of fibreglass or wood. ....
d A large vehicle whose skirts inflate to allow it to travel across land or water. ....
e A type of ship whose main purpose is to move secretly underwater. ....
f A bicycle whose twin seats allow two people to ride it. ....
g A South American animal whose hair is very thick. ....

4 Join the two sentences in a–f, using *whose*.

EXAMPLE: *Johnson is going to sail around the world alone. His yacht is sponsored by a leading British firm.*

Johnson, whose yacht is sponsored by a leading British firm, is going to sail around the world alone.

a The Regent's Canal in London runs between Camden and Islington. Its towpath is increasingly used by cyclists.

b This new jetski has a top speed of over 100 kph. Its seating accommodates four people easily.

c The hot air balloon was designed by the Montgolfier brothers. Its first flight was made in 1783.

d From 1983 to 1987, the number of cars and trucks in the United States increased by 20.1 million. The population in that period grew by only 9.2 million.

e The Brox, a new four-wheel cycle trailer, is being trialled by the Royal Mail. It has seven gears to allow it to go up hills, and even steps, easily.

f The American space shuttle can be used again and again. It has heat-proof tiles to allow it to re-enter the earth's atmosphere safely.

G ···⟩ **page 208**

5 Below are several words for parts of different means of transport. Put them into the correct columns. Sometimes, words can go into more than one column. Explain why.

> bonnet boot brake cab cabin
> dashboard exhaust flap funnel gearbox
> hull indicator jet engine mast oar
> paddle porthole propeller radiator rudder
> steering wheel tyre undercarriage windscreen

Cars and trucks	Boats and ships	Aircraft

6 Now use *whose* to describe problems with some of these things, choosing a suitable adjective from the ones below.

> bent broken faulty flat
> jammed missing stuck

The canoe, whose paddle was bent, was difficult to steer.

7 Read this text, about the film actor Robert Carlyle. If a line has a word that should not be there, write the word at the end of the line. If a line is correct, put a tick (✓) next to it. There are two examples (0 and 00).

Me and my wheels

0	Ken Loach was visiting at Glasgow and we went out for something	*at*
00	to eat. I knew he was looking for people for his new film *Carla's*	✓
1	*Song*. A couple of weeks later than he asked me to do a day's work	....
2	with some of other actors. Shortly after that I got the part. All Ken	....
3	told me about the character I had to play was 'Your name's George.	....
4	You drive a bus in Glasgow. Maybe it would and be a good idea if	....
5	you learned to drive a bus.' So I went to the Knightwood bus depot,	....
6	whose driver training programme has been you out on the streets	....
7	of Glasgow within one hour! You don't to know what a bus is like,	....
8	until you've driven one. I was scared stiff at the first, driving this big	....
9	red bus with an L-plate on it. You soon calm down enough, though,	....
10	because everyone gets out of your way when you're driving a bus.	....
11	The more important thing to remember is that the front wheels on a	....
12	bus are going behind you, so you need to go beyond the turning	....
13	point before you move the steering wheel. If you didn't, pedestrians	....
14	would be squished. Anyway, I got across my Passenger Service	....
15	Vehicle Licence, so I could always fall back on it, unless you know, start the Unemployed Actors' Bus!	....

Writing folder 13

Compositions 2

See also Writing folder 4, Compositions 1, which dealt with organisation and linkers.

1 The composition below is a poor attempt! Read it and try to decide which statement it addresses: A, B or C.

A Not enough is being done to encourage people to leave their cars at home.
B Cycling is a cheap and enjoyable alternative to the car.
C Traffic congestion threatens our health and the government must develop new policies urgently.

There is a lot of truth in this statement. Nowadays there are more and more cars on the roads, causing traffic congestion in city centres and outside, too. This clearly endangers our health. If we're driving, the stress of waiting in a traffic jam is, oh god, unbearable. As walkers or cyclists we're put at risk by motorists, whose only concern is to get where they want to be fast. I think cycling is healthier because you have to make an effort and it's exercise.
It is less expensive, because you don't have to buy petrol or pay for many repairs. A car, on the other hand, goes wrong and as I don't understand how it works, mine has to be fixed at the garage. Although I don't have one myself, I think it would be fun to use, why not, and it might be quicker than the car. You can choose different routes that avoid the main roads and follow beautiful places, like canals or rivers. Yes, it is definitely better than driving.

2 The five points in the Advice section are important to remember when writing a composition. Has the writer done any of them? Underline the parts of the composition that could be improved.

3 The article in Unit 26 had some useful neutral phrases, which could be used in a composition. Here are some of them, with variations.

The key to solving/reducing/dealing with ... is ...
One of the biggest questions/challenges/problems in the short-term will be ...
It is essential/vital/important that ...

Which of the following ideas (a–j) would be relevant as part of an answer to statement A in 1? Expand these ideas using one of the three phrases above, and including a reason.

a tax motorists more
b improve public transport
c give cyclists free helmets
d restrict parking in cities
e build more motorways
f set lower speed limits
g put up petrol prices
h ban car advertising
i develop solar-powered cars
j issue driving permits for use on certain days

EXAMPLE: *It is essential that motorists are taxed more, so that their cars become a less attractive option.*

4 Statement C includes a time indicator, *urgently*. There is often some reference to time in a composition task.

Some of the phrases below are used in jumbled sentences a–c. Reorder these sentences, adding commas where necessary.

> in the short-term/medium-term/long-term
> within the next five years/our lifetime
> urgent/ immediate/instant action
> of major importance/high priority/the utmost urgency

EXAMPLE: *which cannot be justified / take urgent action / the government should / to cancel new road-building*
The government should take urgent action to cancel new road-building, which cannot be justified.

a whose exhaust fumes / is the introduction of tighter laws / cause greater pollution / on older vehicles / of high priority
b to consult the public / in the short-term / whose concerns have never been fully aired / it is essential
c is needed / while in the medium-term / to reduce the volume of cars / instant action / in our cities / alternative forms of transport / further research should be done on

5 Now answer this exam question, in 120–180 words.

You have had a class discussion on transport. Now your teacher has asked you to write a composition, giving your opinion on the following statement.

The key to solving traffic problems is a better public transport system.

Write your **composition**.

UNIT 27 Material girl

Listening

1 🎧 Before you listen write down everything you know about Madonna and share the information with the rest of the class.

Now listen to a student journalist called Jonas Day being interviewed about Madonna. As you listen, make notes about Madonna on the following:

> Born:
> Place:
> Family:
> Education:

2 🎧 Listen again. Write down the word or phrase which the men use when they are:

taking charge of the conversation
correcting some information
changing subject
apologising
partly agreeing
making a generalisation
giving some information which may not be reliable
thinking
explaining

3 Work with a partner for this activity. Try to use some of the words and phrases you heard in the interview.

One of you is A and the other B. B chooses a famous person and A then interviews B to find out more information about the person B has chosen. When you run out of things to say, swap roles.

EXAMPLE:
Student A: *So, William Shakespeare, I believe you were born in London?*
Student B: *Actually in a place called Stratford-upon-Avon.*
Student A: *Okay, right, now can you tell me a little bit about your career?*

4 🎧 Listen to the rest of the interview with Jonas about his article on Madonna.

For Questions 1–7, choose the best answer A, B or C.

1 One surprising thing about Madonna is that she
  A prefers making records to films.
  B has extensive business interests.
  C is unconcerned about media attention.

2 How did Madonna get into the pop music business?
  A She worked in New York clubs.
  B She wrote to record producers.
  C She found out about the people in control.

3 She wanted to have Michael Jackson's manager because
  A he only looked after one pop star.
  B she admired what he'd done for Michael Jackson.
  C she wanted to be more famous than Michael Jackson.

4 According to Jonas, Madonna's main quality is her
  A cleverness. B ability. C persistence.

5 What does Jonas say about Madonna's acting career?
- **A** It has been disappointing so far.
- **B** It has been more profitable than singing.
- **C** She has upset too many people for it to succeed.

6 Jonas says that in the nineties Madonna
- **A** had better luck with her films than her records.
- **B** preferred singing with other people.
- **C** tried to widen her business interests.

7 Jonas thinks Madonna will succeed because she
- **A** is determined.
- **B** is still producing great songs.
- **C** challenges people to think.

Pronunciation *Intonation patterns*

5 🎧 Listen again to Jonas talking about Madonna.

Anyway, she did ballet, singing and piano lessons.

Notice how his voice goes **up** when he says *ballet* and *singing* and **down** when he says *piano lessons*.

Now you do the same.
One person in the class says:
I've been to Moscow.
The next student says:
I've been to Moscow and Washington.
The next student says:
I've been to Moscow, London and Washington.

Continue round the class, adding new places and making sure that you get your intonation right.

6 🎧 Now listen to the interviewer.

'A scholarship?'

He sounds surprised and so his voice goes **up**. Now you do the same in groups of four.

- **A** I saw Stephen cycling to school this morning.
- **B** Stephen?
- **C** Cycling?
- **D** This morning?

Now make up sentences of your own and the others show surprise at what you've said.

7 🎧 Listen to the interviewer again.

What about her family?

When he asks a question beginning with *Wh-* or *How*, then his voice goes down at the end.

In pairs, practise asking and answering these questions.

Where do you live?
What do you do?
When were you born?
How do you get to work?

Think of some more *Wh-* questions you can ask your partner.

If you didn't hear the question properly you can repeat it using a different intonation pattern. In this case your voice goes up at the end. Normally you insert 'did you say' in the question.

🎧 **Where** did you say you live?
What did you say you do?

Now you do the same.

8 🎧 In English our voices rise and fall to show interest or friendliness. When this does not happen, the speaker can appear indifferent or even rude. Often it's not **what** we say, it's **how** we say it that's important.

Listen to this man speaking and decide if he's being friendly.

- **a** It's over there.
- **b** Make me a cup of coffee.
- **c** Thank you.
- **d** Hello.
- **e** Excuse me.
- **f** See you soon.

Revision of tenses

1   What are the differences in meaning between *a* and *b*?

   1 a I believe Madonna has asked you to write about her.

     b I believe Madonna asked you to write about her.

   2 a She sees quite well without glasses.

     b She is seeing her manager this afternoon.

   3 a He agreed when he saw her.

     b He agreed when he had seen her.

   4 a She was making an album when she met her producer.

     b She made an album when she met her producer.

   5 a She believed her life to be totally under control.

     b She had believed her life to be totally under control.

   6 a Her records haven't done very well.

     b Her records haven't been doing very well.

   7 a It will probably sell 20 million copies.

     b It is going to sell 20 million copies.

2   Match the two parts of these sentences so that every sentence is correct and makes sense.

1 I've been waiting for you	**a** before.
2 I went to the cinema	**b** over 100 years ago.
3 I didn't have breakfast	**c** for the time being.
4 My grandfather was born	**d** last night.
5 He has given up buying CDs	**e** for two years.
6 I haven't done my homework	**f** this morning.
7 I go clubbing	**g** recently.
8 She got married	**h** yet.
9 I haven't had a holiday	**i** once a month.
10 I think I've heard this record	**j** since three o'clock.

3   Put these sentences into the correct tense. Sometimes there is more than one possibility.

a Where .... (you born)?

b I .... (fly) to Hong Kong tomorrow.

c I .... (play) football when President Kennedy .... (shoot).

d What .... (you do) this weekend?

e I .... (go) phone you, but I lost your number.

f Shakespeare .... (be) the greatest English playwright.

g It was the first time I .... (go) to the theatre.

h It is the first time I .... (hear) that record.

i I .... (believe) that homework .... (abolish) by the year 2010.

j The painter .... (paint) the ceiling, while the plumber .... (fix) the pipes.

k After the film .... (finish), everyone clapped.

l I wonder who .... (make) more money – Michael Jackson or Madonna?

m I .... (try) to explain how to do it for the past ten minutes!

n This time next week I .... (sit) on a ride in Disneyland.

o What time do you think the plane .... (arrive)?

p He arrived at the party late because he .... (work).

q Madonna .... (produce) some great records recently.

r I .... (not see) you for ages. What .... (you do)?

s This time last week I .... (be) in New York.

t Where you .... (live) before you .... (move) here?

G ⋯⟡ page 208

Vocabulary

4 🎧 Listen to the whole interview again and complete these sentences with the phrasal verbs and expressions that you hear.

a I guess she didn't want to .... the moment of stardom .... any longer.

b I'm afraid I never .... of that story.

c Right, OK, now tell us how her career ....

d Especially when she married Sean Penn – the newspapers really .... her ....

e She said at the time that what they said in the newspapers .... her ....

f Also she .... a lot of people's .... with her desire to shock.

g I think she's very good at ....

h She's the type who will get on whatever she ....

Rewrite the sentences using one of the alternative words or phrases from the box below.

decide to do postpone begin	
criticise upset communicate	
astonish find out the truth	

5 In pairs, ask and answer these questions. Use an English-English dictionary to help you.

a Do you ever put off doing things? If yes, which sort of things?

b Have you ever put someone's back up? If yes, how?

c Would you be put out if someone told you your English accent wasn't very good?

d What would put you off buying a Porsche?

e Do you put anything by for a rainy day?

f Have you ever read a book you couldn't put down?

g What sort of things do your family do that you can't put up with?

h Would you be able to put someone up if they came to visit you?

6 For Questions 1–10, read the text below. Use the word given in capitals to form a word that fits in the space. There is an example at the beginning (0).

SINGING AND ENGLISH

Standard English is **(0)** <u>independent</u> of accent. As long as you use Standard English words and Standard English **(1)** .... forms, you're still speaking Standard English. However, singing disrupts **(2)** .... patterns to some **(3)** .... People usually sing more slowly than they speak and so the tempo is disrupted. As the **(4)** .... must hit the notes, in key, so the ordinary intonation patterns are **(5)** .... obscured.

Other **(6)** .... of accent are clearly not destroyed. You can usually tell the **(7)** .... between someone from England and an American singing because the latter pronounces all the 'R's. That being said, there does appear to be a **(8)** .... for many pop and jazz stars, **(9)** .... opera stars for example, to make some **(10)** .... in their singing style towards some kind of mid-Atlantic compromise, not quite either British or American.

INDEPENDENCE

GRAMMAR

SPEAK
EXTEND

SONG
LARGE

CHARACTER
DIFFERENT

TEND
LIKE
ADJUST

7 Make nouns from these verbs which you heard in the listening.

to associate	to act (two forms)
to believe (two forms)	to die
to know	to announce (two forms)
to manage (two forms)	to operate (two forms)
to decide	to choose

Make adjectives from these nouns which you heard in the listening.

occasions	intelligence
a responsibility	talent
fame	a success
determination	harm

Exam folder 14

Paper 5 Speaking

The Speaking Test is an opportunity to demonstrate your level of English. Don't be too worried about making mistakes – you are not only assessed on your accuracy, but on your range of grammar and vocabulary, your pronunciation, and your ability to communicate with other people in discussion.

Advice

- Try to be relaxed and cheerful – it will take less than 15 minutes!
- Ask the examiner if you are unclear about an instruction.
- Don't be afraid to spend a few seconds thinking, in order to plan what you are going to say.
- Give detailed answers in Part 1, rather than answering the examiner's questions in a single word.
- Listen carefully to the other candidate's long turn in Part 2, so that you can make a comment when asked.
- Keep going during your own long turn, remembering to compare and contrast, rather than describe an individual picture.
- Be sensitive to the other candidate in Part 3 and use turn-taking skills to ensure you both work towards completion of the task.
- Interact both with the other candidate and the examiner in Part 4. Here, you have the chance to broaden the discussion, so take the initiative and show them what you know.

Now put all the advice into practice in this complete Speaking Test.

Part 1: Answer these questions.

How do you like to spend your free time?
Do you go shopping because you have to, or because you enjoy it?
What kind of music do you prefer to listen to?
Can you describe a work of art that is special for you?

Part 2: Look at these pictures, which show a famous person.

Student A: Compare and contrast these pictures, saying what sort of lifestyle you would want to have if you were famous.
Student B: Talk briefly about how your life differs from that of a famous person.

Now look at these pictures, which show two different parts of the world.

> **Student A:** Compare and contrast these pictures, saying which place you think would be more difficult to live in, and why.
> **Student B:** Comment briefly on which place you would prefer.

Part 3: Look at the picture together.
It shows a living room which doesn't have enough furniture in it. Talk about the problems with the room and decide together on which *three* things you would buy to improve it.

Part 4: Now discuss these questions.
How important is it for a room to be comfortable?
Which of your possessions are particularly special to you?
Is it useful to have a computer at home? Why?/Why not?
Will more people work from home in the future? Why?/Why not?
What are the advantages and disadvantages of having an office at home?

1 **In pairs talk about these questions.**

a Which of the rooms above do you prefer? Why?

b What's your favourite colour? Why?

c What colour do you dislike? How does it make you feel?

d What colour do you think is best for
a bedroom?   a bathroom?
a kitchen?   a living room?

e If you are not sure exactly what the name of a colour is in English you can say, for example, that the curtains are 'light' or 'dark' blue, or 'bluish'. What shade is:
sky blue?   off white?
navy blue?   pea green?
deep blue?

f Match the colours on the left with the feelings on the right.

red	jealousy
blue	cowardice
green	depression
yellow	anger

g Would the answers be the same in your country?

Reading

2 **You are going to read an article about people who have a very strange gift. Seven paragraphs have been removed from the article. Choose from the paragraphs A–H the one which fits each gap (1–6). There is one extra paragraph which you do not need to use. There is an example at the beginning (0).**

Remember to read the example, as it will help you to understand the passage.

Listening to colour

Colour has a deep impact on each and every one of us. In both offices and factories, shops and homes, the management of colour is used to improve the environment.

0 | **H**

In the early part of the twentieth century Rudolf Steiner studied these effects of colour on individuals. He developed a theory from which he produced colour schemes for a learning environment.

1 |

Although learning to integrate information from different senses is vital, for the majority of people sight, touch, taste, smell and hearing are fundamentally separate. Yet there is evidence, some anecdotal, some more scientific, to suggest that they are, in fact, linked. This idea of sensory unity is a very old one.

2 |

In more modern times, many individuals have reported experiencing what is normally felt through one sense via another, and have described occasions when experiences of one sense also trigger experiences of another. Many respected scholars have reported the linking of the senses, known as *synaesthesia*.

3 |

More recent studies include the case of a girl who associated colours with the notes of bird song. There was also a boy who felt pressure sensations in his teeth when cold compresses were applied to his arms. Among a group of college students it was found that more than 13 per cent consciously summoned up images of colour when they were listening to music, claiming that this made the experience more enjoyable.

4 |

The author Vladimir Nabokov was once interviewed for a magazine article. He told the story of his 'rather freakish gift of seeing letters in colour'.

5 |

In his autobiography, he remembered the time when he was seven years old. He was using old black and white alphabet blocks to build a tower, while his mother was watching.

6 |

This gift for seeing letters or hearing music in colour is not yet understood. There are probably more people out there who have the gift, but feel embarrassed or awkward about admitting it.

3 In small groups answer the following questions about some of the words and phrases in the article. Use an English-English dictionary to help you.

a What's another way of saying 'a deep impact'?
b What is a 'colour scheme'?
c What do we call people who can't see? who can't hear?
d Do you know another word for 'fundamentally'?
e What is an 'anecdote'?
f What's the difference between a biography and an autobiography?
g What colour is scarlet?
h What's the difference between 'sensitive' and 'sensible'?

Phrasal verbs

4 Replace the phrasal verb with *out* with the correct form of one of the verbs or verb phrases in the box.

It turned out that she could also see the letters in different colours.
… excess red brings out our aggression

to turn out = to transpire
to bring out = to emphasise

solve	produce	put a line through
bloom	prolong	last	distinguish	lose

(handwritten in left margin: long dead.)

EXAMPLE: *The men broke out of the gaol in the night.*
The men escaped from the gaol in the night.

a Her work was a mess because she kept crossing things out.
b The flowers are all coming out, now that it's spring.
c He drew out the speech until it was time to go home.
d They held out for two months on very little food.
e In the fog it was just about possible to make out the cliff edge.
f I was late so I missed out on the chance to be in the choir.
g After spending a long time thinking about it, I finally worked out how to do the maths problem.
h They turn out plastic bags at that factory.

Grammar extra
Verbs and adjectives followed by prepositions

Complete these sentences with a preposition from the box. A preposition can be used more than once.

*listening **to** music*
*embarrassed **about** admitting it*

from	for	away	with	on
to	in	about		

a I prevented her .... throwing the old table ....
b I congratulated them .... their marriage.
c Throw the ball .... me!
d We need a government we can believe ....
e I agreed .... my mother to come home early.
f He apologised .... kicking the ball into my garden.
g I'm fairly keen .... canoeing.
h You can't compare musicians like the Beatles .... Mozart.
i The teacher was very annoyed .... me .... losing my textbook.
j I don't object .... people smoking so long as it isn't in restaurants.
k I'm worried .... doing my music exams.
l Could you explain this word .... me, please?
m I don't think this drink is very different .... that one.

A One such, the physicist Sir Isaac Newton wrote that, for him, each note of the musical scale corresponded to a particular colour of the spectrum: when he saw a colour, he sometimes heard the note. And the philosopher John Locke reported the case of a blind man who claimed that he had had a revelation of what the colour scarlet looked like when he heard the sound of a trumpet for the first time.

B Interestingly, he stated that his wife and son both have the gift of colour hearing and that their son's colours sometimes appear to be a mix of those of his parents. For example, the letter M, for him was pink, and to his wife it was blue and in their son they found it to be purple.

C The scheme of colours that he recommended for each age group was intended to reflect a child's stage of development. The younger children had pink/red, while the older ones had yellow/green.

D As each child develops, he or she learns to use all the senses co-operatively. What the child learns from one sense can be transferred to another.

E The ancient Greek philosopher Aristotle argued that the five senses were drawn together by a 'common sense' located in the heart. Later we see that the anatomical drawings of Leonardo da Vinci reflect the 15th century belief that the senses have a common mechanism.

F When their tutor asked them to draw what they 'saw' when they heard a note rise and fall on a clarinet, their images included lips, lines and triangles. One even drew a house nestling amid hills.

G He casually remarked to her that the colours of the letters were all wrong. It turned out that she could also see the letters in different colours and that she also heard musical notes in colour.

H Apparently, green helps people relax, whereas red is good for getting people to talk and produce ideas. However, too much colour can have a different effect from the one intended – excess red brings out our aggression, for example, while too much green makes staff lazy.

finished ✓

Number and concord

1 Complete these sentences with either a singular or plural form of the verb in brackets. You will also need to decide which tense to use – sometimes there is more than one possibility.

 a No-one .... (have) a black and white TV any more.
 b One of the boys at school .... (play) football very well.
 c Everybody .... (watch) international sporting events, like the World Cup.
 d The majority of politicians .... (believe) they are doing the right thing.
 e Every advertiser .... (want) to sell as much of their product as possible.
 f The police .... (be) trained to deal with crowd violence.
 g Go straight along this road until you come to a crossroads which .... (have) a hotel on one corner.
 h My family .... (be) extremely artistic.
 i You'll find the scissors .... (be) in the drawer.
 j Five pounds .... (not seem) very much money these days.
 k Neither my brother nor my husband .... (enjoy) golf.
 l The United States .... (form) in 1792.
 m More than one pop group .... (find) success too difficult to handle.
 n A group of us .... (go) to France on a camping holiday every year.
 o Neither of the doctors .... (be) available.
 p Neither child .... (like) ice-cream very much.
 q Politics .... (be) something I've always been interested in.
 r Forty kilometres .... (be) too far for me to cycle in a day.

 G ⋯⟩ **page 208**

2 Put the words in the box below in the right section A or B (some of the words can go in both sections).

 A Words which take a singular verb
 B Words which take a plural verb

each	every	a group of	all	none	neither
either	both	staff	no-one	one of	the majority of
everybody	more than one	the police	people		
the news	sunglasses	jeans	a series		

3 Complete these sentences using *each, every, both, none, either, neither* or *all*.

 a Those apples are thirty-five pence ....
 b He sings .... of the time he is in the car.
 c .... of my parents speak English better than I do.
 d Which of these three cars do you prefer? – .... of them.
 e I bought two hats last week, but haven't worn .... of them.
 f Do you want a cheese or a chicken sandwich? – ...., I'm on a diet.
 g .... mother worries about her children.
 h .... side of the garden had flowerbeds.
 i She took quite a few photos but .... looked any good.
 j .... time I see my grandmother she gives me roses.
 k I tried to phone Jane two or three times, but .... time there was no answer.

4 What is the difference between this pair of sentences?

 a My family are not very good at posing for photos.
 b The family nowadays is much smaller than it used to be.

 Do you know any other words which follow the same rule?

 G ⋯⟩ **page 208**

Listening

5 🎧 Listen to this journalist talking about hair colour and the effect it can have on personality. For questions 1–6, complete the sentences.

1 New research has found that brunettes are sensible and ....

2 Dyed blondes are apparently less concerned about ....

3 People dye their hair blonde as a sign of ....

4 A personality test was done on .... who had dyed their hair.

5 One red-haired actress was called .... at school.

6 Peter Jameson believes that stereotyping also affects men and causes ....

6 Read the text. If a line has a word that should not be there, write the word at the end of the line. If a line is correct put a tick (✓) next to it. There are two examples (0 and 00).

Colour in the workplace

0	Companies study and make the use of our colour associations and	*the*
00	preferences in order to sell us their products. The packing, for	✓
1	example, relies heavily on colour, both to carry an information and to	....
2	make the product attractive. While sugar is sold in packets coloured in	....
3	bluey-pinks and blue because of, unlike green, these colours are	....
4	associated to with sweetness. In experiments with washing powders,	....
5	the colour of the packet has been shown to have a profound influence on	....
6	every choice. Even though the powder in three sample packets – coloured	....
7	yellow, blue and yellow-blue, was the same, customers both thought the	....
8	powder in the yellow packet was too strong, that in the blue packet too	....
9	weak. The most popular powder was still in the yellow-blue packet. In	....
10	any similar research, coffee in a brown jar was thought too strong and in	....
11	a red jar too rich, in a blue jar too mild, and in a yellow jar too weak – even	....
12	though the coffee was the same. Fast-food outlets which are often	....
13	decorated with reds, yellows and whites. Red makes up the place warm and	....
14	inviting. Yellow, together with white, emphasises hygiene. This must	....
15	creates a place where customers can relax themselves and enjoy their food but do not linger too long.	....

Writing folder 14

Applications 2

1 Look at this advertisement and decide what information you should include in your letter of application.

WANTED

FAMILY TO SPEND A MONTH ON A DESERT ISLAND

IPK Magazines is looking for a family who would be willing to spend a whole month by themselves on a desert island.

Write and tell us
- why you think your family would be suitable
- what qualities you think would be particularly useful
- any special experience anyone in your family has

Contact Dave O'Hare

2 Now read this letter of application. Correct any grammar, punctuation, spelling or vocabulary mistakes that you find in the letter.

Dear Mr O'Hare,
   I saw your advertisment for a family to spend a month on a dessert island and I would like suggest my own family. My family is six persons – my parents, myself (I have 22 years), my two sisters (12 and 16), and my brother (8). We are coming from Iceland. My father is doctor and my mother is sports teacher. I study Economical course on the university, and my brother and sisters are still studing at school.
   I think we would really enjoy to spend a month by our own, as we all get on very good with each other. We aren't the kind of person wich watches TV all day or needs to be entertain all time. We are a sociable and sympathetic family who is capable of taking care themself.
   The last year we spent in the mountains camping on ourselves wich was useful experience for being on a dessert island. As my father is doctor he can look after some emergencies that would happen. My mother is very interesting in sport and we are all very fit and in a good condition. I have attended lessons in fishing two years ago and I have a good knowledge of wich plants are good eating and wich poisonous.
   I wish you will consider my aplication and look forward to hear from you.
Yours faithfully
Magnus Magnusson

3   Read this advertisement and then look at the plan below.

WANTED

Judges for the Most Interesting Hobby competition

Do you have a hobby?
Do you think you could join a panel to judge other people's hobbies?
Write and tell us about

- your hobby
- why you think you would make a good judge
- any relevant experience you have

Write to Mr P. Crispin

Planning a formal letter

Remember NO address needed!
Beginning and Ending? Dear Who?, Yours?
Good first sentence!
Important points
1 ?
2 ?
3 ?
My hobby – stamp collecting
Useful vocabulary
1 to collect, a collection, an album, to swap stamps, first day covers and ?
2 my personal qualities – (be positive) – enthusiastic, fair, polite, tactful, energetic and ?
3 competitors, a panel of judges, to make a decision, to choose a winner, to decide between, and ?

---

4   Here is the application that the student wrote, based on the plan. Complete the gaps with a verb from the box below using the correct tense.

try	hold	make	write
see	help	criticise	ask
consider	collect	know	
enjoy			

Dear Mr Crispin,

I (1) .... your advertisement for people to judge the Most Interesting Hobby competition. I am a 24-year old Norwegian boy and I (2) .... stamps for the past ten years. I (3) .... it may seem like a boring hobby to some people, but I really (4) .... it. I have eight stamp albums to keep my collection in and collecting stamps (5) .... me to find out more about the world. I also practise my English as I have pen friends all over the world and we (6) .... to each other in English.

I think I (7) .... a good judge of other people's hobbies because I'm so enthusiastic about my own. I (8) .... to be tactful and fair, because it is so easy to hurt someone's feelings if you (9) .... something as personal as a person's hobby.

I (10) .... to be a judge when I was at school. We (11) .... an art competition and four of us students had to judge the best picture. We had to spend a long time discussing who to pick and it was very difficult to choose between the best ones!

I do hope you (12) .... my application and I look forward to hearing from you in the near future.

Yours sincerely,

Ole Olafson

---

5   Write **a letter plan and the letter of application** for either:

a the family on the desert island
or
b a judge in the hobby competition.

1 What do you think these headlines are about? Is it fair to talk about people in this way? Give examples of recent stories where the press has invaded people's privacy.

¹ **SEXY STAR'S SHOPLIFTING SHAME**

² *Footballer turns wife-beater*
★ shock pics on page 5 ★

³ **Boss stands down after bribery charge**

⁴ **MINISTER'S TEENAGE SON IN DRUGS SCANDAL**

⁵ **Judge's secret love nest**

2 Describe what is happening in this photo and say who is involved, choosing from the people listed below.

agent	bodyguard	cameraman	editor
journalist	manager	paparazzo	star

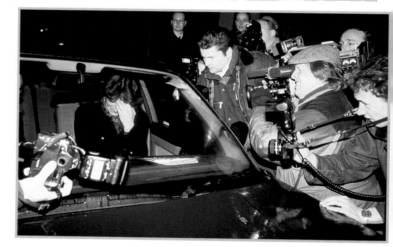

3 🎧 You are going to hear five speakers talking about a newspaper story which involves a teenage girl and a rock band. For Questions 1–5, decide which of the opinions A–F each speaker expresses. Use the letters only once. There is one extra letter which you do not need to use.

A Journalists create scandal that is only remembered in the short-term.
B Journalists should check their facts more carefully than they do.
C Journalists are insensitive towards the people they deal with.
D Journalists face difficulties when trying to research a story.
E Journalists concentrate their efforts on people who are well-known.
F Journalists have to invent things to get a good story.

Speaker 1 ⬜ 1
Speaker 2 ⬜ 2
Speaker 3 ⬜ 3
Speaker 4 ⬜ 4
Speaker 5 ⬜ 5

4 🎧 Listen to the five speakers again and tick all the idioms you hear, noting which speaker (1–5) said them. Explain what you think the idioms mean, by referring back to the people and events in the news story.

break new ground
a change of tune
flavour of the month
get sick to the back teeth with
go to someone's head
in the public eye
keep a low profile
out of the blue
put a brave face on something
the rest is history
a three-day wonder
turn something on its head

5 What do you think the newspaper actually printed? Look at these three headlines then discuss ideas in groups, using the information in the tapescript and your own imagination.

PARENTS' AGONY AS ONLY DAUGHTER RUNS AWAY WITH ROCK STAR

BLONDE SCHOOLGIRL HELD ON BAND'S YACHT AGAINST HER WILL

BAD BOYS OF ROCK ARE AT IT AGAIN – WILD PARTY EXCLUSIVE

6 Read the article about tabloid reporting on the royal family. For Questions 1–15, decide which answer, A, B, C or D, best fits each space. There is an example at the beginning (0).

Example:

0 **A** turned   **B** put   **C** set   **D** moved

0	A	B	C	D

Royal press coverage

Royal reporting has been **(0)** ..... on its head recently. On Thursday July 9, *The Sun* newspaper had a 'world exclusive' headlined 'Camilla meets Wills', **(1)** ..... how William, the son of the Prince of Wales, had finally met his father's close friend, Camilla Parker Bowles. The article was full of the details that would **(2)** ..... any reader of its truth. A week later, *The Sun* **(3)** ..... about a 'royal world exclusive' under the headline 'Prince Charles writes in The Sun'. This was **(4)** ..... strangely enough, **(5)** ..... to a letter with Charles's signature on page four. It stated how grateful he was to Sun readers for helping to **(6)** ..... money for a Nepalese hostel. Exactly a week later came **(7)** ..... another 'world exclusive': 'When Harry met Cammi'. This story **(8)** ..... that Camilla, in an 'historic encounter', had now met Prince Harry, Charles's younger son.

The Express, a rival newspaper to *The Sun*, **(9)** ..... a story about Charles's deputy private secretary Mark Bolland, which described him being **(10)** ..... 'out on the town with one of *The Sun's* female executives.' To outraged competitors like *The Express*, it was **(11)** ..... what was going on. Charles's press **(12)** ..... were cosying up to the very newspaper which had **(13)** ..... him such pain with its years of intrusive reporting. In other words, *The Sun* was getting leaks from his own **(14)** ..... . This change of heart towards the media may be down to Mark Bolland himself, who, as the son of a former bricklayer and **(15)** ..... at a comprehensive school, is as different from the establishment as chalk and cheese. These are indeed interesting times for the media.

	A	B	C	D
1	speaking	talking	explaining	insisting
2	conclude	prove	fulfil	convince
3	boasted	applauded	congratulated	greeted
4	precise	accurate	careful	faithful
5	sending	referring	bringing	pointing
6	develop	grow	raise	lift
7	yet	just	since	even
8	demanded	believed	requested	claimed
9	directed	spread	stood	ran
10	looked	regarded	spotted	realised
11	actual	obvious	certain	sure
12	team	crew	band	group
13	produced	created	resulted	caused
14	office	company	business	party
15	instructed	learned	educated	studied

English idioms

Do not attempt to change any of the vocabulary in an English idiom. Similar idioms in your own language may use a different word – for example, in one Swedish idiom, you say you have a chicken in your throat, whereas in the English one, it's a frog!

Be careful when you use idioms in your own writing. They are effective if used sparingly, but the writing becomes unnatural if too many are included. See Writing folder 15 for more information.

Parts of the body

1 Many common idioms contain a part of the body, like the ones used in 29.1, for example *a change of heart*. It's usually quite easy to work out the meaning of these idioms. Start by thinking of the literal meaning of the words, even forming a picture in your head, like the ones above.

In this way, match idioms 1–20 to meanings a–t.

eye
1 see eye to eye with someone
2 raise eyebrows
3 cast your eye over something
4 turn a blind eye to something
head
5 turn something on its head
6 get your head round something
7 keep your head above water
8 lose your head
hand
9 have a hand in something
10 be given a free hand
11 have the upper hand
12 wash your hands of something
feet
13 find your feet
14 have your feet on the ground
15 get cold feet
16 vote with your feet
fingers
17 put your finger on something
18 get your fingers burned
19 keep your fingers crossed
20 point the finger at someone

a ignore
b agree
c surprise
d check

e panic
f survive
g change
h understand

i be in control
j refuse responsibility
k make the decisions
l help create

m reject
n become anxious
o gain confidence
p be sensible

q be unsuccessful
r accuse
s identify
t hope for good news

Common verbs in idioms

2 You know the meaning of the verbs used below, but can you work out the meaning of the idioms? Check in a dictionary if necessary.

break new ground	get your act together
make your mark	take somewhere by storm
get to grips with something	put your oar in
come out of your shell	catch someone off guard
tighten your belt	go out of the window
keep a low profile	put something on ice

3 Decide which idiom you would use for the situations a–k and include it in a suitable sentence, changing pronouns and tenses where necessary.

EXAMPLE: *Company executives were advised to make budget cuts because of a shortfall in profits.*
Company executives were advised to tighten their belts because of a shortfall in profits.

a The paparazzi managed to surprise them unexpectedly in their hideaway cottage.

b The government has delayed many of its proposals for new road development.

c She forgot all her promises to her parents about studying hard when she met Danny.

d The software uses an innovative technique that requires much less memory.

e Some town councils have dealt seriously with traffic problems.

f Kevin has done a lot in his new job in a short period of time.

g The British film *The Full Monty* went down very well in America.

h The argumentative politician could not resist adding his views.

i John hid in the back row of the cinema, hoping he wouldn't be seen by his teacher.

j On the first day at a new school, children are very nervous, but they soon begin to open up.

k Caroline's always letting people down – she really needs to improve her behaviour.

Idioms and prepositions

4 Many common idioms, including some of the ones above, feature a preposition. Choose the correct preposition from the ones below to fill in the spaces in a–m and suggest what these idioms mean.

at	for	in	off
on	out	to	with

a the icing .... the cake

b .... full swing

c .... a nutshell

d .... the count

e shocked .... the core

f .... a loose end

g .... a tight corner

h .... a limb

i economical .... the truth

j thin .... the ground

k .... loggerheads .... someone

l pie .... the sky

m quick .... the mark

5 **Select one of the idioms above to illustrate cartoons 1–4. Now use the remaining idioms in a–h.**

EXAMPLE: *I've had some lovely presents, but this one is truly* <u>the icing on the cake</u> .

a Tickets for *Radiohead's* concert next month are very ....

b I'm going to go .... and say that France will win the World Cup in 2002.

c Faye's always having ridiculous ideas – they're all .... !

d If you're .... , why not come round and see us this evening?

e To put the problem .... , my boss wants to fire me.

f The press was really .... and there was full coverage of the scandal the next day.

g Politicians can be rather .... , preferring not to give any bad news.

h I was .... by what Gerry said, as I had absolutely no idea of what had been going on.

Exam folder 15

Paper 2 Writing

In the Writing paper you will have 1 hour 30 minutes to answer two questions. Make sure you use the time well, planning each answer, and leaving a few minutes at the end to check what you have written.

1   Read the exam question below.

You have had a class discussion on the media. Now you have to write a composition, giving your opinion on the following statement.

Newspapers used to carry real news, but their main role today is to shock and entertain us.

Write your **composition**.

2   The answer opposite could be improved in a number of ways, some of which are given in the teacher's notes. Read through the answer and the notes. Then make the changes suggested and add any improvements of your own. Your final answer should be 180 words long.

Advice

- Read the question carefully, underlining key words.
- Make a quick paragraph plan for each answer.
- Write legibly and leave a line between paragraphs.
- Don't copy out phrases from the question – you must use your own words as far as possible.
- Try to use a variety of structures and a range of vocabulary.
- Check you have included all the points in Part 1.
- Choose a Part 2 question that you know something about, and use your imagination if you run out of ideas.
- Write at least 120 words – for a fully-developed answer, you are more likely to need 180 words.
- Make sure you write in a consistent style, that is appropriate for the target reader.
- Correct any spelling or grammatical errors clearly.

Where is the introduction?
Very unclear beginning

Join the ideas in the first three sentences to make one complex sentence.

I think it depends which newspapers you read. Some of them still report the news. Others don't do it much. I think it's important for any newspaper to report what (had) happened, but people like to read other things too. I think it's good to expose scandal occasionally. Famous people are in the public eye and they cannot turn a blind eye to this.

Incorrect tense

Develop your ideas here – give an example of what you mean re scandal.

Lose the second idiom – very unnatural. You haven't commented on newspapers 'entertaining us' (see question) – add something on this.

Who does 'their' refer to? Avoid the repetition here.

Check spelling

Expand your ideas on television news.

I don't think it's (their) main role though. (Their) main role is to inform and this means (writting) reports on current news and events. I think television can do this too, but with a newspaper it's not the same. You have time to read and think about it. That's what I think.

116 words

Very sudden end – summarise your views in a final paragraph.
You have used 'think' seven times!
Reword in different ways.

UNIT 30 Anything for a laugh

1 Say what the word 'funny' means to you. Then
   compare and contrast the types of comedy shown
   in the pictures, and explain which you would
   rather see and why. Talk for about a minute each.

2 You are going to read four 'urban myths'. These
   are modern-day stories, usually humorous, which
   people enjoy telling each other at parties or at the
   pub. First, read questions 1–15. There is an
   example at the beginning (0).

In which urban myth does someone

receive praise for their cooking?	**0** A
need to withdraw money?	**1**
have an injured pet?	**2**
appear unconcerned?	**3**
mistake a person for a criminal?	**4**
have urgent treatment?	**5**
have a conversation in an elevator?	**6**
go to a restaurant?	**7**
intend to use public transport?	**8**
disobey a request?	**9**
have to make a hard decision?	**10**
break the rules?	**11**
try to hide something?	**12**
give a person the sack?	**13**
receive an apology?	**14**
have something taken from them?	**15**

A A woman was looking forward to an important dinner party
where her guests would include her husband's new boss. She
wanted to serve a really special meal, so she bought a whole
salmon, which she cooked and prepared beautifully. The dinner
party started well, and the woman received many compliments
about the starters she served. At a suitable moment, she slipped
out to get the fish from the kitchen, where she found a rather
horrifying sight: her cat was sitting on the work surface, tucking
into the fish <u>with gusto</u>. She <u>shooed the cat away</u> and, in a state of
total panic, hastily disguised the damage with some carefully-
placed slices of lemon and cucumber. Then she took the salmon
through, to gasps of admiration. However, when the woman went
to the kitchen to make the coffee, she found her cat <u>writhing
around</u> on the floor in agony. Convinced that the salmon was to
blame, the poor woman went back in to tell her guests the truth.
They all rushed off to hospital to have their stomachs pumped.
The woman had only just returned home when the doorbell rang.
It was the milkman, who explained that he was just calling to see
if the cat was all right. Apparently, he'd dropped a metal milk
crate on its head that morning.

B A young man had been out for the evening in central
London. When the pubs closed, he went to Charing Cross station
to catch his train home, but then decided he would rather have
something to eat first. Checking his pocket, he found he only had
about £2. It was a difficult choice: go home or get a
quarterpounder with <u>all the trimmings</u>. Then he remembered he
had his cash card, so all was well. He bought himself a burger,
which he had already started to eat when he reached the cashpoint
machine. He put in his card, set the snack down next to the
keypad, punched in his numbers and waited for the cash to come
out. Instead, the screen flashed up: 'Sorry, you have used the
wrong number. Do you wish to try again?' A bit nervous, he keyed
in another number. Again the message appeared. He was
convinced that the first number was right, so he keyed it in
carefully. No sooner had he finished than a message came up,
saying his card had been <u>retained</u>. This was not the only thing he
lost, either, for the glass shield came down, locking away his
delicious burger.

3 Now scan the four texts for the answers, ignoring the underlined words. Compare your answers with another student.

4 Which do you think is the funniest of the four urban myths? Are any of them not funny at all, in your view? Explain your reasons to another student.

5 You may not know the underlined words, but you were still able to answer the questions. Try to work out their meaning now by looking at the surrounding context. Then use some in a–h.

a They sensed movement in the trees and suddenly, a huge bear .... in front of them.

b It was West's favourite role in Shakespeare and he played the part ....

c Take that .... look off your face – it's me in disguise!

d Rafter .... the ball in the air badly and, apologising to his opponent, decided not to play the serve.

e Jane's father .... everyone .... , so that she could get some rest.

f Their large wedding, which had .... , cost a fortune.

g We .... the cost of Gregor's meal between us, as it was his birthday.

h The TV news showed thousands of villagers .... their homes.

6 🎧 Listen to another urban myth about driving. Then retell the story.

An English couple who were driving around America were spending a few days in New York. They'd had some great evenings out on the town, including a show on Broadway and an Italian meal on the Lower East Side. They'd been a bit anxious at first, having seen all those violent shoot-'em-up cop shows on TV, but by the final evening, they were really enjoying themselves. They drove back to the hotel, parked in the basement car park, and waited for the lift up to reception. It was quite dark and rather scary. Suddenly, a huge man with a Rottweiler <u>loomed</u> out of the shadows. The lift came and the couple hurried in, followed by the man and his dog. As the doors closed, the man shouted 'Get down, lady'. Rather than put up a fight, the petrified couple <u>tossed</u> all their money at him and threw themselves on the floor. When the lift arrived, they scrambled to their feet and ran out in a panic. To their surprise, when they checked out the next day the receptionist explained that a man had already <u>settled</u> their bill, and handed them an envelope. Inside was all the money they'd given the 'mugger', and a note saying: 'I'm real sorry about scaring you yesterday, and I hope paying your bill has made up for your <u>ordeal</u>. By the way, Lady is the name of my dog …'

One day at his Mirror Group headquarters in London, Robert Maxwell, who lived in the luxurious <u>penthouse</u> flat at the top, was coming down in the lift. At the next floor he was joined by a young lad in a <u>scruffy</u> suit, who happened to be smoking. Maxwell was furious to find one of his employees ignoring the company's no-smoking policy. The lad was promptly told to extinguish the cigarette, but paid no attention, and indeed started blowing smoke in Maxwell's face. Maxwell angrily insisted that he put it out immediately. 'No way,' said the lad, and carried on puffing. At this, Maxwell demanded to know how much the lad earned a week. On being told £200, he took £400 in cash from his pocket and handed it to the <u>bewildered</u> lad, saying, 'I'm giving you two weeks' notice. You're fired! Get out of my offices now.' 'Don't worry, mate,' said the lad, <u>fleeing</u> through the lift doors with his wad of cash, 'I'm going – I work for Telecom anyway!'

Ⓖ rammar extra

rather

Look at these examples from the five urban myths and then answer questions a–c below.

1 So, rather than standing around waiting at the garage, he went off to the local pub …
2 Rather shaken, the man drove off the motorway …
3 … but then decided he would rather have something to eat first.
4 It was quite dark and rather scary.
  a In which example could you use 'instead of'? Which word apart from 'rather' would you also have to omit?
  b In which example is 'rather' used to mean 'prefer'? Which word has to be used as well? What word could be added to these words to give the opposite meaning?
  c In which two examples is 'rather' used in the same way? What similar word is also used in one of these examples?
    Turn to the Grammar folder for a summary of the uses of *rather*.

Ⓖ ⋯⟩ page 208

The grammar of phrasal verbs

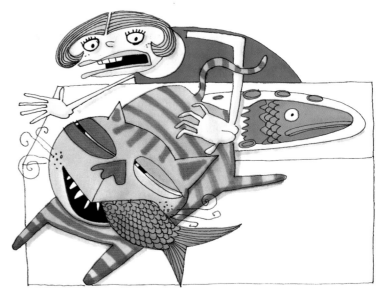

1 Look at these examples from 30.1. First, say which two contain intransitive phrasal verbs (verbs which have no object). Then, look carefully at the word order used with the remaining phrasal verbs. Can the position of the object be changed in any of the examples? If so, give the alternative word order.

EXAMPLE: She shooed the cat away. ✓
She shooed away the cat.

a A woman was looking forward to an important dinner party.
b She slipped out to get the fish from the kitchen.
c He set the snack down next to the keypad.
d He keyed it in carefully.
e No sooner had he finished than a message came up.
f Rather than put up a fight, the petrified couple …
g I hope paying your bill has made up for your ordeal.
h Maxwell insisted that he put it out immediately.
i They offered to clean the car up.
j I've just ploughed into a herd of cows with my lorry.

Which of these general rules are true, in your view? Use the examples a–j to back up your opinions.

1 When a phrasal verb is intransitive (has no object), the verb and the particle cannot be separated by other words.
2 When a noun is used as the object of a phrasal verb, it can always come before or after the particle.
3 When a pronoun is used as the object of a phrasal verb, it always comes before the particle.
4 In a three-part phrasal verb, the object cannot come between the two particles.

2 With some phrasal verbs, the particular meaning alters the rule on word order. Compare these examples. In which ones is it possible to change the word order?

a He put a sign up to show them the way.
b The soldiers put up fierce resistance to the attack.

c I'm sorry to have kept you up so late.
d Jenny couldn't keep up the payments on her flat.

3 Complete these sentences using the phrasal verb given in brackets in a suitable tense, and including a suitable noun or pronoun.

EXAMPLE: I *turned the car round* and headed home, with my foot on the accelerator all the way! (turn round)

a Please .... – you've watched far too much already. (turn off)
b Sooner or later you'll have to tell me the truth, so let's ...., shall we? (get over with)
c It was getting foggy, but they .... in the distance, which had its lights on. (make out)
d That story .... driving in an open car for life! (put off)
e While we were living in Sweden, we .... quite well. (pick up)
f If there are any words you don't understand, ... in a dictionary. (look up)
g Why don't we ....? It'll be warmer down on the sand. (make for)
h Everyone ...., who really appreciated their support. (get behind)
i I've just .... to that question! (work out)
j You really should ...., you know – they're really fattening. (cut down on)

G ···⟩ page 208

4 Match the first lines (1–15) and second lines (a–o) of these jokes. Then take a vote to decide on the three funniest ones, giving reasons for your choices.

1 What do you call someone who hangs around with musicians?
2 Every time I drink coffee I get a stabbing pain in my left eye.
3 When a man has a birthday he takes the day off.
4 What's the definition of a modern artist?
5 I ended up as the teacher's pet.
6 What's the best way to make the landlord paint your apartment?
7 Did you start out as an actor?
8 What's the best way to stay out of the army?
9 Why did you wake me up? It's still dark.
10 My brother and I are inseparable.
11 What are you doing in my tree, young lad?
12 A Hollywood couple have finally worked out their divorce settlement.
13 Would you please open up the piano?
14 Old pickpockets never die.
15 What would you do if you were in my shoes?

a One of your apples fell down and I'm putting it back.
b No, as a little boy.
c Clean them up.
d She couldn't afford a dog.
e In fact, it takes six people to pull us apart.
f I can't – the keys are inside.
g Take the spoon out of the cup.
h Join the navy.
i Someone who tosses paint on a canvas, wipes it off with a cloth and sells the cloth.
j A drummer.
k Well, open your eyes!
l Now they can get married.
m Move out.
n They just steal away.
o When a woman has one, she takes a year off.

5 Read this biography of Jim Carrey. For Questions 1–15, fill each space with one word only. There is an example at the beginning (0).

A funny man with a funny face

Jim Carrey's humour is very **(0)** <u>much</u> his own brand. It is often slapstick, sometimes a **(1)** .... tasteless, but always hilarious. Carrey, who **(2)** .... born in 1962, believes that his sense of humour developed **(3)** .... his teenage years. This was his way of dealing **(4)** .... a difficult period in his life. His father had lost his job and Carrey junior had to earn money and study **(5)** .... the same time. He took a job **(6)** .... a janitor and somehow managed to fit the schooling in too.

When he was only 15, Carrey performed live at Yuk Yuks, **(7)** .... famous club in Toronto. He later moved to Los Angeles to tour the club circuit there. From 1990, he starred regularly in the TV sketch show In Living Color, **(8)** .... one of the many characters he played was Fire Marshall Bill, who always went **(9)** .... in smoke! Sadly, this character finally had to **(10)** .... laid to rest because of complaints that his fire act **(11)** .... have a bad influence on children.

Carrey's first feature film was Ace Ventura: Pet Detective, one of 1994's **(12)** .... popular films. The Mask, his next film, was the perfect vehicle **(13)** .... his oddball humour and was hugely successful. Other films **(14)** .... then have included Batman Forever and Liar, Liar. His current salary **(15)** .... estimated at around $20 million per film.

Writing folder 15

Transactional letters 3

1 In one type of transactional letter, you have to correct facts (see also Writing folder 4). Read this article and the notes made on it. Decide on the five main points that need to be covered in a letter to the editor.

NO GREAT LAUGHS AT FESTIVAL OF FUN!

The comedy on offer at this year's Festival of Fun has been very disappointing indeed. I cannot think of a single performance that has been memorable, in contrast to last year's wonderful line-up of stars from stage and screen. It seems that the organisers have tightened their belts considerably this year, selecting unknown and second-rate acts on the cheap!

    There have been just too many dull and predictable performances: the pathetic slapstick routines of Forbes and Company, the very unfunny stand-up comedian Linda Ritson, whose jokes were very thin on the ground, and the dreadful comedy duo Holmes and Watson, who were clearly under-rehearsed.

    Saturday's audience was shocked to the core by Ted Grainger's rude and offensive jokes. To make him top of the bill was a big mistake and it was interesting to see how many people voted with their feet soon after he came on stage.

    This year's event was a total disaster. Let's hope the organisers get their own act together next year!

[Notes on article:]
- I can! eg La[rry] Hatfield on pm?
- unfair!
- what's wrong with political jokes?
- it's called improvisation
- not true (summarise my impression[s])

2 Now read this sample answer. Apart from the opening paragraph, it is a well-written letter. However, it has missed out a major content point and would therefore get a low mark. Which point has been omitted?

Dear Editor

I want to point the finger on the reporter who wrote the article about the Festival of Fun, which breaks new ground, published in yesterday's Daily News. The article raised my eyebrows and I couldn't get your head round it. Your reporter has been economical of the truth and I don't see eye by eye with him.

For a start, the reporter says there were no memorable performances. Perhaps he was absent on Friday evening, when some excellent acts were on offer. The well-known comedian Larry Hatfield, for example, was superb.

To call other performers 'second-rate' is very unfair and I have to say that I found the acts singled out in the article rather good. In addition, to criticise them as 'unknown' surely misses the point of a festival like this, which is to give talented new acts the opportunity to perform?

Your reporter described Ted Grainger's witty political humour as 'offensive', but the majority of the audience found him very entertaining and I didn't notice many people walking out, either!

It cannot be called a disaster. In a nutshell, the organisers have done a brilliant job this year and will, I'm sure, do the same again next year.

Yours faithfully
Izzy Edwards

d Please turn off it at once – you're making too much noise.

e The police is available twenty-four hours a day.

f Neither my father nor my mother has blond hair.

g It's the first time I had been to the Paris Motor Show.

h The office block had been standing on this street for more than a decade when they decided to demolish it.

i I am believing in the trustworthiness of our police force.

j What time do you think the train is arriving?

k Seldom we see new ideas on saving energy.

l The building which roof had been blown off by the gales is on the next street.

m If we all share a car to work, then the motorways wouldn't have been necessary.

Vocabulary

Idioms and expressions

4   Fill in the spaces with one of the words in the box.

eye	keep	end	tune	ice	feet
eyebrows	hands				

a She'll soon change her .... when she realises people have stopped going to her films.

b I've been at a loose .... all summer, now that I've got no studying to do.

c If I became famous, then I think I'd prefer to .... a low profile.

d My father got so fed up with my brother's laziness that he washed his .... of him.

e We can't afford a new car at the moment so we've decided to put that particular plan on ....

f It took me some time to find my .... when I arrived in Tokyo.

g The dress she turned up to the wedding in raised a few ...., I can tell you!

h It must be very difficult for people in the public .... to get any peace and quiet.

Phrasal verb story

5   Complete the story with the right form of a phrasal verb from the box.

end up	take aback	call up	bring in
put off	miss out on	work out	take on

If the Royal Marines had drummed one thing into Sergeant Ken Murgatroyd during his twenty-two years of service, it was the importance of seizing opportunities. After he left the Royal Marines, his new job in telesales involved (1) .... computer companies. However, one morning he rang the direct line of Neil Corbould, a senior assistant to the film director Steven Spielberg, by mistake. Within minutes Mr Murgatroyd had been (2) .... for a leading role in the war film *Saving Private Ryan*.

No one was more (3) .... than Mr Murgatroyd. Mr Spielberg needed to (4) .... someone who could (5) .... how to make the scenes as realistic as possible. Mr Murgatroyd, who was one of the navy's foremost authorities on landing manoeuvres, was perfect.

'I hadn't even heard of the film when they gave me the job. I was trying to sell an Internet database, when I pressed a wrong button and (6) .... talking to a man at a special effects company. I told him I had made a mistake, but out of curiosity asked him what kind of work he did. When he told me, I thought, I can help with that.'

Working with celebrities didn't (7) .... Mr Murgatroyd at all. 'In fact, I found all the Hollywood types very pleasant. I don't think they had ever worked with someone like me before. I wouldn't have wanted to (8) .... an opportunity like that.'

Grammar folder

Unit 1
Comparison

There are various ways of making comparisons in English.

1 **Comparative and superlative adjectives**

Regular adjectives of one syllable have forms like these:

Adjective	Comparative	Superlative
young	young**er**	(the) young**est**
large	larg**er**	(the) larg**est**
slim	slim**mer**	(the) slim**mest**

Note that if an adjective ends in a single vowel and consonant (not *w*), the final letter is doubled, as in *slim* above. Some common examples are:
sad, big, thin, fat, hot, wet.

Two-syllable adjectives ending in a consonant followed by the letter *y* are formed like this:

Adjective	Comparative	Superlative
dirty	dirt**ier**	(the) dirt**iest**

Some common examples are:
angry, busy, easy, funny, happy, heavy, silly, tiny.

Most other two-syllable adjectives and all longer adjectives form their comparative and superlative forms like this:

Adjective	Comparative	Superlative
careful	**more** careful	(the) **most** careful
casual	**more** casual	(the) **most** casual
outrageous	**more** outrageous	(the) **most** outrageous

Some common two-syllable adjectives have both forms:

Adjective	Comparative	Superlative
simple	simpl**er** OR **more** simple	(the) simpl**est** OR (the) **most** simple

Other examples are:
clever, common, cruel, gentle, likely, narrow, pleasant, polite.

Irregular adjectives have the following forms:

Adjective	Comparative	Superlative
good	better	(the) best
bad	worse	(the) worst
far	farther/ further	(the) farthest/ furthest
old	older/ elder	(the) oldest/ eldest

2 **Adverbs of degree**

These adverbs of degree can be used in front of comparative adjectives:
a bit, a good deal, a great deal, a little, a lot, much, rather, slightly.
This T-shirt is a bit cheaper than the others because it's last year's design.
Helen is much more intelligent than the rest of the group.

These adverbs of degree can be used in front of superlative adjectives:
by far, easily, much, quite.
You're easily the cleverest person I know!

3 *not as … as*

This structure is used to compare two things or people. A less common form is *not so … as*.
Sally is not as tall as her brother.
Most adverbs have regular comparative and superlative forms, where *more* and *most* are added to the verb, like this:
seriously   more seriously   most seriously
A few adverbs are irregular:
well   better   best
badly   worse   worst
The irregular adverbs far and old have the same form as their related adjectives.

Unit 2
Adverbs

Most regular adverbs are formed by adding *-ly* to a related adjective:
quick → quickly, endless → endlessly
Adjectives ending in double *ll* just add *y*:
full → fully
However, there are sometimes spelling changes when an adverb is formed in this way:
-le becomes -ly: gentle → gently, remarkable → remarkably
-y becomes -ily: easy → easily, cosy → cosily
-ic becomes -ically: tragic → tragically, automatic → automatically
-ue becomes -uly: true → truly

Some irregular adverbs do not end in *-ly*:
fast, hard, late, well.

The adverbs *hardly* and *lately* have different meanings from *hard* and *late*:
I worked hard on the project all day.
I hardly had time to stop for a coffee all day.

I finished the work late in the evening.
I've put in some long hours at work lately.

Review of present tenses

Uses of present simple tense

- Permanent situations
  Most people access the Internet for information.
- Habitual situations
  I check my e-mails twice a day.
- In time clauses
  Once you finish your work, give me a ring.
  We usually play tennis until it gets dark.
- In zero conditionals
  If you use all seven letters in the board game Scrabble, you get fifty extra points.
  Steam forms when water boils.

Uses of present continuous tense

- Temporary situations
  I'm living at home until I find my own flat.
- Developing situations
  Traffic is becoming heavier and heavier.
- Events happening now
  Sit still while I'm talking to you!
- Events in the near future
  Tim's leaving for Hanover next week.

See Unit 10, Review of future tenses (page 202), for further information about the present simple and present continuous tenses.

Stative verbs are not normally used in continuous tenses. The commonest of these are:

admire be believe belong consist dislike doubt
fit forget guess hate hear imagine include
keep know like love mean prefer realise
recognise remember seem smell sound suppose
taste understand want wish

I keep forgetting to pay the phone bill.
We wish we could be with you right now.

Unit 3
Modals 1: Obligation, necessity and permission

Strong obligation *must* and *have to, have got to* (Informal)

Present and future	*must*	*have to*	*have got to*
Past		*had to*	

1 **must**
   Must is used to talk about strong obligations in the present and future that are imposed by the speaker.
   You must brush your teeth before you go to bed.
   I must arrange to have my windows cleaned.
   (It is also used to talk about laws: *Drivers must obey traffic signals.*)

2 **have to/have got to**
   Have to/have got to are used to talk about strong obligations in the present and future that are not imposed by the speaker.
   I've got to do some homework tonight. (My teacher says so.)
   If in doubt whether to use *must* or *have to*, use *have to*. Do not use *I've to*, which is incorrect.

3 **had to**
   Had to is used to talk about past and reported obligations:
   I had to help on the farm when I was young.
   We were told we had to get a visa before we left on holiday.
   There are also other ways to express obligation:
   to make someone do something
   to be compulsory

Weak obligation *should, ought to*

Present and Future	*should do* *ought to do*
Past	*should have done*
	ought to have done

There is no difference in meaning between *should* and *ought to*.
You ought to/should write home more frequently.
In the past *should have done* and *ought to have done* are often used for criticism or regret, because an action didn't happen:
We should have bought/ought to have bought your sister a card for her birthday.

There is no difference in meaning in the following uses.

Lack of obligation *needn't*
             doesn't/don't need to
             doesn't/don't have to

Present and future	*needn't* *don't need to*
	don't have to

She doesn't need to/needn't come to the meeting if she doesn't want to.
You don't have to wear a uniform at our school.

The following past uses express different meanings.

Past	*didn't have to*
	needn't have done
	didn't need to do

Needn't have done is used when something is done but it was unnecessary:
I went to the bank but I needn't have done as I had some money in my coat pocket.
Didn't need to is used when doing something is not necessary:
I didn't need to have an injection to go to the USA.

You can also use the expression *to be optional* to express lack of obligation:
Going to lectures was optional at my university.

Asking for and giving permission *can could may*

Can is the more usual way of asking for and giving permission.
Could is a bit more polite and *may* is quite formal:
Can/may/could I borrow your bike?
Yes, you can/may.

Other ways of asking for and giving permission are:
to allow someone to do
to permit someone to do
to let someone do

Prohibition *mustn't can't*

Present and future	*mustn't*	*can't*
Past	*was not to*	*couldn't*

Mustn't and *can't* are used when something is forbidden:
You mustn't cross the road without looking.
Elizabeth can't go out this evening – her father says so.

Other verbs which can be used are:
to forbid someone to do something
to ban someone from doing something
to not allow someone to do something
to not permit someone to do something
to not let someone do something.

It is also possible to use an imperative: *Don't cycle on the pavement!*

Unit 4
as and *like*

(See also grammar summary in Unit 4)

Like can be used as a preposition and is followed by a noun (*like a house*), a pronoun (*like it*), or a gerund (*like swimming*). It is used to give a comparison:
Your house is like our house/ours. (Is similar to ours.)
My bed is so hard it's like sleeping on the ground.

As can be used as a preposition to tell you what job or function a person or thing has:
As a chef, I have to cook one hundred meals a day.
I used the tin as a cup to drink out of.

Please note these other uses of *as* and *like*.
It's like living in a palace, living in your house. (It's not a palace.)
As a palace, Windsor is very impressive. (It is a palace.)

As is used in prepositional phrases:
At my school, as at most schools, pupils were expected to respect their teachers.

Some verbs can be followed by an object and *as*:
He is known as a generous person.
I don't regard learning a language as optional.

Like and *such as* can be used to mean 'for example':
I enjoy films like/such as thrillers.
I dislike sports such as/like skiing.

As can be a conjunction and is followed by a subject and verb:
She cut up the vegetables as I had taught her. (In the way I had taught her.)

In British English it is becoming more common to hear *like* followed by a subject and verb. *Like* followed by a subject and verb is acceptable in American English:
I don't speak like he does.

Unit 5
Table of common irregular verbs

INFINITIVE	PAST TENSE	PAST PARTICIPLE
become	became	(has/had) become
bet	bet	bet
burst	burst	burst
buy	bought	bought
creep	crept	crept
cut	cut	cut
draw	drew	drawn
drive	drove	driven
eat	ate	eaten
feel	felt	felt
find	found	found
get	got	got
hear	heard	heard
hold	held	held
hit	hit	hit
keep	kept	kept
know	knew	known
leave	left	left
lose	lost	lost
put	put	put
run	ran	run
say	said	said
see	saw	seen
send	sent	sent
set	set	set
shake	shook	shaken
shut	shut	shut
sink	sank	sunk
speak	spoke	spoken
spend	spent	spent
swim	swam	swum
take	took	taken
tell	told	told
think	thought	thought
weep	wept	wept

Review of past tenses
Past simple
This is used to talk about events in the past which:
- occurred at a particular time
  The Titanic sank in 1912.
  I drove back from London last night.
  This indicates a completed action in the past with a fixed time phrase.
- happened regularly
  Matthew spent most weekends at tennis tournaments.
  She burst into tears every time she heard his name.
  Note that *would* and *used to* are also used to talk about the past in this way – this is dealt with in Unit 8 (page 201).

Past continuous
This is used to talk about events in the past which:
- had a longer duration than another action
  I was cutting up vegetables in the kitchen when I heard it on the six o'clock news.
- were temporary
  Norwich were losing two-nil, with only five minutes to go.
  It is also used to set the scene in a story: *The sun was shining when the old man set off from the cottage.*

Present perfect
This is used to talk about events or a period of time which:
- started in the past but are still true or are still continuing
  We've lived here for eight years.
  Ellen has eaten no meat since she was six.
- happened in the past but have an effect in the present
  They've cancelled tonight's concert so we'll have to do something else.
  I've heard from Iain again.

Past perfect
This is used to talk about events which:
- happened earlier than something else
  Ken sat in the dark miserably and thought about what he had said to his girlfriend.
  Once I had finished my exams, I started clubbing again.

  Note that the past perfect needs to be used when it is important to show a time difference.

  Unit 14 deals with the perfect tenses in more detail (page 203).

Unit 6
Adverbs of frequency
always, never, often, normally, seldom, sometimes, usually
These adverbs describe how often an event happens. They go in different places in a sentence, as follows:
- after the verb *be*
  The post is always late on Saturdays.
- before the verb in simple present or past tenses
  I normally start work at nine.
  We usually swam in the local pool, but we sometimes went to a different one further away.
- after the first auxiliary verb in other tenses
  I'll never forget his look of absolute horror.
  Helen has seldom seen her mother.
- at the beginning of the sentence for emphasis
  Sometimes we walked home along the river.
  Never had I felt so alone.
  (Units 24 and 26 deal with inversion.)

Conditionals with *if*
These are normally used to talk about possible events and the effects of them. There are four main types:
- Zero conditional
  Not a true conditional, as the events described both happen.
  If I stay up late, I feel awful the next day.
  When the moon passes between the earth and the sun, there is an eclipse.
  If/When + present tense | present tense
- First conditional
  Used to talk about likely events in the future if something happens.
  If I pass FCE, I'll have a big party!
  If you don't stop talking, I'll send you to the head teacher.
  If + present tense | future tense will

- Second conditional
  Used to talk about unlikely or impossible situations.
  If I won the lottery, I'd give all the money to Oxfam.
  People might behave differently if they had the chance to repeat their lives.
  If + past tense | would, could, might
- Third conditional
  Used to speculate about the past.
  If we'd had more money, we'd have gone to the States last year.
  If you'd told me the truth in the first place, I wouldn't have asked the teacher.
  If Tom had taken his guitar, he could have played with the band that night.
  If + past perfect | would have, could have, might have + past participle
  (Unit 25 deals with mixed conditionals.)

Unit 7
Gerunds and infinitives 1
The gerund
The gerund is a verb which is used as a noun. It can be the subject of a clause or sentence: *Climbing the hill took them all day*, or the object: *I consider learning to save to be an essential part of growing up.*

You use the gerund after certain verbs and expressions, especially those expressing liking/disliking:
I don't mind getting up early in the morning.

Common examples:
like   love   enjoy   adore   fancy   feel like   detest
hate   loathe   can't stand   dislike   don't mind   finish
avoid   give up   keep   suggest   consider   miss
imagine   it's not worth   it's/there's no use
there's no point (in)

A **Gerunds are used after all prepositions except for *to***
(Some exceptions to this rule are: *to look forward to doing, to object to doing, to get used to doing.*)
On hearing the news, she burst into tears.

B **After adjective and preposition combinations**
Steven is fantastic at cooking Thai food.

Common examples:
good/wonderful/fantastic/bad/awful/ terrible at
happy/pleased/glad/anxious/sad/worried about
afraid/frightened/scared/terrified of
interested in
keen on
capable of
proud of

A common use is with the noun *difficulty* (to have difficulty in).

C **After verb and preposition combinations**
I don't approve of people drinking and driving.

Common examples:
insist on   approve of   apologise for
consist of   believe in   succeed in
accuse someone of   congratulate someone on

D **After phrasal verbs**
I gave up playing tennis when I hurt my knee.

The infinitive
A **The infinitive is used after certain verbs**
I learnt to speak Spanish in Valencia.

Common examples:
afford   agree   ask   choose   help   hope   want
intend   pretend   promise   expect   prefer   used

B **After certain adjectives**
I was surprised to see him at the party.

Common examples:
difficult   possible   happy   certain   simple

C **After verbs which follow the pattern verb + someone + *to do* + something**
I asked her to open the window.

Common examples:
encourage   permit   allow   persuade   teach   force

D **To express purpose**
I went to the shops to get some bread.

E **The infinitive without *to***
This is also used after modal auxiliaries (*can, must*), after *let, had better* and *would rather*. *Make* has no *to* in the active, but adds *to* in the passive:
I made him go to school /He was made to go to school.

Unit 8
used to and *would*
Used to and *would* express habitual actions in the past.
1 *Used to* is followed by the infinitive and is used for actions which no longer happen. It is used for permanent situations as well as habitual actions.
   I used to have a tricycle when I was five years old.
   John used to have long hair before he joined the army.

   The negative is *didn't use to.*
   I didn't use to go abroad for my holidays before I won the lottery.

2 *Would* is used for past habitual actions which were repeated. *Would* takes an infinitive without *to.*
   I would get up for work at seven, then get the bus at seven-thirty.

3 *Get/Be used to doing* means to be or to get accustomed to. It can be used with all tenses and is always followed by a gerund (an *-ing* word).

Unit 9
Modals 2: Speculation and deduction
- *could, might, may* are used to speculate about something the speaker or writer is unsure about:
  It could be a sea eagle, though the feathers look too dark.
  That star you're looking at might in fact be Jupiter.
  The answer may be to readvertise the job.
- *must* is used to indicate certainty:
  That car must be doing over 50 mph at least!
  It must be possible to make a booking on the Internet.
- *can't/cannot* and *couldn't/could not* are also used to indicate certainty, in relation to impossible ideas and situations:
  It can't be her birthday – she had a party in August.
  You cannot be serious!
  They couldn't possibly be here before lunchtime.

- *couldn't/could not* can also be used in questions, sometimes with *possibly*, to speculate about something:
  It couldn't possibly be a case of mistaken identity, could it?
  Couldn't it be a computer error?
- *could have, might have, may have* are used to express uncertainty about something in the past:
  It could have been Greg you saw on the bus – he often catches the 206.
  The dinosaurs might have survived without the meteor impact.
  I think I may have met you before.
- *couldn't have/can't have* is used to express certainty that something in the past was impossible or didn't happen:
  He couldn't have damaged your bike – he was with me all evening.
  It can't have been raining, as the path is completely dry.
- *must have* is used to express near-certainty about something in the past:
  It must have been cold that winter.
  Jan must have arrived home by now.

Order of adjectives

Opinion adjectives always come before descriptive adjectives:
the brilliant French film 'Le Bossu'
an appalling old brown tracksuit
Descriptive adjectives generally follow this order:
size shape age colour nationality material
a small oval brooch
the young American film star
It is unusual to have four or more adjectives together – a separate phrase is more commonly used:
a slim-cut black leather jacket with a classic Italian look

Unit 10

Review of future tenses

There are many ways of talking about the future in English. Sometimes, more than one tense is possible, with no change of meaning.

The future simple tense *shall/will* can be used for:
- future plans
  I'll give you a ring sometime.
- definite future events
  Our representative will meet you at the airport.
- predictions based on general beliefs
  Mass space travel will soon become possible.
- offers or promises relating to the future
  I'll prepare some salads for the party.
  I'll do my homework after this episode of the Simpsons.

  Remember that the future simple is also used in the first conditional (page 200).

The 'going to' future can be used for:
- future plans, particularly if they are likely to happen soon
  I'm going to clear out the kitchen cupboards at the weekend.
- intentions
  James says he's going to work harder.
- predictions based on facts or events in the present
  It's going to snow tonight.

The present continuous tense can be used for:
- imminent future events
  I'm having a meeting with Charlotte at two o'clock.
- definite future arrangements
  Johnny's starting school next September.

The present simple can be used for:
- events based on a timetable or known date
  The plane leaves at 09.45.
  'Twelfth Night' opens on Saturday at the Arts Theatre.
- future intentions
  NASA plans to send further rockets to Mars.
- definite planned events
  The new pool is due to open in April.

The future continuous tense is used to indicate certainty, when we are thinking ahead to a certain point in the future:
Tom will be sharing an office with Fran.

The future perfect simple is used to refer to events that have not yet happened but will definitely do so at a given time. This tense also conveys the idea of completion at some point in the future:
This time next year I'll have finished my course.
Space tourism will have become a reality by 2010.

The future perfect continuous tense is used to indicate duration:
At the end of June, Henry will have been working here for sixteen years.

Unit 11

Past and present: participles

The past participles *bored, interested, thrilled*, etc. are used when we want to talk about how people feel:
I was thrilled when I received her birthday invitation.

The present participles *boring, interesting, thrilling*, etc. are used to describe what causes the feeling:
The film was so boring that I fell asleep.

Unit 12

The passive

The passive is used:

1 When the action is more important than the person doing it:
   The film is loaded into the camera automatically.
2 When we don't know who did something:
   The camera was put together in a factory.
3 Very frequently, in reporting the news, scientific writing and other kinds of writing where we are more interested in events and processes than in the person doing the action:
   A factory was set alight during the weekend and two million pounds' worth of damage was caused.

Formation of the passive

The passive is formed with the verb *to be* and the past participle of a transitive verb. For modals it is formed with the modal + *be* + past participle.
Get can sometimes be used informally instead of *be*.
It is used with all tenses except for the present perfect continuous and the future continuous.
Compare these sentences:
A *George Eastman invented the Kodak camera.*
B *The Kodak camera was invented by George Eastman.*

Sentence A is active and follows the pattern of Subject (George Eastman), Verb (invented) and Object (the Kodak camera).
Sentence B is passive and the pattern is Subject (the Kodak Camera), Verb (was invented) and Agent (by George Eastman).
Sometimes there are two objects:
My uncle gave me some money for my birthday.
It is more common to say:
I was given some money by my uncle.
rather than
Some money was given to me by my uncle.

The agent *by*

It is sometimes unnecessary to include the agent – if for example we don't know who did something or it is obvious from the context of the sentence who did it:
She was arrested for speeding. (It's obviously going to be by a policeman so it's not necessary to include it.)

The infinitive

For sentences where the situation is in the present and need to have an impersonal sentence you can use the passive form of the verb plus the infinitive:
The President is believed to be in contact with the astronauts.
In the past we use the passive plus the past infinitive:
He is said to have poisoned his opponents in order to gain power.

Unit 13
Reporting

When direct speech is reported, it becomes indirect speech. There is usually a change of tense in the indirect speech, which is called 'backshift':
'I want to go home straightaway,' said Jennifer.
Jennifer said that she wanted to go home straightaway.

'Can I show you my stamp collection?' asked Billy.
Billy asked if he could show me his stamp collection.

'After Robert left primary school, he grew up very quickly,' said his mother.
Robert's mother said that after he had left primary school, he had grown up very quickly.

When something is reported that is a general truth, there is often no tense change:
"Girls' exam results are generally better than boys'," the head teacher admitted.
The head teacher admitted that girls' exam results are generally better than boys'.

There are a number of different reporting verbs in English. Here is a list of common ones, showing the structures they can take:

accuse + of + -ing
Mary accused Nick of deliberately forgetting to tell her.
admit + to (optional) + -ing; + that (optional)
The company admitted to selling banned products.
I admit that I was to blame.
apologise + for + -ing
James apologised for being late.
argue + for + -ing; that (optional)
The department argued convincingly for having extra staff.
Sally argued that it was unnecessary to delay the expedition.
claim + that (optional)
Newspapers are claiming that Mr Blair was told in advance.
deny + that (optional); + -ing
He denied his part in the crime.
Kirsty denied hiding the files.
explain + that (optional)
Geoff explained that there was no more money available.
insist + on + -ing; + that (optional)
The children insisted on staying up late.
Keith insisted that the project was too difficult.
promise + that (optional); + to + infinitive
Mum promised she would pick me up at 4pm.
Jackie has promised to look after the cats while we're away.
refuse + to + infinitive
The MP has refused to comment on these rumours.
say + that (optional); in passive, 'is said' + to + infinitive
People said that the flames were visible ten miles away.
The CD is said to include many new songs.

suggest + that (optional); + -ing
Vera suggested that they should seek sponsorship for the exhibition.
Hugh suggested contacting everyone by phone.
urge + to + infinitive
Owen urged them to keep calm.
warn + that (optional); + to + infinitive
His sister warned us that he might not come.
The police warned people not to use that part of the motorway.

Unit 14
Perfect tenses

See other units for information about:
- the present perfect tense, the past perfect simple tense (Unit 5)
- the future perfect simple and continuous tenses (Unit 10)

Present perfect continuous tense

This is used to emphasise the duration of a recent or ongoing event:
Lars has been talking about his own experience – does anyone share his views?
I've been learning Italian for six years.

Past perfect continuous tense

This is used to emphasise the duration of a past event:
I'd been working for the same company for twelve years and it was time to move on.

all/the whole

All is used with plural nouns and cannot be used on its own with a singular noun. You cannot say *All company is moving*, instead you say *The whole company is moving*.

The whole is not used with plurals. You cannot say *The whole businesses are affected by computerisation*. Instead you say *All businesses are affected by computerisation*.

Note that it is possible to say *Whole businesses are affected …* without the definite article, but this gives a change of meaning: you are now referring to each individual business.

Possessive pronouns are also used with *whole*:

Your whole career has been ruined.

You can use *of the* with both *all* and *the whole*:

All of us were sad to leave.
The whole of the world is watching the event.

Unit 15
Countable and uncountable nouns

1   A noun can either be countable or uncountable. Uncountable nouns cannot be made plural, and they only have one form. They take a singular verb. Uncountable nouns are often the names of things or substances or abstract ideas which cannot be counted.
Examples of common uncountable nouns: accommodation, traffic, news, bread, milk, wine, information, advice, electricity

2   Some nouns can be countable and uncountable and have a difference in meaning:
a   *Her hair is very long.* Uncountable noun meaning the hair on her head.
b   *There's a hair in this sandwich!* Countable noun.

a *Coffee grows in Brazil.* Uncountable noun for the product.
b *Would you like to come round for a coffee?* Countable noun meaning 'a cup of coffee'.

a *I haven't got enough paper left to finish this composition.* Uncountable noun.
b *Run out and buy me a paper will you?* Countable noun meaning a newspaper.

3 Uncountable nouns can be limited by using a countable expression. *A bit* or *a piece* are often used with uncountable nouns, although it is usually better to use a more specific expression.
a piece/slice of cake
a clap of thunder
an item of news
a loaf of bread

4 Determiners can be used with countable and uncountable nouns.
Singular countable nouns can use *a/an* and *the*.
A new table was delivered this morning.
The man next door is a chef.

Uncountable nouns	Countable plurals
how much	how many
a lot of	a lot of
lots of	lots of
little	few
a little	a few
some/any/no	several
the	some/any/no
plenty of	the
a large amount of	plenty of
a great deal of	a large number of

5 There is an important difference in meaning between *a few/few* and *a little/little*:
a *I've seen little improvement in your work recently.*
b *I've seen a little improvement in your work recently.*
a is considerably more negative than *b* in tone.
Compare:
a *There were few people at the meeting.* (It was disappointing because not many people were there)
b *There were a few people at the meeting.* (There weren't many people there, but there is no suggestion that more were expected).

some/any/no

In general we use *some* in positive sentences and *any* in negative sentences and questions:
I bought some new CDs this morning.
Did you get any bread at the supermarket?
I haven't had any breakfast this morning.

However, *some* is also used in questions when we offer something to someone:
Would you like some cake?

Also when we expect the answer to be 'yes':
(In a tourist office) *Do you have some information about the museum?*

Any is often used to show we don't have a preference:
You can take me to see any film at the cinema – I don't mind which.

When you use *no, nothing* or *nobody/no one* you use a positive verb:
I saw nobody when I went swimming this morning.

Unit 16
The article

1 We use the indefinite article *a/an* before a singular, countable noun. It is used when we are talking about something in general or when it is mentioned for the first time:
I saw a man outside the bank selling watches.
A pet can be a good companion for the elderly.
It is also used for jobs:
My aunt is a doctor.

2 The definite article *the* is used in the following ways:
a When something has been referred to before or is common knowledge:
I wouldn't buy a watch from the man standing outside the bank.
b When there is only one of something:
the Earth, the Sydney Opera House.
c With rivers, seas, oceans, mountains, regions, national groups and countries which are groups of states:
the United States, the Netherlands, the Atlantic, the Himalayas, the Irish
d With buildings:
I'm going to the prison to visit a prisoner.
He's in the office at the moment.
e With species:
the cat, the polar bear
f With superlatives:
the biggest tower in the world, the greatest sportsperson, the most important question
g With musical instruments:
I play the piano.
h When talking specifically about something:
The life of an airline pilot is hard.

3 There is no article:
a With most streets (except for *the High Street*), countries, single mountains, towns, cities (except for *The Hague*), lakes:
Austria, Mont Blanc, Tokyo
b When talking about sports:
I play football well.
c When a noun is used generally:
Life is hard.
d With illnesses:
She's off school with chickenpox.

4 Expressions
You go *to prison* if you have been found guilty of a crime. You go *to hospital* if you are ill.
You go *to the prison* or *to the hospital* to visit someone there or to work.
Other expressions which don't take an article include:
to go to bed, to have lunch, dinner, breakfast, to go on holiday, to go to work, in October, to hold office, etc.

Unit 17
Relative clauses

There are two types of relative clause: **defining** and **non-defining**. A defining relative clause gives essential information about the subject of the sentence. A non-defining relative clause gives additional but non-essential information. In other words, this information could be omitted without affecting the sense of the sentence:
The girl who is studying to become a vet is called Sarah.
Sarah, who is 20, is studying to become a vet.

As these examples show, punctuation is used in non-defining clauses but is absent from defining clauses. It is very important to use commas accurately in relative clauses, as inaccurate use may change the meaning of the sentence:

The sports facilities which are not in regular use will be sold.
The sports facilities, which are not in regular use, will be sold.

In the first example, only the sports facilities which are not being used will be sold, whereas in the second example, all the facilities will be sold, as none are being used.

Relative pronouns

In defining relative clauses, you can use:

- *who* or *that* when talking about people
  The boy who is playing is county champion.
  The teacher that I met is Head of Maths.
- *which* or *that* when talking about things
  Colours which can be worn are black, navy and grey.
  The book that I recommend costs £8.50.

The relative pronoun can be left out when it is the object of the sentence, as in the second example of each pair above. It must be included when it is the subject of the sentence.

In non-defining clauses, you use:

- *who* when talking about people
  Ned, who plays the violin, is living above a music shop.
- *which* when talking about things
  The new brand of shampoo, which is selling well, contains only natural ingredients.

That cannot be used, because there is no linking of the clauses, unlike in sentences containing a defining relative clause.

See also Unit 26 for information about the relative pronouns *whom* and *whose* in defining and non-defining clauses (page 208).

Instead of using a relative pronoun, *where*, *when* or *why* can be used after a noun. It is possible to omit *when* and *why* in defining relative clauses as in the following examples:

The hotel where we stayed had a beautiful garden.
Christmas is the time when many people start thinking about their next holiday.
That's the reason why she's so upset.

In non-defining relative clauses, *when* and *why* cannot be omitted:
I moved to London in 1975, when I started teaching.

Unit 18
enough, too, very, so, such

The word *enough* can be used:

- after an adjective or adverb
  The room wasn't large enough to hold everyone.
  You haven't worked hard enough this term.
- before an uncountable or plural countable noun
  The car has enough space for five people and their luggage.
  There are not enough girls doing science subjects.
- as a pronoun
  Enough has been made of this in all the papers.
- with a modifying adverb
  There is hardly enough memory in the computer.
- with certain adverbs for emphasis
  Funnily enough, we heard from him only last week.

too and *very*

These words are often confused. Here are the main uses.

- each can be used in front of an adjective or adverb, but *too* indicates an excessive amount of something, whereas *very* is just an intensifier:
  It is too cold in winter for many plants to survive.
  It is very cold in winter but a few plants do manage to survive.

- *too* can be used to show that two things or people have something in common:
  Dictionaries are useful at school and in the home too.
  You're Swedish too, aren't you?
  Note that here *too* always comes at the end of a clause.
- *too* can be used for emphasis:
  Computers are much more powerful than they were, and less expensive too.
- *too* can be used with a quantifier:
  There are too many loose ends to this story.
  A lot of people earn too little money to pay tax.

so and *such*

These words are also confused sometimes. The main uses are:

- both can be used for emphasis and to express the same idea, but in different grammatical structures.
  It rained so much that most of the area was flooded.
  There was such a lot of rain that most of the area was flooded.
- *such* is used with *as* in giving an example of something
  Dairy ingredients such as cheese and milk are best avoided.
  See also Unit 21 for uses of *so* and *such* in purpose, reason and result clauses (page 206).

Unit 19
Modals 3: Advice and suggestion

Giving advice

You should	try to watch what you eat.
You ought	to get some rest.
You'd better	book a place in the gym.
If I were you,	I'd try to do more exercise.
My advice to you is	to go to the doctor's.

Making a suggestion

I suggest	(that) you (should) cut down on coffee.
	cutting down on coffee.
I recommend	(that) you (should) relax a little more.
	relaxing.
	you to relax.
What about/How about	doing some reading?
Why don't you try	doing some reading?
Have you thought of	playing a musical instrument?

It's time …, It's about time …, It's high time …

After these phrases we use the past simple tense, even when we are talking about the present or the future:
It's time you went to bed.   You need to go to bed now.

It is also possible to use an infinitive with *to* after *It's time* if we are speaking in general terms rather than to particular people:
It's time to go.   Everybody needs to go now.

to have/get something done

Compare: *I cut my hair.*   I did it myself.
        I had my hair cut.   Someone else did it for me.

A *have* + object + past participle
B *get* + object + past participle

Both of these forms are used, but B is more informal than A.

Unit 20
Gerunds and infinitives 2

Some verbs can be followed by both a gerund and an infinitive. Depending on the verb, this can result in a change in meaning.

No change in meaning

Verbs such as *start, begin, continue, attempt, intend, be accustomed to, be committed to, can't bear*.
These can be used with either a gerund or an infinitive with no real change in meaning:
The audience started to clap when the performance finished.
The audience started clapping when the performance finished.

Slight change in meaning

Verbs such as *like, prefer, hate, love*.
Compare:
I like swimming. In general.
I like to swim in the morning. Talking about a habit.

Note that in American English, the infinitive is used more often than the gerund for both meanings.

After *would like, would prefer, would hate* and *would love* an infinitive is used for a particular occasion or event:
Would you like to dance?

A change in meaning

Verbs such as *try, stop, regret, remember, forget, mean, go on*.

Try

I tried to open the window, but it was stuck. I couldn't do it as it was too difficult.
It was hot, so I tried opening the window. I did it as an experiment to see if some fresh air would help.

Stop

I stopped the car to get some petrol. Purpose.
I stopped going to that garage when they put their prices up. I didn't go there any more.

Regret

I regret to tell you that we have no more rooms available. Giving bad news.
I regret not making more friends when I was at school. For past events.

Remember and forget

I remember/never forget going to New York by Concorde when I was quite small. This happened in the past.
I must remember/mustn't forget to buy a newspaper while I'm out shopping. Events that still haven't happened.

Mean

I mean to work hard at university. Intention.
It will mean going to the library more often. Involve/this is the result.

Go on

When I've finished shopping, I think I'll go on to see a film. A change of activity.
Please don't stop, go on showing us your photos. Continue.

Unit 21
Concessive clauses

Concessive: yielding, making or implying concession (≡ conceding, granting, admitting)

These are used in English to give contrasting information to the information in the main part of the sentence.
James insisted on playing in the match, despite feeling ill.
A number of different conjunctions can be used in front of the concessive clause:
although despite even if even though
in spite of much as though whereas while
Much as and *whereas* are less commonly used and occur mainly in formal written English.
I prefer to buy free-range eggs, even though they are more expensive.
Although we were very tired, we watched the whole of the play.

Sometimes it is possible to reduce the concessive clause by leaving out the main verb. So, in the second example, you could say:
Although very tired, we watched the whole of the play.
You should only do this when the concessive clause refers to the subject of the main clause. So, for example, you would not say:
Although very boring, we watched the whole of the play.
Remember that *despite* and *in spite of* cannot be followed by a main verb. You cannot say:
Despite he was late, John had another cup of coffee.
Both can be followed by a gerund or a noun:
In spite of being late, John had another cup of coffee.
Despite the time, John had another cup of coffee.
You can add *the fact that* and follow this by a verb clause:
Despite the fact that he was late, John had another cup of coffee.

Purpose, reason and result clauses

A purpose clause explains information given in the main clause:
I looked the meaning up in a dictionary to see if I was right.
The conjunctions used at the front of a purpose clause are:
because in case just in case so so as to
so that in order to in order that to

A reason clause also explains information in the main clause, for example why something happened:
At midnight, we could still see perfectly well, because there was a full moon.
The conjunctions used are:
as because for since

A result clause explains the effect of a situation or action that is mentioned in the main clause:
The dress was very expensive, so I didn't buy it.
The conjunctions used are:
so so … that such such … that
That can often be omitted:
I've had such a lot of bills (that) I can't afford a holiday.
See Unit 18 (page 205) for other uses of *so* and *such*.

Unit 22
Complex sentences

Here are more examples of some of the complex sentence types covered in the unit.
Prepositional phrase
Besides jazz and hip-hop, I also enjoy baroque chamber music.
Adjectival phrase
Elegantly dressed in red velvet, the pianist adjusted the stool and began to play.
Concessive clause
Despite the fact that he is world-famous, Keith Gregory earns relatively little from his live performances.

Reason clause
Mark turned the amp up fully, so as to be heard at the back of the hall.
-ing clause
Having played together for more than eighteen years, the quartet rarely disagree on interpretation.

Rhetorical question
How he ever managed to carry that tuba round as a child, I'll never know.

Unit 23
Intensifiers
Gradable adjectives

A gradable adjective is one which can be used in the comparative, such as *sad* (*sadder*). You can use *very* to make it stronger:
I was very happy when my friends held a surprise party for me.

Non-gradable adjectives

These are extreme or absolute adjectives such as *gorgeous, fantastic, marvellous*. You can use *absolutely* or *really* to intensify them:
The weather yesterday was absolutely gorgeous.

I wish/If only
Talking about the past – things you regret doing/not doing:
Wish/If only + past perfect
I wish I hadn't been so rude to my mother last night.

Talking about the present – things that haven't come true now and things that might come true in the future:
Wish/If only + past simple
I wish I were/was lying on a beach somewhere instead of being here.
I wish I could speak Japanese.
Both *were* and *was* are acceptable but *were* is more formal.

Talking about irritating habits – things which are annoying you:
Wish/If only + would
He wishes his daughter would wear smarter clothes.

as if/as though
Both *as if* and *as though* mean the same.
To talk about 'unreal' situations you use the past tense after both *as if* and *as though*:
He looks as if he's tired. He is tired.
He looks as if he was/were exhausted. He isn't.

would rather
Would rather + past simple is used to talk about the present or future:
I'd rather you didn't go to the disco tonight.

Would rather + past perfect is used to talk about the past:
She'd rather they had gone to an Italian restaurant.

Would rather + infinitive without *to* is used to talk generally about the present and future:
The government would rather not give out too many benefits to young people.
Do not confuse this phrase with *had better*, which means 'should'.

Unit 24
Adverbs and word order
At the beginning, usually for emphasis

- Time adverbs – *tomorrow, yesterday evening* – can go at the beginning or the end of a sentence.
  Tomorrow I'm going swimming.
  We had a curry last night.

- Most negative adverbs can be placed at the beginning of a sentence but the word order changes as a result. This is called inversion.
  seldom, never, rarely, under no circumstances, no sooner, hardly.
  Never have I seen such a wonderful sunset!
  Notice the change in word order. The meaning is the same as '*I have never seen such a wonderful sunset*', but the inversion gives the sentence more emphasis.

- Adverbs of frequency – *sometimes, often*, etc.– can start a sentence for emphasis, but they usually go between the subject and the verb. There is no inversion after them.
  Sometimes I go shopping after work.

- Adverbs of manner – *suddenly, quietly*, etc. – can start a sentence for emphasis.
  Quietly she stepped into the cellar.

- Adverbs of opinion – *actually, surprisingly*, etc. – are often placed at the beginning of a sentence for emphasis.
  Actually, I'm older than you think.

In the middle

- Adverbs of frequency – *sometimes, often, always, usually*, etc. – are placed:
  before the verb in simple sentences – *We often play tennis.*
  after the first auxiliary verb – *I have always been fond of chocolate.*
  after the verb 'to be' – *I am never ill.*
- Adverbs of degree – *almost, very, quite* – are placed before the word they modify:
  It was very dark outside.
- Adverbs of manner – *suddenly, quietly*, etc.
  They suddenly appeared from behind the wall.
- Adverbs of opinion – *obviously, stupidly*, etc.
  I obviously forgot to tell you where I would be.

End position
Adverbs of Manner (*How*), Place (*Where*) and Time (*When*) usually go in the end position. Never place one of these adverbs between a verb and its object. You cannot say *They gave generously the present.*
If there are two or three adverbs of manner, place and time they are placed in this order:
Manner – Place – Time
Valerie behaved badly at her aunt's yesterday.

Unit 25
Mixed conditionals

- *If* + past tense (second form) with *would(n't)/might(n't)/could(n't)/should(n't)* (third form):
  If I weren't so busy all the time, I could have come along.
  Used when a change in a present situation would have affected a past situation.

- *If* + past perfect tense (third form) with *would(n't)/might(n't)/could(n't)/should(n't)* + infinitive (second form):
  If you had told me about the skiing trip, I would be there with you now!
  Used when a change in a past situation would have caused a different present situation.

Unit 26
Relative pronouns

See also Unit 17 on relative clauses (page 204).

who or whom?

Both pronouns are used in relative clauses. *Whom* is a formal word, which can only be used as the object of a verb or with a preposition:

Ruth Gresham, who cannot sell her house as a result of this new rail route, says she will seek compensation.

The people for whom this new housing development is planned are unhappy about the lack of public transport.

whose

This pronoun is used to refer to both people and things:

Professor Newton, whose latest book on urban sprawl has had excellent reviews, will open the conference.

This revolutionary new car, whose energy comes from solar panels, is expected to go into production shortly.

Unit 27

Refer to the sections for Units 2 (present tenses), 5 (past tenses), 10 (future tenses) and 14 (perfect tenses).

Unit 28
Number and concord
Singular verbs

The following all take a singular verb:
crossroads, headquarters, series, news
Thirty kilometres *is a long way to go.*
Four pounds *isn't enough to buy a meal with.*
More than one *voter is going to be disappointed.*
One of *my friends is from Russia.*
The United States *is governed from Capitol Hill.*
*Your **hair** is too long. (and all **uncountable nouns**)*
Athletics *has become very popular in schools. (**politics, mathematics**)*
Every *house has its own garage.*
Everybody/everyone *in the room agrees more housing should be built.*
No one *likes eating blue food.*

Plural verbs

The following all take a plural verb:
jeans, scissors, the police, sunglasses, premises, stairs, clothes
A group of *girls were dancing in the disco.*
The majority of *people I know don't smoke.*
A lot of *builders try to cut corners.*
A number of people *had to stand at the concert.*
All of *us believe in freedom of speech.*
Both of *the students were late handing in their homework.*

The following take either a singular or a plural verb – usually a singular verb is more formal:

Family, staff, team, government, committee, firm, public
Neither *the Prime Minister nor his Deputy has/have replied to the ultimatum.*
None of *us is/are going to the party.*
Each of *them eats/eat an apple a day.*

Unit 30
Uses of *rather*

- Used as an adverb, in the same way as *quite*:
  Eddie Izzard's humour is rather surreal at times – elephants on skis, that sort of thing.
  Some comedians are quite direct and indeed rather rude to their audiences.

- Used with *would* to mean *prefer*:
  I'd rather go to a live show than watch a video.
  John says he'd rather not come with us, as he's very tired.

- Used as a prepositional phrase to contrast two things or situations:
  The jokes were about society in general rather than being purely political.
  Rather than stay at home watching TV, he got changed and went off to the party.

- *Rather* can also be used as an adverb immediately before a verb of thought or feeling, to express an opinion politely:
  I rather think his recent success has gone to his head.
  I rather like your hair cut short.

The grammar of phrasal verbs

Phrasal verbs consist of a main verb and a particle (which is an adverb or a preposition).

- When used intransitively (that is, without an object), the verb and particle of a phrasal verb cannot be separated:
  The engine cut out and they drifted on the waves.

- When the particle is an adverb, transitive phrasal verbs can either be separated or followed by a noun as object; they are always separated by a pronoun as object:
  He keyed the number in carefully.
  He keyed in the number carefully.
  He keyed it in carefully.

  Could you set the drinks down on that table?
  Could you set down the drinks on that table?
  Could you set them down on that table?

- When the particle is a preposition, no separation is possible:
  The lorry ploughed into a barrier.
  My older sister keeps getting at me!

- For three-part phrasal verbs, no separation is possible:
  The sparkling blue sea more than made up for their difficult journey.
  I was really looking forward to that concert – what a shame it's been cancelled.